INSTANITY!™

D1572279

INSTANITY!™

Desperation for "hope" and "change" prompts a state of <u>instant</u>, selective, and intentional <u>insanity</u>!

KEVIN MCGARY

TATE PUBLISHING & Enterprises

Published by Tate Publishing & Enterprises, LLC
127 E. Trade Center Terrace | Mustang, Oklahoma 73064 USA
1.888.361.9473 | www.tatepublishing.com

Tate Publishing is committed to excellence in the publishing industry. The company reflects the philosophy established by the founders, based on Psalm 68:11,
"The LORD *gave the word and great was the company of those who published it."*

Published in the United States of America

ISBN: 978-1-61663-461-2
1. Political Science, General
2. Political Science, Government, General
10.11.09

DEDICATION

It would be a gross misrepresentation for me to take any credit for this book, as proper dedication must be given to my Father.

Father, you have provided me with the will, ability, inspiration, and complete perspective for this book. You make all things possible! This book is just another example of your divine wisdom being displayed as your handiwork is accomplished through me, and I thank you for the privilege. There is nothing more pleasing than for you to receive all the accolades and fullness of any glory that may result. I humbly submit this book to you, and I pray you use it to accomplish whatever you will.

Your son,
Kevin

ACKNOWLEDGMENTS

I want to express a special thanks to all my friends and family, as you have extended me grace over the past several months while I have been generally aloof and have not called, visited, or been accessible. You have been very gracious and forgiving; I do not take for granted your extension of grace toward me, and I thank you!

A special thanks is also extended to my good friends David Wetzel, Vincent and Mel Engobor, and Ms. Jeral Davis. Each of you provided inspiration and encouragement as I embarked on this work. Your encouragement gave me strength and motivation, which prevented me from growing faint and faltering. I thank you!

Many thanks to Ms. Donna Chumley and the entirety of the Tate Publishing team. You have been incredible to work with! You are all high quality professionals with commitment to excellence, and I thank you for seeing the possibilities and trusting me with this vital work. If not for your commitment and encouragement, I don't know where, when, or how this book would have been possible.

My Rotary colleagues—Paul Martin, Ed Bullock, Andy Krake, Linda Horner, Lee Tompkins, William Roberts, and Professor Jay Tontz—have been especially helpful in reading and providing valuable input that helped shape this work. I am humbled and very thankful for your input and commitment.

A special thanks is also extended to Duane and Sharon Ferrell and Robert Greenslade from the East Bay Freedom Fighters, and Michael Archer, and Professor Annette Hoffman-Walker for help and support while working diligently to proofread the final manuscript.

Anything good that comes from me would not be even remotely possible without the help and support of my wife, Tracey. Tracey, you are my best friend and soul mate, and we are a team with a special assignment—He is doing a new thing. You provided invaluable input while provoking and inspiring me. Thank you for the much-needed grace you extended to me during this project.

To my children, Sean and Lauren—Daddy's finished! Thanks for your encouragement and support.

TABLE OF CONTENTS

PREFACE

As an avid reader, I know that unless you receive a strong recommendation and endorsement from someone you know and trust, there are several questions you ask yourself before investing valuable time into reading a new book. One of the first questions is simply: *Why* should I read this book? The next questions are: *Who* is the author, and *what* qualifies him? One of the final considerations has to do with timing. You may ask, *why* should I spend my time reading this book *now?* These are all great questions, and each deserves an answer right up front.

I will begin by explaining why this book is a worthwhile read. The short answer is that reading this book will help stop the expansion of what can only be described as irrational new policies and initiatives that will seriously, negatively impact our country. By reading this book, you will have the capacity to make a difference. By gaining new vantage points and observations of new policies and initiatives, you are likely to become more enthused about participating in this new era of government. No doubt, one of the primary factors that has limited our participation thus far is that we have somehow allowed ourselves to blindly trust our government. This has shaped us into non-thinkers, and therefore non-participants, in the political process. This book, however, is designed as a wake-up call; it is written for average, "thinking" Americans.

The term "thinking" is specifically noted because I have met many Americans who blindly believe that the current administration is fully capable of doing the right thing and looking out for everyone's best interests, while saving our country's economic future and also saving the planet. These people possess blind faith and employ wishful thinking; they are not independent thinkers grounded in reality. While our government and leaders may be well-intentioned, putting blind faith in them during this most pivotal point in history will likely produce consequences to the detriment of our country.

There are many who would celebrate Obama's presidency and our historic moment throughout the next four years, and just allow whatever happens to happen! Regardless of the logical facts, the mind-set of people is to believe that Obama can do it all, that he can handle anything, or that he's got it all under control. Full disclosure: If you are of this mind-set, this book is probably not for you!

This book is suited for people who are concerned about the new era of U.S. government. In recognition of the unprecedented challenges we face, this era is marked by what most should consider irrational initiatives that greatly accelerate an increase in government spending, burgeoning budget deficits, and an apparent weak and naive foreign policy. How can we begin to objectively analyze, then appropriately intervene where there seem to be relatively illogical policies and initiatives? This book is designed for those of us who have a healthy respect for the "hope" and "change," but are hoping to see change by instilling old-fashioned common sense back into our policies. It is written for people like me, who are no longer willing to continue blindly trusting the government and are ready to begin thinking for ourselves while holding leaders and politicians fully accountable for the direction of our country.

I have been told many times that I am a "facts man," so this book is not intended to emotionally charge readers so much as it is to appropriately inform about what I would describe as insane new realities. It allows readers to draw clear, prudent, rational, and logical conclusions. In the end, I expect that the veil will be lifted, and we will see our government and its respective leadership clearly and objectively. Readers will gain a much more powerful understanding of how to begin to greatly impact America's future just by thinking independently and rolling up their sleeves to participate in charting the country's pathway for success.

Now you are probably asking, "Who are you?" You should know that I am a reluctant author! I have been provoked and inspired to write this book because of what I can only describe as the state of "instant insanity" of people who I otherwise consider very sane, rational, logical, and moral. These people include my family members, some of my closest friends, and my business and professional associates. I have noticed a state of instant insanity when I attempt to have thoughtful dialogue about our current government and the direction of our country. It seems that when I am involved in any dialogue that requires thoughtful introspection about our blind faith and undying love and support of Barack Obama and his administration, most people—whom I know to be perfectly sane—seem to instantly become irrational and illogical and in complete contradiction to their own confessed values and beliefs! Therefore, since millions of other Americans have great difficulty participating in rational and thoughtful conversations about our current government and leadership, I wrote this book.

We have always pointed fingers and been overly critical of one political party versus another. Right now, however, is not a time to point fingers; it is time to stand together in a collective commitment to common sense. You should know that I am an African-American who considers himself neither Democrat nor Republican. Because of my background and family tradition however, I have voted Democrat most often. But, over the years, I have cast votes for candidates in both parties. Though now I tend to lean more conservatively in my thinking, for all intents and purposes, I am just an American who thinks and votes according to the issues and candidates who most closely align to my principles and beliefs. This book is written chiefly from the perspective of one American citizen making an urgent appeal to another to commit to thinking and reasoning together.

Why the urgent appeal? Why now? We made a difference during our last election cycle; we voted for "change," and in doing so, we made history together. The fact is, however, that we chose to elect an inexperienced administration at one of the most critical times in U.S. history. We are formidably challenged with fighting multiple wars while combating the most devastating economic collapse in decades. In response to some of the challenges we face, there has been a major shift in policy and the emergence of a completely new era in politics. The new era will be marked by many unprecedented changes to our country and society. We have the capacity to help ensure our government administration successfully moves forward, but it requires we urgently renew a commitment to accountability and common sense.

Since we all bear collective responsibility for ensuring that our country remains successful and viable, this means we can no longer excuse ourselves from critical thinking as it relates to our government. This is easier said than done, however, because we have come to a point in history when we have begun to rely too heavily on unreliable and corrupt media outlets, along with a persuasive popular culture. We've allowed them to shape and define our reality. Unfortunately, unhealthy reliance on these outlets has promoted what I call a cycle of insanity.

As you read, you will find that the state of insanity described herein can be fully cured simply through objective observation and thoughtful consideration of actions and consequences. By the end of the book, you will find that we can maintain success as a great nation after we intervene in order to immediately halt; then, we can go further to prevent our government's propensity for insanity along the way.

PART ONE

Management of Our Enterprise

"Democracy is always temporary in nature; it simply cannot exist as a permanent form of government. A democracy will continue to exist up until the time that voters discover that they can vote themselves generous gifts from the public treasury. From that moment on, the majority always votes for the candidates who promise the most benefits from the public treasury, with the result that every democracy will finally collapse due to loose fiscal policy, which is always followed by a dictatorship. The average age of the world's greatest civilizations from the beginning of history has been about 200 years. During those 200 years, these nations always progressed through the following sequence:

- From bondage to spiritual faith;
- From spiritual faith to great courage;
- From courage to liberty;
- From liberty to abundance;
- *From abundance to complacency;*
- *From complacency to apathy;*
- *From apathy to dependence;*
- From dependence back into bondage

Introducing ... Instanity: Our "new era"

- Instant: an almost imperceptible space of time; an infinitesimal or very short space of time; a moment.

- Insane: foolish, irrational; not of sound mind; mentally deranged; crazed, maniacal.

- Instanity: the state of becoming instantly and selectively illogical and irrational or insane.

For the purposes of this book, "insanity" should not be viewed as a loaded or derogatory term. It should primarily be viewed as a descriptive term, which is being used because it most appropriately describes thoughts and actions that seem to lack logic, reason, and rationality. The fundamental characteristics used to depict a relative state of insanity are:

A. When "we the people" demonstrate a lack of logic and reason and make irrational choices and decisions.

B. When government leadership demonstrates a lack of

logic, reason, and prudence in the pursuit of irrational policies and initiatives

C. When history is overlooked, and we are doing the same thing over again but expecting a different result.

D. All of the above.

Albert Einstein's definition of insanity is doing the same thing—in our case, making the same mistakes—over and over again, and expecting different results. This is a good working definition of insanity, and after looking at current policies and intentions, it seems to directly apply to the current era of U.S. government. Many policies and initiatives being pursued by our new era of government leadership, like increased taxation schemes and expanded government management and control, have been tried many times and have been proven unsuccessful.

After reflecting on Einstein's definition of insanity while also attempting to put our current government policies and initiatives in some coherent context, I was reminded of a quote written by Alexander Tytler over 200 years ago; this quote is profoundly prophetic today as it conveys a cycle of insanity within the context of government. The quote is as follows:

> "Democracy is always temporary in nature; it simply cannot exist as a permanent form of government. A democracy will continue to exist up until the time that voters discover that they can vote themselves generous gifts from the public treasury. From that moment on, the majority always votes for the candidates who promise the most benefits from the public treasury, with the result that every democracy will finally collapse due to loose fiscal policy, which is always followed by a dictatorship. The average age of the world's greatest civilizations from the beginning of history has been about 200 years. During those 200 years, these nations always progressed through the following sequence:
>
> • From bondage to spiritual faith;

- From spiritual faith to great courage;
- From courage to liberty;
- From liberty to abundance;
- From abundance to complacency;
- From complacency to apathy;
- From apathy to dependence;
- From dependence back into bondage.

Yikes! Does this cycle sound vaguely familiar? Does it strike you as somewhat surreal based on the apparent cycle we are currently experiencing in America?

Models of governance representative of variations of socialism, Marxism, communism, fascism, and others have been tried over thousands of years, and invariably, they have all failed. Conversely, free market capitalism absolutely works and has been proven quite successful for America. Regardless, there seems to be a tendency to reject logic and prudence and embark on another cycle of experimentation with models of governance that have already proven deficient. Reflecting on Einstein's definition, what do we expect to achieve from renewed efforts to infuse variations of failed governmental models? Is the expectation that it is wholly possible to infuse variations of failed models of governance and actually achieve success? This is a classic example of insanity.

This book is offered to help confirm the existence of a phenomenon that robs foresight and an objective perspective, generating a state of irrationality. Actions and decisions rooted in irrational, illogical, and indefensible mindsets represent a general state of what I can only describe as insanity, and it seems to have spread throughout the nation's government.

Unfortunately, the current strain of insanity is not limited to members of our government, as it seems to have grown quite contagious. It has aggressively spread throughout our major media outlets and permeated our majority two-party political system. This can only mean that it is just a matter of time before all Americans run the risk of catching it. If we can confirm that a form of insanity exists, we can look at remedies and antidotes to help overcome it. In the end, we will be surprised to learn that the best remedy is quite simple: We must begin to think for ourselves and exercise our own common sense.

Since this book declares the existence of an actual, contagious state of insanity, it would be irresponsible to not clarify and provide examples. First, let's understand that our United States government has a very long history of waste and inefficiency throughout all branches of government, divisions, and offices—in, and throughout, all levels. We also know that, even though our government may be well-intentioned, it has a track record of amassing huge debt and of allowing undisciplined and completely out-of-control spending. With our experience and understanding of our government's track record, shouldn't we consider it absolutely insane to actually expect and believe in a government strategy that dramatically increases deficit spending during an economic cycle already encumbered with trillion-dollar deficits? Do we think it is rational to believe our government actually works in our best interest when they don't even take time to read the bills and legislation they sign? Does it make any sense to believe and expect that our government, with its well-documented, gross inefficiency and mismanagement—the Postal Service, IRS, and Social Security—should own and manage some of the world's largest banks, financial institutions, insurance companies, and auto manufacturers? Isn't it insane to actually want, expect, and believe that we should allow almost 10,000 new "pork barrel" projects and "pork barrel" spending, totaling hundreds of billions of dollars, during one of the worst economic downturns in history?

Is it just me, or is it completely irresponsible and insane to actually believe that the U.S. is dutifully protected from its many enemies while we leave our porous borders on the north and south unsecured? We advertise our CIA methods and secrets, and we have stopped the very interrogation—and methods—that kept us safe for over eight years. No doubt about it, these issues are problematic *and* insane.

Since there is minimal outrage about irrational, major policy issues and too few voices holding our elected leaders accountable, there is indication we have entered into a state of instant insanity. Here's the issue: If we do not force ourselves to look beyond the blur of media rhetoric and high-gloss politics, we will think that current governmental policies actually make sense and are in our best interest. With overwhelming evidence of patterns of government incompetence, however, common sense should dictate an expectation of more erroneous policies. Our lack of reaction to these illogical and irrational policies demonstrates that we experience bouts of selective and instant insanity—instanity!

Thinking independently and objectively is critical. If we objectively ponder the direction of our government and its policies, yet continue to endorse and defend them, perhaps we lack objectivity. This is very common. When it comes to Barack Obama and his administration and policies, we generally defend him to such an extent that we seem to lose our sanity. What is interesting about this phenomenon is that we willingly, selectively, and intentionally disregard logic in order to embrace "hope." When it comes to this administration, our zeal for "hope" and "change" has prompted a state of instant insanity. We all know many average Americans who typically live by making rational assessments based on standards, criteria, and accountability, but when it comes to this government, it seems these people flip a switch and become instantly irrational and illogical. They make excuses and defend our new leadership and government.

Why? This is a prime illustration that people allow themselves to become instantly insane—or to become non-thinkers about government and policy—as though it's a patriotic duty to practice blind faith and unwavering support. It is never fashionable to become a non-thinker in *any* domain, let alone the domain of government and policy; this only further propagates a state of instanity while undermining a democratic Republic upheld by the system of checks and balances. One of the ways the system works is that we, the people, are supposed to provide oversight and demand accountability, and our government is supposed to appropriately respond by balancing the will of the people in conjunction with the best interest of the country.

We truly live in historic times. As Americans, we can now celebrate a presidency that has broken racial barriers while also receiving generous support from the majority of media and the American public. Our zeal for "hope" and "change" has provided new impetus for our elected officials and politicians to begin to think and act differently toward America.

This sounds like good news, right? Well, what if our new paradigm was brought about due to sheer insanity? Would we still feel our politicians and our country are headed in the right direction if we come to realize that—individually and collectively—we have been riding a wave of insanity? Should we at least be willing to interrogate our individual thought processes and decision-making to see if perhaps our zeal and desperation for hope and change provide objective criteria and rationale for holding our politicians accountable? When we allow the media, prevailing culture, image makers, and personal popularity to dictate important decisions, we enter into a state of imprudence and irrationality reflective of instanity.

As you know, instanity is not officially a word. Unofficial status notwithstanding, I believe it's the best word to properly characterize what happened during our last election cycle and what is still spreading. Americans instantly embraced, and still wholeheartedly believe in, the mantra of hope and change without regard to any indication of past competencies, track record, or criteria for success. The very act of instantly and selectively believing in someone or something just because we are desperate for change is crazy and irrational, or insane.

Before going any further, you should know that although I have a degree in Sociology and Psychology, I am by no means a psychologist. I know there are many aspects and facets of insanity, and I do not want to diminish the term or malign its relevance by using it in conjunction with our current political climate. Therefore, for the purposes of this book, I define "insanity" as a state of being foolish and irrational or not thoughtful; crazed and maniacal. We are quite familiar with "temporary insanity," which is used heavily as a defense in criminal cases. In general, this is the state at which someone temporarily loses their mind as a result of sudden trauma or a series of events. I needed a new word that conveys instant, selective, and continuous irrational responses from people who willfully and purposefully reject the idea of having thoughtful criteria and rationale for actions; thus, instanity!

Obviously, I do not believe that most Americans are suffering from actual, clinical insanity. For the purposes of this book, however, I hope that we can begin to see that, at this point in history, in the very specific domain of American politics, we are seeing something that is appropriately described as instanity. When we see our government conveniently overlook constitutional freedoms, dramatically increase spending at a time of massive deficits, increase expansion in entitlements and spending, and take over entire industries, one can't help but say we've lost our minds.

Make no mistake; this book is not a referendum on Barack Obama and his administration. However, he, his administration, and the entire cast of government leadership offer the best and most relevant examples of instanity. While at times this book may offer critical analysis of our president, his administration, his background and foundations, and his policies, these issues are only being used as examples to help us observe how we have veered from the path of decision making based on logic and objectivity and are now on an uncertain path wrought with irrationality. The intent is not to critique, rebuke, or condemn our president. He played by the rules, took full advantage of all the resources afforded him, and got elected. That's the American way. God bless him!

Rather than offer a referendum, this book is very much intended to be about us—individually and collectively—as Americans! It is for those of us who are wise or seeking to be wise and objective and not to be ideologues. Ideologues who purport to be on the right like radical, Republican conservatives; or on the left, like radical, Democrat liberals, will be disappointed. This book will demonstrate that fervent ideology on either side of the political spectrum presents illogical, irrational, and insane barriers that prevent us from thinking and using our innate capability to pursue wisdom. Ultimately, this is an appeal that wisdom, understanding, and common sense be infused into the current political climate.

Proverbs 4:7 reads, "Getting wisdom is the most important thing you can do. Whatever else you get, get insight" (GNB).

This is appropriately poignant within the context of our current political climate, because it helps confirm the precious value of wisdom and insight, which lead to logic and prudence.

One of the biggest challenges we face is the rapid pace of change. Because things are moving so quickly and changes happen daily, trying to remain vigilant is a huge challenge. Gaining wisdom and objectivity in a rapid-paced and ever-changing environment is almost impossible without spending time observing and reflecting. This book will help present a more objective window—through which you can observe and reflect—by providing careful observation and analysis of the many policies and personalities of all of our elected leaders, who will profoundly affect us.

Ultimately, when we gain the capacity for observation, we will be prodded and provoked to overlay current policy and direction and compare and contrast them to our individual thought processes. This will bring clarity to our beliefs and principles. The critical first step is becoming thoughtful, rational, logical people who are willing to interrogate and make thoughtful comparisons based on what we fundamentally stand for.

It seems to me that, during the past election cycle, our heartfelt desire for change had us desperately seeking someone who spoke our language. The question this book will attempt to help answer is: Did we forgo our rationality and in an instant become insane because of a good-looking, vibrant, new personality? Are we now so committed to our voting decisions that we willingly ignore facts and give the administration a pass, even as we begin to see our Constitution undermined, our country socially reengineered, and our freedoms infringed upon by government? In the end, we will likely conclude that, when it comes to Barack Obama and his administration, we as a nation have entered a state of instanity.

There is now a tremendous opportunity for real hope, which will definitely produce big change. This book will help confirm that our hope for successfully maneuvering this country through this incredible period starts with us. This book is written to help us—average American citizens—move beyond the rhetoric and fancy packaging of Washington politicians into an era of common sense and accountability.

We need to be able to formulate our individual, rational criteria and precisely identify the reasons for our support—or lack of support—for our current leadership in Washington. Through this type of genuine introspection, we will be able to gain strength and move forward with resolve and conviction. We can then tell the people we hired how we want them to run our country and assert that we will hold them fully accountable to our principles and criteria. They will have two choices: Comply, or not get re-elected!

Due to media mania and all the moment-by-moment policy and initiative changes, this book is designed to provide multiple vantage points that will enable logical and rational assessment of our leaders in Washington and the direction of our country. Being able to observe our government and policies from multiple vantage points allows for increased objectivity and provides clarity about how to make assessments based on rational criteria and principles. The vantage points will be thoroughly analyzed in three parts.

In the first vantage point (Part 1), we will use the very appropriate analogy of viewing our country as a fledgling world business enterprise. In this scenario, U.S. citizens make up the board of directors, and President Obama and his newly-formed administration are our new executives. Their job will be objectively assessed based on whether our enterprise—in this case, the U.S.—is achieving success based on the many promises and commitments made to us.

The next vantage point (Part 2) will contrast the new era policies and societal direction in comparison with our American heritage and traditions.

Lastly, since most Americans view themselves as people of faith, the final vantage point (Part 3) will compare and contrast America's founding principles of faith with new policies and practical realities being generated out of Washington.

By the end of this book, we will have objectively assessed the direction of our country, and arrived at logical conclusions about how we can produce real change. It's up to us; we are the enforcers of our freedoms! Together we can produce real commitment to a new and vibrant country filled with hope and change, but this is a collective effort! Come … let's begin by putting a stop to the state of instanity.

CHAPTER TWO

The Management of our Enterprise: New Era of Policy, Practices, and Leadership

We all want progress, but if you're on the wrong road, progress means doing an about-turn and walking back to the right road; in that case, the man who turns back soonest is the most progressive.

—C. S. Lewis

Urgent Memo: Change Is Here!

We live in a great nation! We have been given rights and liberties that allow us to actively participate in our government and politics and help set the direction of our country. Imagine that—we actually have the opportunity to assist in charting the direction of the country! This great liberty is significant because we know that there are many countries that do not allow freedom and forms of democracy, and, as a result, their citizens suffer.

What happens to our country when we don't take full advantage of our liberty to participate? First, we see zealous politicians, ideologues, and the major media begin to frame policies and shape the country's direction for us. Then, we notice policy decisions that we would deem crazy, illogical, and irrational dominate the thinking in Washington.

Basically, if we defer our liberties by putting blind faith in our government officials, we grant them a license to pursue their own initiatives without accountability. This means that instead of forcing our government to exercise common sense on our behalf in policies and decisions, we will see policies initiated based on political favors, partisan rule, and as a means to strengthen political power. Does this mean our politicians purposely disregard us? No, it just means that because we have not exercised our liberty to participate; we have simply deferred via blind faith. They tend to make fast decisions, not common sense ones.

In order for our nation to thrive and continue to succeed, common sense must prevail. We are facing some of the most chaotic times in our nation's history. We are fighting multiple wars, investing in alternate energy sources and strategies, and combating social ills at a time when we are also dealing with a worldwide recession and budget deficits. With so much at stake while massive change is taking place, the decisions we make and the direction we take are critical; there is little doubt that we are at a fulcrum in history, and our decisions will either make us hugely successful or tremendous failures. Needless to say, we have an ominous future facing us. Fortunately, America has a great history of success, so failure is not an option. How do we help America succeed?

America's success is highly dependent upon the engagement of its citizens. American citizens are the collective consciousness of America. If we are the collective consciousness, we can no longer afford to be passively unconscious. By simply using our individual thought processes, critically assessing our government's direction, and engaging in the political process by making our voices heard, we can assure success as we implement "hope" and "change".

The collective liberties to be used help shape this country must count, and this requires that we are willing to think individually and critically! When we choose to defer to others—media, political parties, personalities—instead of thinking for ourselves, we unwittingly foster an environment where selective and instant insanity can prevail. Again, this is an environment where illogical, irrational—even crazy—decisions are made based on a variety of factors, most of which seemingly exclude common sense.

In this state of instanity, there is no consideration of past performance or anticipation of future performance; there is just an irrational desire to exercise blind faith. The danger of instanity is that it prevents us from seeing past political party affiliations, media bias and deceptions, and the cult of personality in order to critically think about how decisions align with our principles. It also prevents us from having standards of accountability. In other words, if we blindly trust and rely on the biased media—which strongly supports the current of agenda of government and politicians—to frame and shape our political reality, how will we really know when things go awry? Instanity is a huge impediment to our success, and it has to stop!

Fundamentally, it doesn't matter where you stand on the political spectrum; everybody loves winning, and everybody wants to be successful! Since we all want to win and have our country perpetuate success, we must begin to collectively think and act like winners. The key term here is "think." One of the most telling characteristics of winners is their ability to make and receive critical assessments, make corrections and refinements, and redo based on input and refinements. Our democratic government is designed to function in the same way: American citizens are empowered to offer input through elected officials in order to help make critical refinements so we achieve collective success. Because each individual American plays such a critical role in the success of our country, we cannot afford to blindly trust and allow ourselves to be gripped by and swept into a state of instanity.

One of the most empowering revelations for us at this juncture is to recognize that our government was hired to work for us. "We, the people ... " This factual revelation and the responsibilities and ramifications that result from it require that we begin to think and act like the employers we are. The U.S. government, including the president and all of Congress, are our employees and are dedicated to serve us—the American people. As elected officials, their primary mission is to serve Americans; they are public servants!

This means our leaders' primary mission is to carry out our wants, needs, and desires—not their own. They are to look to us to make critical assessments, corrections, and refinements so they change direction to improve their ability to govern. This is fundamental to our system of checks and balances. Government leaders require our input in order to stay on track with fulfilling our collective vision. They then weigh our input in relation to the country's direction, and we collectively move the country forward. The bottom line is that since we have the responsibility to provide guidance, we are forced to think outside of our political parties and blind trust in order to hold our administration fully accountable to perform the job we hired them to perform.

I realize that attempting to observe all the nuances and complexities of our government and politics can be overwhelming. Even with a desire to understand and engage in critical thinking about our government, unless there is an easy way to wrap our brains around it, we will fall back into a pattern of deferring to others. This is a huge issue—probably one of the biggest deterrents to political engagement. An easier way to make observations and assessments is to use an analogy. An analogy provides appropriate parallels that we can relate to while also providing congruent context for understanding, observing, and making assessments.

To help us become better observers of what is happening in America, we need to view the country as a business enterprise. I find that using the analogy of our country as a fledging business enterprise is easier to understand and is an appropriate analogy. View President Obama as the president and CEO of the enterprise. Congress—the House of Representatives and Senate—should then be viewed as managers. Since all these people work for us, the only appropriate parallel is to view the American people as the board of directors. Now, let's observe what begins to happen when we, as fully-vested board members, begin to closely analyze the pattern and progression of our business under our new president.

We should understand that there is a relationship and communication that takes place between the board of directors and the president. Let's imagine that, as a member of the board, you are privy to communication and updates from other board members and from the president of our business—Obama. Board members are always concerned about the success of the business and how it's performing in relation to the business plan, so updates are encouraged. As you can imagine, various communications can sometimes conflict, depending on who is providing the updates. This is understandable.

Due to the high demands and risks associated with running our enterprise, there will always be some degree of mixed messages. It is the board members' responsibility, however, to validate what has been communicated and make assessments based on the vision, strategy, and goals of the enterprise. The bottom line is that the paradigm of communications between the president and the board of directors is essential to running the business enterprise. It provides the appropriate level of checks and balances that measure progress against the agreed-upon business plan. This kind of input allows the enterprise to stay on track and achieve its anticipated success!

We have seen that when our president updates us, his communications tend to be very general and seem to have just enough information to placate the board members. By conversing with other board members, however, we are able to access more information and get more specific. While it is in the best interest of everyone to hope our new president succeeds, most board members seem to be cautiously optimistic at this point. Because our president is new and has been hired into a chaotic mess, we must be his co-laborers in order to get this business back on track. Our job is to look closely for warning signs and risks that could undermine our ability to achieve success. When we see potential obstacles, we should warn the other board members about areas where our enterprise may be at risk. This provides an appropriate level of early intervention so we can anticipate and mitigate potential problem areas.

With that in mind, and in keeping with our analogy of viewing America as a business enterprise, the following is an example of an interoffice memo to all board members that updates and summarizes areas of concern and potential risks posed early in this new administration.

MEMO

To: All Board Members
From: Fellow Board Member
Re: Change is here!

Change is here! We have hired our new president and CEO, and he is already making strides towards changing the current and future direction our enterprise.

We know our new leader has been hired during a time of innumerable, daunting challenges. Though the challenges are huge, we should keep in mind we are still recognized as world leaders! The world still sees us as standard bearers of innovation and leadership, and anticipates that we will continue dominance as successful world leaders. While we are revered the world over, we must also remember we have many enemies who would love to see our enterprise fail. It seems everyone is waiting to see how our new president will combat our exploding budget and deficits; gross inefficiencies; legacy costs; and new, board-directed initiatives. Make no mistake—in order for us to succeed, these are the primary directives to which we will hold him and his administration accountable, as our challenges will require his immediate attention and focus.

Our new president and his administration certainly energize our high hopes and eagerness for change. While we will do all we can to fully support this new, energetic administration, this memo is provided to help keep everyone abreast of early signs and patterns that, if left unchecked, could pose significant risks and pitfalls to the continued success of our enterprise. Though we are still admittedly early in this new administration, awareness of some key policies and new initiatives will help us assess progress against our stated objectives, and if necessary, provide guidance to our new administration.

With that said, I have noted some areas I think require special attention, as they reflect unanticipated actions or new policy priorities and proposals. Please carefully consider these issues, as they provide us with early insight into our new administration's leadership and management style and vision—or lack thereof—for the future of our business enterprise!

First, we should note that our new president has had great difficulty attempting to fill key roles in his administration. He has personally interviewed—and subsequently proposed—several people for hire, but due to sketchy backgrounds and a general lack of ethics, many of these people failed to pass our basic employment standards. This wouldn't even be worth noting, except there has already been a pattern of far too many of these mistakes in judgment early in this administration. Additionally, instead of achieving results by unifying management ranks—as he exclaimed he would, prior to being hired—we have actually noticed a marked increase in polarization and intense bickering among members of our management teams.

On balance, these issues are seemingly small, but we cannot ignore them. They indicate we should look out for areas of overconfidence and naiveté with our new president. Since strong and unwavering leadership has proven a critical factor to our success, we need to be aware that there seems to be only a minimal competence in our current administration's leadership ability.

Another area that is critical to the success of any enterprise is finance. This is also an area that, due to recent patterns, raises potentially huge concern. Our new administration has proposed emergency spending plans and irrationally high budgets that have accelerated our spending and increased our deficits to the highest levels in our history. This is quite problematic, because it seems completely illogical that anyone would believe it prudent to significantly increase spending while we are experiencing ever-increasing budget deficits and one of the worst economic downturns in history.

In periods like this, rational and prudent strategies would require reduced spending and budget cuts instead of increased spending. Somehow, though, our new administration seems to think the opposite, and believes it is prudent to significantly increase our liabilities while also spending tens of billions of dollars on failing businesses and industries.

It seems we will have much to ponder, as some of our new administration's initiatives get underway. Early patterns are potentially problematic; it seems that, instead of focusing on budget efficiencies and improvements to our core services, there is a general lack of vision and focus. This administration's current leadership seems to be motivated to expand into more markets and buy more businesses without addressing our current business infrastructure, already wrought with huge inefficiencies. We cannot ignore that, at present, we have an unfocused administration with an incoherent vision and business strategy.

In summary, the foundations of any viable and successful business enterprise require unparalleled leadership, exceptional finance and accounting skills, and constant improvements and efficiencies derived from an intense commitment to vision and focus. What's disconcerting is that, when we begin to look objectively at the early days of this administration, we see that there is an emerging lack of leadership ability, worsening finances, and no apparent vision or focus. We can choose to simply dismiss these early warning patterns as part of the normal learning curve, or we can begin to pay close attention. As board members, the enclosed information is provided as simply an update on the state of our business. These facts will help us appropriately anticipate the future of our business, while also providing appropriate guidance to our administration's leadership and management team.

We have now been summarily advised about emerging patterns of seemingly illogical policies and irrational actions that could derail the success of our enterprise. Surely, we should support our administration any way we can, but current economic conditions require immediate action and a concerted strategy, and—unfortunately—"hope" is not a strategy! We should reject our propensity to extend blind faith and confirm to our leaders that we expect them to implement common sense approaches to our current crises in order to preserve and extend our leadership and success!

God bless us all,
Fellow Board Member

Still Too Early, or Far Too Late?

As we begin to look intently and make assessments about the issues confronting our country, we may be tempted to excuse patterns, policies, and behaviors by saying it's too early. I have had many discussions with people who are unwilling to engage in any serious thought about our current administration due to this mindset. While we may think it's still too early to even have an opinion about this new era, our new government is making dramatic policy changes on critical and pressing economic and social issues. Many of these changes are permanently altering the direction of our country, which may actually mean we are too late to express opinions. Since there is so much at stake, it would be irrational and imprudent to continue the claim of it being "too early" to have and express opinions about this new era. It is never too early for an opinion. While it may still be too early to draw definitive conclusions about the success or failure of our new era of government, making rational assessments based on what we see as emerging patterns is actually prudent and logical. It marks a genuine first step to overcoming the state of instanity.

To help illustrate the importance of looking objectively at early patterns and behaviors, we should consider the following analogy.

Let's imagine you are a frequent traveler on a particular bus route. You have taken this particular route many times over the decades and are quite familiar with its various twists, turns, and road hazards. Because it is a chaotic route, it requires only the most experienced driver. You have experienced many bus drivers over the years, and you have become quite familiar with their inclinations and nuances. You found some of the drivers had personality quirks, but the bottom line is that, regardless of their issues, they always appropriately navigated the twists, turns, and hazards, allowing you to safely arrive at your destination.

One day, you get on the bus and realize there is a new driver, and this happens to be his first day. You notice the driver seems very personable, charismatic, and well-intentioned, but he is obviously also new. You soon realize that he is not only new to this route, but he is also new to driving a bus. Since you know the route, you sit in the front of the bus to perhaps help or guide him. As he gets going, you realize he received many accolades from colleagues and high scores from his superiors where he received his training; his high marks, combined with his looks, charm, and confidence seem to somehow relax you into thinking that perhaps he is competent.

Soon after he starts driving, you notice he is making calls on his BlackBerry, sending text messages, primping in the mirror, and making charming conversation with other riders. He is obviously unfocused, but in deference to his personality and with knowledge that he is new, you overlook these early warnings.

You soon realize your driver is constantly partaking in various activities without proper focus on the journey and its many imminent road hazards. Since you want to successfully arrive at your destination, when should you begin to make assessments about his driving ability and provide guidance and input about the road ahead? Is it logical, reasonable, and prudent to excuse him because he is new, even though you know the road is tenuous, and that there are major hazards ahead?

Let's say you know there is a sharp turn ahead that requires decreased speed and extreme caution because of a cliff with a huge drop. Wouldn't it be an act of instant insanity to not warn him of the impending hazard? Would common sense tell you to excuse his patterns and behaviors, which put everyone at risk, by rationalizing that it's too early to assess his ability? It isn't reasonable or logical to wait until you take a sharp turn and go off of cliff; by then, it's too late! You have to assess driving ability early and sound a cautionary alarm based on patterns of behavior and known risks. In other words, it is wise and prudent to make early objective assessments, or everyone will be at risk.

Hopefully, you recognize through this analogy that if we see potential problems, it is our right and responsibility to make early objective assessments in order to prevent potentially disastrous consequences. This is exactly the predicament we face in America; we are on a critical and chaotic path that could present dire consequences to our Republic. At this juncture, America's pathway is wrought with many twists, turns, and hazards, and we need a driver who is focused and committed to getting us to our destination safely. We cannot allow media mania, the cult of personality, or even our zeal for hope and change to distract us from reality—what we really need is extreme competence and expertise.

As candidate Hillary Clinton said in a speech in Columbus during the presidential campaign, "When that phone rings ... There is no time for speeches or on-the-job training!" Impassioned rhetoric and soothing talk may make us feel good, but in this new era, all levels of our government leadership need to be highly competent and committed to success.

The prior analogy demonstrates what happens if we fail to exercise our common sense; the ultimate consequence is that we put everyone at risk. It also provides justification and credence as to why it's never too early to make assessments. Our country, our core principles, and our very souls depend on it. With that in mind, what should our response be? Our country is experiencing the worst economic downturn in many decades, and our leaders pursue policies that:

- increase taxation
- dramatically increase government budgets and spending
- encourage government dependence via significant increase in entitlements
- increase government expansion
- dramatically increase influence of unions and "special interests" on policy
- increase in bribes, fraud and corruption throughout White House and Congress
- increase government intervention and takeover of private companies
- increase appointments of rouge and nefarious characters to "key" policy positions
- reduce liberty and freedoms
- reduce strict adherence to the U.S. Constitution

Is it prudent, logical, and rational to simply defer to our government leaders as they confront these important issues?

Can it be described as anything but insane when we refuse to form opinions about these critical matters at this most critical juncture, simply because our government is new? These issues, in and of themselves, represent our pathway filled with extreme hazards. Do we sound early warnings or wait until we go over a cliff? We can choose selective instanity, or we can choose to exercise our responsibility to common sense, but since these choices mutually exclude one another, we can't do both. The bottom line is that America needs us to sound the alarm, and we must act!

We share a collective responsibility for America. America is our enterprise. We have been given the responsibility for helping steward her while keeping her successful and great as we navigate a new and uncertain path. Since America's structure is similar to that of a business enterprise—organizational hierarchy, vision and goals, ethics, budgets—we should make observations and assessments from the perspective of running a business. In this new era in government, keeping up with the many nuances and complexities is overwhelming, and it complicates our ability to make logical and rational assessments. If we can begin to view our government from the perspective of a business enterprise, however, we will have the capacity to make assessments based on appropriate and analogous business ethics and principles. Powerful new observations and assessments will ensue, and we will have the capacity to hold our leaders accountable. Then, real change, which will perpetuate the success of our country, can again take hold.

Let's begin to rebuild our enterprise.

Enterprising America

> "Nothing is more essential to the establishment of manners in a State than that all persons employed in places of power and trust must be men of unexceptionable characters."
>
> —Samuel Adams

The analogy of America as a business enterprise and our government officials as our employees is powerful. It provides an appropriate method to better comprehend how our government is supposed to work for us, while also providing a coherent understanding of the various actions and policies being implemented that are irrational, illogical, and rather insane. It allows us to see a firsthand account of instanity, which seems to have swept over our government officials.

Instanity can be very subtle. If we allow ourselves to become gripped by and swept into an irrational fervor without ever contemplating whether actions are helping achieve an anticipated goal, instanity can prevail. Once instanity is present, we begin to make irrational excuses for behavior. We selectively cling to instanity, anticipating that our hope and zeal will manifest into a positive outcome. We all know this way of thinking is just wishful thinking and is completely irrational.

The way to break a cycle of instanity is to commit to objectively look at the facts and make common sense assessments based on those facts. In the case of our current government administration, we should want to see it for what is. Unfortunately, it's a mess!

In the Beginning Was the Word(s) ...

"Here comes the orator! With his flood of words, and his drop of reason."

—Benjamin Franklin

I am sure most—if not all—of us thought a Barack Obama was highly improbable. The likelihood that a new, inexperienced politician of African-American descent would become the new President of the United States was almost unfathomable. The historic significance of someone rising from the ranks of community worker to permanently upsetting the historical and political spectrum has many speaking about Obama in messianic terms. Even now, it seems the current administration arose almost supernaturally! It was an incredible accomplishment, and—at the same time—it provides a good demonstration of our own collective state: We were quite desperate.

Let us not forget, we were in a period of American history when we were experiencing disenchantment, disenfranchisement, and an overall feeling of disappointment with the prior administration. Wars, burgeoning deficits, out of control spending, and other missteps made the Bush administration unpopular and the need for change inevitable. We were looking for someone different, and that meant we were definitely a captive audience for anyone who represented the possibility of real change. Therefore, when Obama capitalized on hope and

44

change, we allowed it to resonate strongly and to transform us. Ultimately, we became resolute in our commitment to it.

Hope and change are powerful words. They are especially powerful during times of desperation. As we have seen, they can provide a rallying call that can unify, captivate, and provide enthusiasm to an entire nation. Since these words were used to captivate us, and we relied on them to dictate our voting decisions, don't you think it's time we find out what they mean? Shouldn't we know what these words represent to our country and our future? What should we expect from an administration that has sold us on this new era?

A full year has elapsed since this new administration took office. During the election process, change was touted as having an immediate impact for all Americans—not gradual or subtle. Now is the perfect time for us, as thinking Americans, to see exactly what kind of hope and change have already begun on our behalf. Additionally, we should look for patterns in the Obama recipe for change; we need to distinguish them so we anticipate how it will impact our future.

The first step to producing any change on a nationwide scale is strong leadership. Leadership is the primary criterion that is the start and finish of major initiatives. In our scenario, it will mean either the beginning of a great new era in governance or the end of what has made America successful and resilient over the years. Barack Obama is our leader, so let's begin to objectively assess his capacity for leadership.

Leading by Leadership

As members of the board of directors, one of our primary duties is to continually assess our new employee—in this case, Barack Obama—and his administration from the perspective of whether or not we have effective leadership. In order to gain confidence about whether we can meet our desired goals and our vision for success, we need to be able to objectively assess the style and substance of our leaders. This provides a window into the future, as strong, competent leadership is more likely to secure a strong and successful future.

Before we can appropriately assess our leader's competence in this arena, let's first understand some of the basic criteria of good leadership. There are many great books that confirm the characteristics of a great leader. In essence, we find that good leaders are expected to have an even greater capacity for personal commitment, strength, integrity, and courage. We refer to a natural leader as one who seems to be the embodiment of these characteristics, naturally. What separates great leaders from all others is that they live their lives with a significantly greater capacity for these leadership traits.

As mentioned, a strong leader is what we will need to help ensure our success as we enter into this new and uncertain era. We should understand that one of the hazards of leadership is there many people who deem themselves leaders but are wholly disqualified because all they have acquired is academic understanding that is theoretical and abstract, with no real life experience; most of their understanding then, comes from abstract philosophy and anecdotal hypothesis developed (primarily) in a classroom.

It is prudent, then, to objectively analyze our current leadership by evaluating actions and policies against what the experts have already confirmed as the necessary traits for competent and strong leaders. This analysis will help logically and rationally assess whether our leaders are likely to be effective and successful while moving us in the right direction.

Since everyone has unique skills and styles, one of the most critical and completely observable functions of a president is his form of leadership. During times of dramatic change, leadership is especially observable, because there are considerable pressures, uncertainty, and chaos. A good example of this is during the 9/11 attacks and their resulting devastation. We were able to get a sense of President Bush's leadership style.

It is important to note that the general style and pattern that characterized him on 9/11 followed him throughout his presidency. Now, President Obama has inherited additional fallout from 9/11, plus huge additional economic challenges, and it is his opportunity to respond. With all that he has inherited, plus historic worldwide chaos and the pressure of trying to prove himself, we should already be getting a sense of general pattern and style of leadership.

If we view America as a business enterprise, strong and determined leadership will determine whether our enterprise will have continued success or become a failure. Leadership is at the core of every successful enterprise, as business experts consistently regard strong leadership as a foundation for any successful venture. So, before looking at the policies and various initiatives of our leader, we must first begin by understanding and assessing his leadership style.

Using noted leadership criteria, while carefully assessing leadership style and overall leadership ability, will help provide the objectivity needed in order to evaluate this important quality.

According to well-known business management author Ken Blanchard, author of *The One Minute Manager*, the best leaders are characterized by strong desire and commitment to serve. The best presidents and CEOs of businesses are fervent in fulfilling their commitment to serve their constituents— board members, employees, customers, and partners. They work hard and sacrifice all to make sure they not only meet, but actually exceed, the demands and expectations of their constituents. They also make many promises about goals, visions, and policies, and they consistently fulfill them. It is all too common that leaders (and especially or current U.S. leadership) have become wholly entranced with the status of leadership rather than object of leadership which is service. This produces an incessant need and struggle to defend the status quo. But if put in its proper perspective with the object of service being the focus of leadership, nobody would struggle to hold to it nor defend it. This is a true commitment to service.

In his book, *The Age of Unreason,* Charles Handy says that "effective leaders have integrity." He goes further to state that integrity means being true to oneself. One of the biggest problems we see with our leaders today is that they are not consistently acting with integrity and are not fully committed to fulfilling promises. It almost seems that their primary commitment—due to their apparent intoxication with power—is their absolute reverence to the platform and position and not to service.

Well-known leadership and management authors and consultants like Ken Blanchard, Stephen Covey (*The Seven Habits of Highly Effective People*), Peter Senge (*The Fifth Discipline*), and Max DePree (*Leadership is an Art*) confirm that leaders who are committed and enthused to serve make the best leaders. Great leaders are people with servants' hearts. They are not only driven by the excitement of meeting challenges and overcoming them, but also by the desire to serve the best interests of their countries, employers, constituents, etc.

Conversely, there are also leaders who can only be deemed as mediocre because they have a tendency to covet position and title rather than a commitment to the service of others. We have seen many examples of these types, who are driven by selfish ambition and are prone to make bad decisions and invite corruption. With these people, the biggest motivation isn't service; instead, it is a strong desire to maintain the status quo. This way, they can hold on to their power and positions. This is typical of what we see today in all aspects of business and government, and it seems to have become an integral part of Washington politics.

Unfortunately, we have many leaders who are career politicians. Many have never held a private sector job or worked in any capacity outside of Washington. They have built entire careers, spanning multiple decades, and are prominently known as career politicians instead of public servants. Washington politics have a tendency to corrupt, so when politicians are in office for decades, they can become smitten with power and will do anything to keep their cushy positions and increase their power and money. Unfortunately, the vicious cycle of power and politics is being played at our expense and demise, and not out of a sincere commitment to serve. Prior to taking his new role, Barack Obama promised to end this cycle, and we optimistically embraced this supposed new era.

We should ask ourselves, are there any indications that we have ushered in a new, positive era in politics? Or are we feeling the consequences of incompetent leaders with the wrong motivations and intentions? If our leaders respond when we demand they change course, we have a good indication that they are listening. How are we to interpret times when our leaders disregard our demands by ramming incoherent health care reforms down our throat instead of immediately cutting spending and deficits? What about when our leaders pretend to know nothing of the thousands of protests about their out-of-control tax burden, and therefore do nothing? If they were committed to serve, wouldn't our leaders at least listen to our concerns about increased government expansion and begin to look for ways to streamline and reduce government intrusion?

Even with slumping poll numbers and our many protests and commentary, we have leaders who are set on forcing their personal agendas onto our enterprise while disregarding our protests.

We are now at a point in history when our lethargy and instanity have emboldened our leaders to completely disregard us, their employers. Though we hired these leaders to serve us by looking out for our best interests, they don't seem to have a commitment to serve us. Their actions and patterns indicate that they are looking to implement strategies that will allow them to take full advantage of this new era of unbridled government dominance in order to fulfill their personal agendas. This pattern confirms that we have many leaders who are wholly committed to being—first and foremost—politicians. Their zeal to get elected was about personal ambition and not about serving us. It is disheartening to realize that, contrary to campaign promises, an entirely new administration has emerged that seems to be committed to being the best politicians they can be. Thus far, we have seen that this new administration is the best at raising money and at power brokering but, unfortunately, they come up woefully short when it comes to being the best public servants they can be.

Knowing that one criterion of great leadership is commitment to service, how would you grade our current leaders? Objectively evaluating the aforementioned leadership issues is a good first step in overcoming the state of instanity. Though we have a propensity to give our leaders high marks, it would be irresponsible and insane to do so after objectively assessing them using standard leadership criteria. I see few policy initiatives that reflect the will of the majority of Americans, and because of that, our leaders thus far deserve a very poor grade. All is not lost, however, as there are other aspects of leadership that should be also objectively considered.

Accolades and "Credit" Earned Through Credibility

Another major aspect of good leadership is establishment of strong credibility. It has been said that credibility is the currency of leadership. Leaders are expected to be straight shooters. Good leaders say what they mean and mean what they say. Regardless of the possible fallout, leaders take full responsibility for their actions and deeds while speaking candidly and from the heart. This builds integrity and allows for an effective foundation for rapidly building trust.

In their book *Leaders,* Warren Bennis and Burt Nanus confirm, "Trust is the emotional glue that binds followers and leaders together."

We find that the ability to quickly build confidence and trust is an essential attribute of a good and effective leader. With that, let's assess how our leaders are doing in the area of credibility.

From the start, our new leaders have produced a credibility deficit. Within our current leadership, we have witnessed many flip-flops and directional changes that seem to indicate indecision and a lack of resolve. There seem to have been more directional changes within this administration than with any other in recent history. Both during and after the campaign, we have seen many unprecedented directional changes. This sends mixed signals, as it indicates confusion, uncertainty, and—in many cases—just plain incompetence.

Promises were made about not allowing earmarks, not hiring lobbyists as executive staff, closing Gitmo within one year, Iraq troop withdrawal deadlines within one year, and assuring that 95% of citizens would receive tax reductions. Unfortunately, none of these commitments were achieved as promised. While these issues are problematic, there is also a very specific instance that confirms a huge leadership deficit exacerbated by credibility issues, and that's the promise of unity.

When Barack Obama campaigned for his position, he promised to shake up the status quo in Washington. He promised "no more business as usual" and vehemently defended his own track record—that his commitment was more indicative of a maverick than John McCain's. He promised he would be just what Washington needed in order to change the direction of our government and its respective politics. Many months have passed since his arrival in Washington. However, there are no indications of a Washington makeover; the political climate shows absolutely no sign of a political shake-up.

We have instead witnessed what most would call the absolute worst and most dire demonstration of politics as usual. The current political climate in Washington is marked by incessant partisan bickering, excessive power brokering, replete with buying votes, kick-backs, scandals, and untoward personal agendas that revolve around money and power. There is an unprecedented and shameful degree of polarity in Washington, with none of the bipartisanship and unity we were promised. Recent Gallup Polls (Jan 25, 2010) confirm Barack Obama is the most polarizing first year president in history! We certainly see commitment, but unfortunately, we see a commitment to maintain the status quo instead of permanently ending it. What happened? Where is the unity we were promised? Where is the bipartisanship, transparency, and change? It boils down to a lack of leadership. Ronald Reagan said it best when he quipped, "Since when do we in America believe that our society is made up of two diametrically opposed classes—one rich, one poor— both in a permanent state of conflict and neither able to get ahead except at the expense of the other? Since when do we in America accept this alien and discredited theory of social and class warfare? Since when do we in America endorse the politics of envy and division?"

In their book *Leaders: Strategies for Taking Charge,* authors Warren Bennis and Burt Nanus confirm that "the leader is responsible for the set of ethics or norms that govern the behaviors of the people in the organization." They go further to state that "in the end, trust, integrity and positioning are all different faces of a common property of leadership." Based on this description, America is facing a lack of leadership.

The American people are left holding onto nothing but broken promises, but we want, expect, and demand change in Washington politics. Our leaders seem to have completely disregarded this issue while taking full advantage of our extension of goodwill. Again, the primary currency of leadership is credibility, and leaders must think and act with integrity at all times by saying what they mean and meaning what they say. Right now, we are witnessing a pattern that demonstrates a lack of integrity, and therefore, a loss of credibility. There have been far too many instances where a strong commitment to leadership could have been exerted in order to follow through on promises, but our leaders have failed. Again, this confirms that fundamentally, we are devoid of leaders who actually know how to lead.

Riding a huge wave of excitement and momentum, it would have been relatively easy for Obama to shake up the status quo in Washington. After all, the whole election was about change, so certainly other leaders would have responded if there had been a push to change the paradigm. It would have taken real leadership and resolve, but certainly it could have been done—what a disappointing lost opportunity!

Instead of using his momentum to produce a big win for us, our leaders seem to have chosen to use our enthusiasm to pursue their own personal and political gain. In the end, we are not getting the change and unity we expected; instead, we have the most bitter and partisan political climate ever witnessed. Since we now know that our leaders lack credibility, how should we assess current leadership? Are they truly looking out for our best interests?

As mentioned, a good leader is committed to serving the interest of his constituents. As a leader, the President of the United Sates has the most visible job in the world; he becomes a de facto world leader. This means that our president not only has to commit himself to serving our interest domestically, but also has to stand up for and serve America's interests when on the world stage with other world leaders.

"Serve" is a key term. Regardless of where he is or what he is doing, our president is elected to serve our collective interests in every situation—24/7! This means when an overwhelming majority of the country rejects current proposed versions of health care reforms, a good leader and president will refrain from forcing his personal vision and agenda, and instead heed to collective voices for *serving* collective interests. Our history confirms that a singular and steadfast commitment to serve the collective interests of all factions of the enterprise—including the board of directors, management teams, employees, and customers—is one of the key traits that separates highly successful CEOs from those who are less successful. This is one trait that made President Ronald Reagan a great president and leader. If our current leader is to succeed, he must learn to serve us by standing firmly on our behalf while consistently reinforcing American values, even in the midst of our enemies and allies.

Our leader has been hired to carry out our strategic vision. A key determinant of whether or not he is doing a good job is whether his purposeful actions align with our vision and goals. That said, one of our primary goals is to protect our interests nationally and internationally so we can enhance our leadership and success around the world. Obviously our enemies and allies are spread throughout the world, so effective leadership requires diplomacy and strength. We should note that sometimes, strong diplomacy demands that we take a tough stance.

When we were deciding the election, Obama's lack of experience dealing with enemies and allies was seen as a huge risk. Since many entities around the world would love to undermine the continued success of our enterprise, a strong leader is definitely needed. This area was a big unknown, as there were no prior experiences that indicated fortitude and mettle when faced with difficult and confrontational situations. We did have early indications, however, as there seemed to be a willingness to have unconditional conversations with enemies. Obama was perceived as soft—one who would squander decades of strong and purposeful leadership with a marginal leadership style that showed lack of resolve and an illogical penchant for appeasement.

True to form, our president defended himself as a naturally strong leader, and when there was speculation that he would be soft, he forcefully commented that he is not an "appeaser," and that his form of diplomacy would entail dialogue—sometimes forceful—but not appeasement.

Now Serving: Appeasement and Apologies ... Come and get it!

Thus far, we have witnessed a leadership style that should give us reason for concern, as it leaves much to be desired. We have already noted that the standard for good leadership is a commitment to serve. A good leader must also be committed to delivering upon our strategic vision, and he must be authoritative and precise while defending our interests on the world stage.

Due to some missteps and transgressions that occasionally occurred within past administrations, our new leadership team is trying very hard to distance itself from prior policies. In doing so, we seem to be producing an irresponsible lapse of leadership and judgment that will likely cause our already fragile enterprise to be even more vulnerable to those who wish us harm. While there may be good and noble reasons for trying to distance ourselves from past transgressions, it should only be entertained as an option if it can be done while maintaining a strong leadership stance. If not, pursuing this direction will not serve the best interests of our enterprise, and will only put us at increased risk. For over one hundred years, our enterprise has successfully maneuvered through worldwide chaos, wars, famine, and innumerable challenges. It is our history of strong and determined leadership that has allowed us to succeed through constant turmoil. We have been the standard bearers of world leadership while protecting freedoms and liberty. We have become the envy of the world, and it seems erroneously arrogant for a new era of leadership to undermine and undo the many decades of strong and successful leadership in order to chart a new—and quite uncertain—era of diplomacy.

Since all world leaders are appointed to also serve their own country's interests, strength and conviction in commitment to serve are vitally important for anyone elected president. As hard as it is to admit, we will unfortunately have to come to grips with the fact that the era of diplomacy our new president has embarked upon is marked by a willful strategy to appease and apologize to our allies and enemies. Ironically, there are no leadership or management books that cite appeasement and apology as effective strategies for world-class leadership ... so why do it? There are no known case studies or historical precedence of any kind that lead us to believe that appeasement is a viable strategy. Is this naiveté, sheer incompetence, or both?

To clarify, I define *appeasement* as the act of yielding or conceding to the demands of others in a conciliatory effort, at the expense of our principles. A good example of appeasement is when our leader dropped a key demand on Iran and allowed it to keep nuclear facilities open, while pursuing nuclear enrichment and missile testing, in order to supposedly explore nuclear energy alternatives, despite the fact that the country has an overabundance of existing energy sources.

A good example of apologizing is when we saw our leader in Strasbourg, France, and he seemingly proudly exclaimed, "In America, there is a failure to appreciate Europe's leading role in the world. Instead of celebrating your dynamic union and seeking to partner with you to meet common challenges, there have been times when America has shown arrogance and been dismissive—even derisive" (CNN Politics, April 2009). Though there are many more examples, these are just two that clearly point to a penchant to appease and apologize.

It has been stated that this president has been more critical of U.S. policy and history in just his first few months in office than any other president in history. The criticisms and apologies are endless, and our enemies are taking full advantage.

Our allies *and* our enemies have a huge appetite for any of our perceived weaknesses. Underestimating our enemies is no virtue, though for them, it is certainly helpful. As we serve up a string of apologies and look for opportunities to appease, we become the conduit to feed our enemies' ravenous appetite to take advantage of weakness as they look to gorge themselves on all the contrition we dish out. For them, it shows that the U.S. admits wrongdoing and failed policy decisions. This presents an ideal environment for their media and propaganda machines to spin stories, take sound bites out of context, and rewrite history to benefit their extreme ideologies. By replaying select portions of apologetic speeches along with scenes of hugs, kisses, and subservient bowing to rogue regimes, we enable new tactics for recruitment of extremists and breed even more fervent ideologues. On the world stage, wrought with enemies who wish to do harm, any sign of contrition and weakness will be used to our detriment.

It seems to me that anyone who has even a basic understanding of leadership can understand this simple concept. Instead of embarking upon and blindly trusting a newfangled and unproven strategy to appease—a strategy that could completely undermine our many decades of world leadership—shouldn't we be at least willing to ask how a strategy to appease and apologize helps further our vision of perpetuating strong leadership around the world? With all that we have at stake, wouldn't it be insane to simply defer to a leader with virtually no experience or expertise in the arena of world leadership?

As board members, we should consider the success of past administrations and weigh our history of strength and resolve against this new, apologetic strategy. Exactly how does this new strategy align with our strategic vision to remain a strong and principled enterprise? How are our best interests served by a strategy that involves appeasement and apologies for past ills? Conventional wisdom and common sense confirm that a strong leader always takes a strong and committed stance on behalf of his constituents. This is how he demonstrates service!

Historically, we have been blessed with strong leaders— Jimmy Carter notwithstanding—who have acted in our best interest while collaborating with other world leaders. What are we to think about our new leader and his administration when they have purposefully and strategically decided that it is now in our best interest to appease and apologize to our allies and enemies? Why is it necessary?

When Nicaragua's Daniel Ortega spends an hour in an anti-American rant, calling our leader the "president of an empire," shouldn't a strong condemnation, or at least leaving the room, have been the response? When a rogue nation like Cuba sends signs that they are willing to have dialogue, then clarifies by saying they are not willing to negotiate human rights as part of any dialogue, shouldn't we stand firm for the principles and values of human rights? Unfortunately, our leader accommodated and acquiesced on these occasions. Instead of contrition and acquiescence, a strong and principled leader is one who is willing to engage others, but not at the expense of his own principles. A good leader is one who will not compromise his commitment to principles, but instead will stand firm on them.

With every new leader, there is hope and expectation for a new beginning. Around the world, our allies and enemies also have high hopes and expectation for new beginnings. This, in most cases, provides for a grace period and an extension of good will. It is most prudent to use this period to renew relationships and establish new beginnings by confirming a break from past administrations—by conveying the new leadership style and mutual expectations.

What style of leadership was being conveyed when our president bowed to King Abdullah of Saudi Arabia at a G-20 meeting in London? Do you think Saudi Arabia will expect that we will have strong or weak leadership?

Saudi Arabia is a country that perpetuates significant human rights atrocities issues, mostly related to mistreatment of women, and our president—who is supposed to stand for our values and principles—bowed to the Saudi king! We should try to understand the ramifications of this, since in the Islamic world, bowing is a sign of subservience.

Our new leader, acting on our behalf and within the scope of power and authority we have granted him, actually appeared to present us as subservient to Saudi Arabia (Islam). Though there was footage of this obvious bow as an act of subservience, how did we withhold outrage? Can it be that we actually believe the White House's assertion that this act wasn't actually a bow, even though our eyes confirm the contrary? Actually, it seems our leader has some sort of "irritable bow syndrome;" he seems to be compelled to bow as a standard greeting. While on his trip to Asia he bowed (deeply and at the hips) to the Emperor of Japan and more recently he even bowed to the mayor of Tampa, Florida! It should be noted that none of these recipients duly reciprocated. In our zeal for new hope, have we become completely blind to obvious insanity?

Let's consider this scenario again, using the analogy of America as a business enterprise, with President Obama as the president and CEO and Saudi Arabia as one of our business partners. In our analogy, let's say that our business has a long history of success and strong business ethics that have actually allowed us to become the dominant leader worldwide. Let's also say that our business partner has a history of weak ethics and unfair and oppressive business practices that are clearly contrary to our successful business practices.

Common sense should indicate that, as the leader, we are in a position to positively impact and influence our partner. Instead, however, our new president decides to acquiesce and appease by actually telling our much smaller and less successful business partner that our practices are subservient to theirs. How does this tactic align with common sense? Would we deem our president as a competent and strong leader if we knew he would represent our company in such an irresponsible way?

Historically, we are perceived as a principled nation with strong values and commitment to freedoms. Over the past several decades, we have become standard bearers—the model of successful world leadership. Though others may disagree with us at times, we have maintained this designation by extolling our virtues and noble efforts without apology. Strength and fortitude have characterized us. As the world becomes even more chaotic and unpredictable, we need even more strength and resolve. Why should we start appeasing and apologizing now? Has this strategy ever worked for a world leader?

Prior to becoming president, our leader promised us there would be no appeasement; specifically, he said, "I am not an appeaser." Regardless of what was said, it is clear that our president's actions are the exact opposite of his pre-election rhetoric. These actions are not trivial, as they actually put us more at risk. We will be perceived as soft, naive, gullible, and weak, which are not positive attributes in this new and chaotic climate. We will all share in suffering consequences of these actions unless we provide guidance.

We cannot afford to have delusions about having strong leadership. Our administration has demonstrated a pattern of selfish and partisan motives instead of servant motives. Our leader believes in an apologetic strategy for past ills instead of looking forward, and he has definite patterns of appeasing our enemies instead of standing firm on principles. Unfortunately, these traits represent the antithesis of acceptable standards for good, common sense leadership. After seriously considering the aforementioned leadership issues, we can only objectively arrive at one logical conclusion and assessment: At best, we have hired a president who is a novice and lacks strength and decisiveness. Unfortunately, we have given our president the most important job in the world during perhaps the most important time in history, and that requires an incredible amount of leadership responsibility. This is another clear example that a state of instanity is prevalent, and we are fully responsible.

We chose who we thought would be a good, competent leader. However, our choice can only be classified as weak, reckless, and quite naive. People who work with or for our leader who are aligned with his ideology try to strongly defend his leadership. Though we have carefully deconstructed what makes a good leader and contrasted patterns, actions, and policies of our president, many will still ardently defend him. Let us understand that since we hired our president as our employee, he works for us; employers are the only ones who can assess employees.

Based on actions, promises, and commitments made to us, we see a pattern of weak leadership. This pattern appears nonexistent for those vested in his success and who work for or with him. What we see goes well beyond political parties, racial politics, and wishful thinking; this now comes down to holding our leader accountable to his own words and deeds. We are the only ones who can assess his leadership—or lack thereof. Assessments of people who work with, for, or around him don't matter!

As employers, we are responsible for evaluating employees to provide help and guidance. When employees begin to show signs of incompetence and difficulty in transitioning to a new job, employers are responsible for providing the guidance needed in order to help them become successful. Our new leader is obviously trying to figure things out with on-the-job training during the most challenging time in our history. Since he has never led at this level, he requires guidance. We run the huge risk of having our employee fail, and in the process, ruining our enterprise, unless we tell him what we expect, and how we expect him to represent us while on the world stage. If we just continue to lavish praise, he will have no way of knowing he is not appropriately meeting our expectations.

How did we get here, anyway? I know there may still be a desire to give our current leadership the benefit of the doubt, since it is early in their tenure. We even may be tempted to dismiss all the aforementioned evidence as too trivial to seriously consider making an assessment of incompetence. Regardless of hope, it is reasonable and prudent to at least look closely at why and how we now are in the predicament of having novice leadership at such a critical time in history.

CHAPTER FOUR

Background to Foreground: The Dawn of An Unprecedented President

"In selecting men for office, let principle be your guide. Regard not the particular sect or denomination of the candidate - look to his character ...."

—Noah Webster, Letters to a Young Gentleman
Commencing His Education, 1789

Being the President of the U.S. is the most important job in the world. This job requires the establishment of a vision and a course for America. It requires the establishment of policy, domestic and foreign, and it requires the establishment of budget and finance priorities. Additionally, it requires providing guidance to Congress concerning social policy and initiatives, while effectively demonstrating strong leadership, commitment, and competence. This would be an ambitious undertaking for anyone, and it would be especially problematic for someone with scant knowledge, experience, and without a proven track record of competence.

After reviewing the rapid progress of our president, we should have suspected he was going to be in well over his head. Though our leader had approximately seven years as an Illinois senator and approximately one year as U.S. senator before beginning his campaign for president, he was still a relative unknown.

How is it possible that someone could serve his state and our nation for eight years without amassing notable achievements, accomplishments, or a good track record? How is it possible to maintain relative obscurity in this environment—a culture that relies on mass information and communication in the instant information age? Voting records and authoring or sponsoring key legislation would tell us much, but we still knew very little about our soon-to-be president. Why?

Our leader's voting track record provided little indication of who he was or what he stood for. Instead of demonstrating commitment to principles and standing up for his convictions, many times our leader choose to defer his voting rights and obligations by simply voting "present" as an Illinois state senator. This ensured there was no record that would provide any indication of who he is or what he represented. Unfortunately, the pattern of leaving a scant voting track record followed him to the U.S. senate as well. After eight years of political participation, we were still left without knowledge of who our new candidate was or what he stood for.

Obama was a politician for several years, yet a very limited political history and a lack of proven success didn't prevent his ascent. He was masterful and calculated in using his exposure in politics to hone his oratory skills. He had enough subtle nuances to produce an air of sincerity. It seems he knew how to speak eloquently and in melodic terms with just enough hype to cloud our thinking. With all the rhetoric and high hopes, we actually thought it made sense to choose a person with no work experience in the private sector, no military service, no executive management experience, and no proven leadership experience. We handed him the most important job on the planet.

When you seriously consider the enormity of it, it would have been remarkable for him to not experience exceptional challenges under these circumstances. In reality, though, it is insane to have expected different results than what we're currently experiencing. When he came on the scene, our new leader was definitely a breath of fresh air. He bounded onto the scene as an outsider, and—almost overnight—provided us optimism for new hopes and dreams. There is no doubt that his rise to the top has been truly remarkable. Perhaps this is what has prompted our willingness to overlook glaring deficiencies while considering him for the job of the presidency.

Throughout the presidential campaign, we saw a world-class marketing campaign that was heavily scripted and seemingly devoid of genuine character and resolve. We experienced image-making with a flair of oratorical spin that was unmatched. Many words were spoken, but they were just nebulous enough to escape real meaning and accountability. Though we all heard the rhetoric and were enthused to participate in a new era of politics, we knew very little about the man we ultimately hired. We were seduced into a rhetorical trance that captivated our high hopes and wishful thinking. Powerful words delivered with grace, charisma, and charm blinded us from looking intently into issues related to competency and commitment.

Prior to our hire of him, there was little known of our president. Even associates who had worked alongside him for years were still somewhat clueless as to whom he really was; we knew nothing of his leadership style or his competency in governing. None came forward to assert his accomplishments and past successes as evidence of his competency and commitment to succeed. The fact is, the closer we came to the election, the more questions we had about who this person was. It is amazing that no one seemed to actually know who he really was and what he fundamentally believed. Until the night of the election, we were quite unsure about what kind of leader we were getting. Irrationality prevailed, however, because for whatever reason, we felt the risk of the unknown was worth taking, especially since we were fed up with the prior administration. We were deluded into believing that anything would be better than the outgoing administration. Unfortunately, our zeal for hope and change ushered in a genuine state of instanity.

How could we have elected someone with absolutely no record? Contrary to what we want to believe about our new leader's experience, he has never run a business, governed a state, or worked in the White House. How could we elect someone with no proven skills and no expertise or competence as our president and world leader? The only logical answer is that we were ambushed by high-gloss marketing that pushed good looks and personality. In the end, we followed a manufactured persona instead of credible experience and proven competence. The tactic was to distract us from looking for substance, and—based on the outcome—it was a perfect strategy. We wholeheartedly fell for it!

Think about it: If we are completely focused on good looks and polished speech, we will overlook and even dismiss the obvious lack of experience. We will tend to overlook the many flip-flops, gaffes, and complete reliance on the teleprompter as trivial and unimportant when compared to our renewed optimism. We were driven by optimism and wishful thinking at a time when our world required leaders grounded in definitive realism. In actuality, there were glaring indicators that confirmed a lack of competence, yet we completely ignored them.

While we were engrossed with personality, we neglected to ask tough questions about experience, proven competency, and accomplishments. We didn't even care to scrutinize his résumé, and now we scratch our heads about what went wrong in our vetting process. The plain and simple answer is this: *We* went wrong. We instantly and willfully neglected our instincts toward logic and allowed a charming new personality to cloud our vetting.

The irony of the predicament we're in is that there were

actually many early signs and indicators we could have used to assess Obama's personality and inclinations. By carefully observing his friends and associates, we could have arrived at early assessments or rational conclusions. He went to the top colleges, and, in addition to professors, he had many friends and associates who helped shape his thinking and who were privy to his personal agenda.

I am sure we all have heard the old cliché, "Show me your friends, and I'll show you your future." In truth, our parents probably referred to this cliché many times as they warned us about hanging out with the wrong people. I use it even now to teach my children about being wary of the company they keep, as their choices can ruin their futures. Our close friends and associates provide a window into our thinking and confirm the pathway of our future. If we would have been willing to apply this truism in order to get a more grounded assessment of our leader, we could have discovered quite a lot about his personality and proclivities.

When questions arose about our president's background, he admonished us to look at those with whom he surrounded himself. He encouraged us to look at his friends and acquaintances to see how he would govern. This was good advice. We should do exactly as he recommended and take a close look at his foundations and relationships to gauge his perspective and world view.

By his own admission, the early foundational influences of our president came from his experiences as a community organizer. During his tenure as a community organizer, he studied, taught, and discipled other community organizers on the radical principles authored and proposed by Saul Alinski. Through a simple analysis and understanding of Saul Alinsky and his basic philosophy, we should gain some insight and perspective on our new leader. Here is an overview of Saul Alinsky's work and philosophy.

· · ·

67

"Barack Obama's training in Chicago by the great community organizers is showing its effectiveness," Alinsky, Jr. wrote to the *Globe.* "It is an amazingly powerful format, and the method of my late father always works to get the message out and get the supporters on board. When executed meticulously and thought-fully, it is a powerful strategy for initiating change and making it really happen. Obama learned his lesson well."

Saul Alinsky was an early community organizer based in Chicago. Alinsky's basic philosophy was to bring about social reform by organizing in mass community power. He was a social reformer who brought together community groups to work with socially aware churches and other organizations who were committed to change. His work should be thought of as a primary reference point for community organizing and community development. To further his work and reach beyond Chicago, Alinsky published a book called *Rules for Radicals.* This book admonished community organizers and young radicals to begin new hope and change through constructive, nonviolent methods. The *Rules* became the de-facto manual for community organizers. *Rules for Radicals* was specifically written for people considered the have-nots. It provided them with specific strategies for how to transfer wealth away from those considered the haves. Fundamentally, Alinsky's book outlines strategies for community organizers to follow when bringing together people bent on what he deemed social and political justice. He espoused principles of sharing wealth, as he believed that if we will not share part of our material wealth, we will lose all of it.

. . .

In the push to immediately remake America, our leader has begun to rapidly implement policy and strategies for higher taxes on the wealthy—transfer wealth from the haves, per Alinsky—while more than tripling deficit and debt for implementing social and political "justice," (another key Alinsky tenet), and burdening an already crippled government with health care—social "change."

Common sense tells us it doesn't make sense to implement any of these initiatives during a time of major, worldwide crises and economic upheaval. However, these policies may make perfect sense to those with an overriding desire to implement community organizing strategies—to immediately level the playing field through redistribution of wealth. In an interview on Chicago Public Radio, Obama spouted, " ... *the Constitution is a charter of negative liberties. Says what the states can't do to you. Says what the Federal government can't do to you, but it doesn't say what the Federal government or State government must do on your behalf, and that hasn't shifted and one of the, I think, the tragedies of the civil rights movement was because the civil rights movement became so court focused I think there was a tendency to lose track of the political and community organizing and activities on the ground that are able to put together the actual coalitions of powers through which you bring about redistributive change ...*"

There is no doubt the Alinsky legacy continues through our president. One of the most troubling aspects of this is, unfortunately the Alinsky model is being learned and passed on in the form of indoctrination on our school- aged children. As it is, our kids are targeted for liberal progressive agendas, now we will have to be even more vigilant about Marxist/Socialist agendas being thrust upon our children. Recent reports confirm our president is using our public school system to recruit for Organizing for America (OFA), which is formerly known as Obama For America. This organization has noted its agenda as "to build on the movement that elected President Obama by empowering students across the country to help us bring about our agenda". Hmm ... What agenda? The Alinsky socialist agenda? It should be noted that the required reading for participants in this program is, among other things, Saul Alinsky's Rules for Radicals.

Our president has been referred to as a Marxist, a socialist, a radical liberal, an extremist, and many other inflammatory descriptions. In light of the policy and actions we are seeing, these descriptions may be harsh, but not necessarily unfair or ungrounded. They may actually be the most accurate way to describe Obama and this new era. To help clarify why these characterizations may be appropriate descriptions, it is necessary to have a basic understanding of the terms.

A socialist can be summarily described "as a person who holds economic and political theories advocating collective or governmental ownership and oversight of the means of production and distribution of goods" (Oxford Dictionary of Politics).

Likewise, a Marxist is a person who holds the theories and practice of socialism with a specific emphasis on class struggle and the class conflicts created by materialism. A Marxist is motivated to pursue an establishment of a classless society. After considering the many new initiatives that mark our new era of governance, coupled with the Marxist tenets of Saul Alinski and the obvious influence of his work on our president, the Marxist and socialist characterizations are not as much insults as they are reasonable descriptions for many of his policies.

Marxist and socialist arguments will mark this presidency. The fact is, the Democratic Party is the majority power in the White House and in Congress, and has historically held policy positions that confirm definitive leanings—some believe not just leanings, but an outright ambition—toward socialism. One good example of socialist tendencies within the Democratic Party was around the turn of the century, when Norman Mattoon Thomas ran for president. He was a leading American socialist, pacifist, and six-time presidential candidate for the Socialist Party of America.

In a 1944 speech, Norman Thomas said, "The American people will never knowingly adopt socialism. But, under the name of 'liberalism,' they will adopt every fragment of the socialist program, until one day America will be a socialist nation, without knowing how it happened. I no longer need to run as a presidential candidate for the Socialist Party. The Democratic Party has adopted our platform."

According to a recent Gallup Poll (Jan 2010), most Democrats have a favorable view of Socialism. Gallup confirmed 61% of people who classify themselves as liberals, have a favorable image of Socialism. This is over three times as many for the number of conservatives (20%). A Newsweek cover (February 2009) proudly declared "We Are All Socialists Now." There is no doubt socialism is taking hold in America. Before we go headlong trading in capitalism for a disastrous embrace of this failed form of governance, we should consider the wisdom of Winston Churchill who commented, "The inherent vice of capitalism is the unequal sharing of blessings; the inherent virtue of socialism is the equal sharing of miseries." Our leader seems to want an equal sharing of miseries!

Whether fair or not, however, socialist characterizations may still actually be a bit too simplistic to describe a person with a background of a community organizer grounded in Alinsky's philosophy. Obama also happens to be the most powerful politician, beholden to political party elite, a polished orator—masterfully skilled at being purposely vague and deceptive—and the first African-American president—with a need to create a legacy. These competing characteristics present a much more complicated picture. We need to look at other potential influences before we can draw a conclusive understanding of our president.

As irrational, illogical, and insane as some of our leader's current policies and actions seem, we now begin to see a possible reason for the instanity. Saul Alinsky's work certainly helped provide a window of understanding into some of the motivating factors that have led to the actions and initiatives our president has taken. However, Alinsky and his respective philosophy were just the beginning of who we can now appreciate as a sophisticated and complex president.

There is little doubt our president is passionate. He's shown passion about increasing the size of government, taxing the rich, leveling the playing field for those he deems the have-nots, and programs for "social justice"—new plans for health care and energy. These issues are very obviously driving the actions of our leader. Unfortunately, as noted previously, none of these issues are what will make a good leader in our current environment, since the majority would rather be served by smaller government, lower taxes, less spending, and less government intervention. We need to ask ourselves, if our leader is not passionate and motivated about serving us in the way we specifically asked him, what drives him? His own agenda, formulated from a steady diet of Alinsky, the teachings of Rev. Wright, and an underlying empathy toward Bill Ayers.

Though we heard much about our president's allegiances prior to hiring him, we were quick to dismiss these as insignificant. Again, high gloss politics and imagery forced us to look at the person and personality instead of proven competency and experience. We failed to recognize how significant relationships—even if casual—can be, as they provide perspective and outlook while helping to shape our paths. Our cavalier desire to dismiss relationships as trivial is what led us to make a decision to hire without enough understanding about our new employee.

If we had examined intently the vetting of our new president, we would have uncovered that our employee has been immersed in relationships with controversial people and questionable theologies. It is perhaps these relationships that prompt some of the seemingly insane rationale for his actions and policies. In his book, *Dreams From My Father*, Barack Obama states, "To avoid being mistaken for a white sellout, I chose my friends carefully. The more politically active black students. The foreign students. The Chicanos. The Marxist professors and structural feminists and punk-rock performance poets. We smoked cigarettes and wore leather jackets. At night, in the dorms, we discussed neocolonialism, Franz Fanon, Eurocentrism, and patriarchy." Maybe I'm an anomaly but, I would venture to guess that most of us who attended college during the early 1980's probably didn't have a single Marxist friend. It seems especially odd that someone attempting to become a political leader would boast of having Marxist professors as friends. I have no doubt our president is very shrewd and calculating while carefully choosing his friends; that said, we should consider the fact that he chose his Marxist friends according to his own mindset and overall disposition.

Our president has spent over twenty years attending a church lead by Reverend Wright. Though we have seen and heard many stories about Wright and his extreme rhetoric, we may not have understood what compels such a person. The fact is, Reverend Wright, his church members, and his followers believe in the tenets of black liberation theology. Prior to the presidential election, Reverend Wright boasted about his allegiance to this theology, and his church's website prominently displayed the commitment of the church to this controversial theology.

In a nutshell, black liberation theology is committed to promoting efforts to liberate African-Americans from multiple forms of bondage, including political, social, economic, and religious. This theology promotes the idea that Jesus was a black man and paints the black race as helpless and constantly victimized by the forces that prevail within societies.

Though it has religious connotations, black theology is primarily focused on freedom and liberation through politics and social change rather than through spiritual salvation through Jesus Christ. Black liberation theology has been criticized for having a heavy emphasis on Marxist tenets and ideas that flow contrary to the stream of American capitalism. If these ideas are embodied by someone who is a proponent, this theology can be used to promote "white guilt," or socio-economic guilt of the wealthy, and they can be used to destroy the capitalist freedoms that exist within America as we know it.

At best, this theology presents highly controversial tactics that are destined to undermine America's capitalistic governance and Constitution. At worst, it provides a point of view laden with prejudice, biases, and the promotion of bigotry—again, the black man is the victim, and others must be held responsible. Either way, it would obviously be dangerous for an American governmental leader to embrace these beliefs.

In our zeal for hope and change, have we been reckless? Did we hire someone we can wholeheartedly trust with all the power and authority we've granted him? Our leader was hired to act in our best interests, but when we see signs of obvious instanity and are silent, we become complicit to irrational and reckless policy and actions.

At some point, we must realize that we are wholly responsible for the actions of our employees. I do not hold our president, his controversial background, or his leaders responsible for this new era in American governance. We are responsible. Our vetting, and now our silence, make us complicit! When we had every opportunity to scrutinize character, actions, intentions, and competencies, we declined and constantly excused irrationality. Perhaps we should've listened when, during the presidential campaign, liberal journalist Chris Matthews called our president "an empty suit." Maybe we should have also paid attention when current Secretary of State Hillary Clinton and Vice President Joe Biden indicated he was "too inexperienced" and in "well over his head."

Instead of some level of scrutiny, we constantly make excuses about it being too early, or needing to allow our leader time to learn his new role. The media is absolutely complicit as well, as they liberally give our leaders a pass on any level of scrutiny. However, when we see policies contradictory to our foundations and beliefs, shouldn't common sense prevail and force us to inquire? How did we miss it?

When I think about our vetting process and current situation with our president, I am reminded of Matthew 12:34–35, which states, "You snakes... how can you say good things when you are evil? *For the mouth speaks what the heart is full of.* A good person brings good things out of a treasure of good things; a bad person brings bad things out of a treasure of bad things" (GNB).

Wow—reflect on the wisdom of these verses! These verses confirm that, as we listen to words, actions, and intentions, we will know the heart of a person. The passions of the heart cannot be betrayed for long. Ultimately, the heart is revealed through actions. Even the most deceitful people are ultimately uncovered as their hearts' passions are manifested through actions. We should use these verses as confirmation of how we failed to properly vet our leader. Though he heavily relied on a scripted presence, marked by almost complete dependence on teleprompters, our president did have many unscripted moments that should have provided clues to his heart. At various times, he spoke of increased taxation of the rich, increasing size of government through increased regulation, and universal health and energy policies. He spoke of leveling the playing field and of meeting with our worst enemies without preconditions. Some of these other notions can be attributed to our leader's background and foundations, but where does the notion of meeting with enemies who want to destroy America come from?

We should recognize that, before we hired him, our president had no foreign policy experience whatsoever. He did try to cover up his inexperience by stating he was partially raised in Indonesia and had some foreign travels, but we completely dismissed his inexperience. Further, we handed him the most complex and demanding foreign policy responsibility in world history. This easily confirms our state of perpetual instanity, but more on this later. Foreign affairs inexperience is one factor, but not the complete answer about where the penchant for weak/ soft policies arose.

During this time, when there is a confirmed need for committed, authoritative, and precise leadership, where do these policies come from that only serve to encourage our enemies' continued irresponsibility? We only need to look a little more intently to discover that perhaps relationships with people with anti-American views have influenced some of the ideas impacting our arguably weak foreign policy.

By his own admission, Obama enjoyed years of friendship with a well-known, self-proclaimed domestic terrorist by the name of William Ayers. William Ayers and his associates were members of a radical left organization based in Chicago called the Weather Underground. We can summarize the Weather Underground as follows.

. . .

The Weather Underground was an organization that embraced tenets of class struggle of oppressed peoples versus the creators of the wealth of empire. They believed in a revolutionary struggle for control and use of this wealth to benefit the oppressed. They hoped to cause social chaos in order to cause the destruction of U.S. imperialism, and to usher in a new era of a classless society—namely, communism. The leadership was made up of very bright people with charm, charisma, and great oratorical skills. They heavily advocated black liberationist, anti-imperialist, and feminist rhetoric. In the seventies, the Weather Underground declared war against the United States government and conducted a series of bombings. The bombing attacks mostly targeted government buildings, including a U.S. capitol building, along with several banks.

. . .

As we can see, trying to observe someone in a well-protected, highly-orchestrated vacuum doesn't allow for transparency. What should be illuminated and now quite obvious to us is the veritable embrace of Marxism, socialism, and Chicago politics that connects, aligns, and seems to appropriately confirm Obama's motivations. When we see inconsistencies, backpedaling, and flip-flops on specific promises and commitments from our leader, we should know that his background and inexperience are what prevent decisive action, which has led to the following failures with keeping his commitment:

- Commitment to no earmarks: There were over 9,000 earmarks, and approximately $450 billion in "pork" in the stimulus and omnibus spending bills.

- Commitment to no lobbyists in his administration: He made seventeen exceptions to this commitment in just his first two weeks in office. By some estimates he now has over 40 ex-lobbyists in his administration.

- Complete transparency in the White House: This administration has been accused of being the most guarded and least transparent of all past administrations.

- A new era of transparency, unity and bipartisanship in the Congress: This is just not reality! We are experiencing the most polarized and inefficient Congress in history.

- Tax cuts for 95% of Americans and no tax increase—in any form—for those making under $250,000 per year: The grim reality is that all Americans will experience additional tax burdens from the policies enacted by this administration. The proposed energy policy alone is noted to be the single largest tax increase on all American households in history.

- Balanced budgets and reduced deficits: Well, we need look no further than current actions to determine the sincerity of this pledge.

- Numerous foreign policy gaffes: Bowing, apologizing, appeasing, re-gifting—you name it.

- Commitments to close Gitmo in twelve months: Hasn't happened, and unless other countries take the imprisoned terrorists, Gitmo may never close.

With this brief overview of some of the factors that impact how our president is perhaps interpreting the world scene, we can now begin to understand him. Among other things, our leader has been referred to as a Marxist, socialist, communist, and even a pacifist. Again, based on his background, all of these descriptions have some merit. We should refrain from strict reliance on these labels, however, as they provide too narrow a view of someone as complex as Obama. To better understand him, we should look beyond the rhetoric and hype that surround him—positive *or* negative—and instead rely on our ability to connect the dots, using the aforementioned wisdom of the Bible. Again, Matthew 12:34 states, "For the mouth speaks what the heart is full of."

The culmination of speaking and actions are what provide understanding of complex individuals. Our leader has an established pattern of relationships that is intricately woven with people, philosophy, and geography. A simple overview of his pattern of relationships can be summarized as follows:

1. In college hangs out with Marxists to avoid being mistaken as a "white sellout"

2. Becomes a community organizer based in Chicago.

3. Embraces Saul Alinksy's Chicago-based teaching and learns Marxist philosophy and strategies for community organizing; disciples others.

4. Meets Reverend Jeremiah Wright and becomes member of his church. Theological emphasis grounded in black liberation theology and Marxist theology.

5. Meets and befriends Bill Ayers, a radical liberal who embraces Marxist philosophies and is involved in domestic terrorism against U.S.

There is no doubt our president has had other notable relationships that have impacted his world view, but in light of the aforementioned relationships, we can start to make sense of his policies and initiatives. We now see that, regardless of his well-polished, closely guarded, and scripted image, it is what his heart is full of that is now clearly speaking.

To summarize, we have a president who is an historic figure, who speaks and acts from the standpoint of an ideologue while having received his foundations and experiences through radical community organizing strategies. He has embraced black liberation theology and inhaled a healthy dose of ideas from a domestic terrorist. Let's also not forget that, even though he has absolutely no experience in world politics, no experience in private business, and no proven competencies in leadership, we have entrusted him to lead us through the most chaotic world scene in history. To his credit, he is a world-class community organizer. This is the epitome of the unprecedented president ... pure instanity!

CHAPTER FIVE

Brilliance Redefined

"The "American Dilemma"... is the ever-raging conflict between, on the one hand, the valuations preserved on the general plane which we shall call the "American Creed", where the American thinks, talks, and acts under the influence of high national and Christian precepts, and, on the other hand, the valuations on specific planes of individual and group living, where personal and local interests... and all sorts of miscellaneous wants, impulses, and habits dominate his outlook."

–Gunnar Myrsal, 1942

"Obama is absolutely brilliant—an incredible man!" By now, we have heard the many accolades, well wishes, high hopes, and enormously high expectations targeted at our president. We have experienced the media hype and almost surreal hoopla about his destiny and greatness. Surely, it is in our collective best interest for him to live up to these expectations, but in light of what we now are beginning to understand about him, is it logical and prudent to have such high expectations for our

leader? Are we being driven by unrealistically high expectations that will lead to dashed hopes and failure—for him, and for us? We have set the bar extremely high for someone with no prior experience. It is insane to expect he will be able to deliver on all our initiatives for hope and change.

We should anticipate that our new leader will likely come up well short of our expectations unless he is truly brilliant. He will need to exhibit brilliance by being committed to learning quickly from early mistakes while also committing to learning while on the job. The key, however, is that this requires a recognition of obvious limitations due to lack of experience—zeal for and commitment to becoming competent.

While I believe our leader has honorable intentions and is sincere about his desire to lead America, I do not understand how we can, at this point, come to the conclusion of brilliance. Webster's Dictionary defines brilliance as "distinguished by unusual mental keenness or alertness." If we overlay this definition on Obama, it would be unfair and irresponsible to label him brilliant. By doing so, we unnecessarily create the additional stress of trying to live up to a term that really doesn't fit.

If labeled brilliant, one would feel compelled to cover up areas of known incompetence and inexperience and take unnecessary risks in order to live up to expectations. Predictably, this would result in making numerous unnecessary mistakes, massive cover-ups, and finger pointing at past administrations. This is indicative of what we have been seeing from our leader since taking office. The actions and reactions from our leader are precipitated by our ungrounded hopes and expectations—it is our fault!

While we want to offer strong encouragement, we should have just used the term "brilliant" in relation to areas of known competence. Then, the term may actually apply. For instance, if we said our president has demonstrated brilliance in community organizing and in politics, the term has merit. The issue here is that, instead of creating additional stress and likelihood of failure by overwhelming our employee with high and unrealistic standards, we should use descriptions that will actually empower him while allowing the appropriate grace period to succeed.

It is unfair and unpatriotic to label our president in unrealistic terms; his office should be distinguished by accolades that are truly indicative of his background and capabilities. Instead of loosely ascribing "brilliance" as a general term that describes Obama's entire existence, it has more meaning if we limit it to the specific domain of politics. It is hard to argue that we have witnessed a brilliant politician. In the specific domain of politics, there is no doubt we witnessed a world-class, first-rate political campaign during the election. We could easily say his entire campaign was brilliant, as it was characterized by forceful and unusually keen strategies that dictated the issues, while alertly putting all other candidates on the defensive. But again, does running a brilliant political campaign and being a brilliant politician automatically translate to being a brilliant person, a brilliant father, teacher, leader, thinker, or businessperson?

No! It is insane for us to simply collapse the many domains of a complex person and blindly ascribe accolades and commendations across someone's entire existence, especially in areas where there is no known competence or experience. We see again that our zeal for hope and change has prompted another example of instanity.

With unprecedented popularity, there are many who believe our president is a man for the ages, who seems to possess an unusual amount of intelligence, personal presence, and an almost godlike understanding about all things. Regardless of facts that may indicate the contrary, for many, our leader is definitely brilliant in all areas and at all times. People have the right to think and believe what they want, so instead of trying to sway opinion, perhaps it would serve us better to look intently at some of Obama's actions, which may provide better grounding for our assessment.

Again, Webster's dictionary defines brilliance as "distinguished by unusual mental keenness or alertness." With that in mind, a brilliant person is one who has the mental keenness and capacity to inspire with eloquent speeches while speaking transparently from the heart. We should consider that we have had difficulty assessing who our leader really is because he is marked by a reliance on speeches, a lack of transparency, and complete dependence on his teleprompters. Ironically, of all the people we would classify as great or brilliant speakers of the past, none solely relied on teleprompters, and they all seemed to have an innate ability to connect, motivate and inspire. This president requires teleprompters while speaking to children at elementary schools, and some have commented he even uses them at the family dinner table!

If we were to shift into again using the metaphor of America as an enterprise, wouldn't we consider it strange for a person to show up for job interviews with cue cards? Would we seriously consider a person for the most important job in the world if all we knew about him was what we could glean from his scripted messaging, passed along by handlers? Doesn't this seem ridiculous and irrational? Before hiring for the most important job in the world, it would have been logical and prudent for us to have a heart-to-heart—a fully transparent meeting. Our president did speak unscripted during some of the town hall meetings, but when he did, we heard him struggle with words, facts, and figures. One glaring example of this is when, while at a town hall meeting, he mentioned having visited "all fifty-seven states." Whoa ... what? Aren't there just fifty states in the U.S.? I don't want to nitpick here, but doesn't this statement seem a little odd for someone who is constantly referred to as brilliant? Isn't it odd for someone who is highly regarded and supposedly steeped in the history and traditions of our country to make such an obvious error?

A complete reliance on the teleprompter, and making a silly mistake about the number of states, may still not be enough evidence to fairly assess someone's brilliance, or lack thereof. After all, long hours on the campaign trail and lack of sleep would cause most anyone to speak incorrectly. If a pattern of mistakes and obvious lack of competency arise, however, we will have appropriate grounding to determine whether the voluminous accolades of brilliance are appropriate. A quick review of some of the important policy and decisions will help us in this regard.

As the chief executive of the United States, the president has a responsibility to make critical and strategic decisions about hiring and firing personnel. He has the ability to choose who he wants on his executive team and White House staff. Depending on position, some of these choices will have to undergo the additional scrutiny of congressional approval. Needless to say, this is a huge task and requires thoughtful analysis and preparation, since key appointments are one of the first indicators of a leader's competency, experience, and preparation for the task. All good leaders must ensure they make good hiring decisions and only extend offers to the most competent individuals; it requires patience and skill to hire the right people.

For the record, our president had two early nominations—Tom Daschle and Bill Richardson—that went nowhere due to improprieties; Richardson is under criminal investigation, and Daschle had tax issues. There was also Timothy Geithner, who was nominated as Secretary of Treasury and was almost unconfirmed after it was discovered he had failed to pay approximately $40,000 in Social Security and Medicare taxes. It was also reported that he employed an illegal immigrant as a housekeeper. Incredibly, Geithner was confirmed anyway—a tax cheat was given the job of Secretary of Treasury. This man now oversees our entire system of taxes ... instanity!

Annette Nazareth, who was nominated for Deputy Treasury Secretary, withdrew her name for undisclosed personal reasons after a probe into her taxes. Caroline Atkinson withdrew as nominee for Undersecretary of International Affairs in Treasury. Then, there was the nomination of Senator Judd Gregg

(R-N.H.), who became the second failed Commerce Secretary nominee. Judd withdrew after realizing there were going to be too many irresolvable conflicts related to policies for stimulus spending and census issues. Sanjay Gupta was in discussions to become Surgeon General; he withdrew after being criticized for lack of political background. Hmm ... is there a pattern here?

If we are to view America as a business enterprise, how many failed new hires will it take for us to begin to seriously question the competence of our new president? The inconvenient truth is that it is his responsibility to make key nominations, and each new hire is supposedly vitally important to our success. If brilliance was innate, this would have been an area where brilliance in leadership and in decision making should have prevailed. Instead, we see a mismanaged process dominated by finger-pointing and a lack of accountability.

Maybe it is naive to expect that any new administration wouldn't have issues with hiring new staff; we should expect nomination issues to plague any administration, especially with public hearings, partisan politics, and congressional oversight. It could be argued, however, that since we had never witnessed so many nomination failures in such a short period of time—there is an obvious leadership issue. To be fair, perhaps we should look further to see if there are other issues that provide a more obvious pattern of inexperience and incompetence. Since there is a huge gap between brilliance and incompetence, we should look for more evidence before concluding either. Since our new president took control of White House and everything that it entails, perhaps we should look at how he manages the White House.

We confirmed that our president was indoctrinated in politics while living in Chicago; there, he learned Chicago politics (affectionately referred to as the "Chicago way"). In all his background dealings, he had exposure to important people and dignitaries of all types. At the White House, there is an expectation that dignitaries from around the world will visit, and as a gracious host, proper protocol and representation must be made on behalf of the American people.

Our president hosted Gordon Brown, who is Prime Minister of the United Kingdom, as one of his first visitors to the White House. As is customary, Mr. Brown came bearing gifts of particular significance to the U.K. that also have some connection to the U.S. These gifts are most often deemed priceless mementos to be exchanged between countries. In exchange, our president provided Mr. Brown with a bag of outdated DVD movies. *What?* Our leader hosts a world leader, we receive priceless gifts, and in exchange we provide five-dollar DVDs to our top ally and world power? That's correct.

To make matters even worse, the DVDs were U.S. versions and don't work on European DVD players. This is not only indicative of obvious insanity but also demonstrates huge lack of leadership, competence, and experience. This should be an outrage to every American. Remember, he works for us: As president, he represents us to the world! What message do you think we sent our friend and ally? Can we excuse this gift fiasco as a just a simple misunderstanding of protocol and inexperience? Or, is there a pattern of sheer incompetence and inexperience?

When invited to participate in the G-20 summit, our president had the opportunity to meet with the Queen of England. This would have been a perfect venue and opportunity to demonstrate his brilliance by correcting the gift fiasco with Gordon Brown—to make amends with an exceptional gift of significance from the U.S. As is customary, our leader came bearing gifts for the queen.

Unfortunately, instead of learning a valuable lesson through earlier embarrassment, our president continued to rely on his instincts and provided the Queen with an iPod. It was a standard iPod, except it was full of his speeches! We have a reputation; we have heard many times from our allies that Americans are narcissistic. I doubt this demonstration of insensitivity and irresponsibility in gift giving did anything except further confirm our reputation while effectively marginalizing our leader as inept and alienating us from key allies.

What about a demonstration of brilliance when considering domestic policy? Domestic policy is certainly an area in which any president has to make and fulfill promises. Because it is close to home, there is an obvious level of scrutiny and account-ability. How would we classify the following policy decisions?

- Extending jihadist terrorist's the ability to use the American Judicial system, at U.S. taxpayer expense (est. $1 billion over 3 years), by providing provisions of Constitution normally reserved for U.S. citizens.

- Instead of appointing people in his administration who would complement his lack of business knowledge, experience and understanding, Obama chooses to appoint people who have similar backgrounds and experiences; this has led to this president being labeled the most anti-business in history. Michael Cembalest, Chief Investment Officer of JP Morgan Private Bank, confirmed less than 10% of the Obama cabinet has private business experience

- Obama is committed to raising taxes on "top wage earners," including small business owners, during a time of a shrinking economic base, increased financial strain, and the worst worldwide economy in decades.

- Obama administration has already quadrupled the budget deficit and spent at levels that exceed all other administrations. This administration has spent more money faster than any other administration in history! Remember, this momentum and velocity of monumental spending is taking place at a time in history when we have accumulated and unbudgeted entitlements—including Social Security and Medicare—estimated at over $50 trillion!

- Stimulus with no stimuli: We spent approximately $800 billion on stimulus funding, with our president promising that such a drastic action would prevent unemployment from rising beyond 8%. He pushed to pass it urgently to prevent a rise to 9%, which he deemed catastrophic. Well, we passed the stimulus plan, and we have gone well beyond 9%—we are over 10% unemployment with the admission that the rate will likely remain unchanged through the end of 2010. In essence, we spent almost a trillion dollars, and unemployment still went well above the promised projections. This is what we should have expected from a person with no business or economic experience!

- The U.S. has no government expertise in running any business successfully. Amtrak loses billions; the Post Office is highly inefficient; and Medicare, Medicaid, and Social Security are grossly mismanaged and inefficient. Yet, we decided to take over a major portion of the U.S. auto industry, the banking industry, and insurance companies. Where is the wisdom behind these decisions? Shouldn't we only attempt to help in areas where we have known expertise and competence? To further our predicament, our president took it upon himself to fire executives within some of these companies! The irony is that he doesn't blame the unions for any of the mess; he actually makes sure the union interests are well-protected before securing the interests of major stakeholders. Perhaps this is what we should have expected as our president has made his allegiances clear; union leaders have been the most frequent White House visitors by far, and he boastfully states, "I owe these unions."

- The president appointed a 31-year-old with no business experience and no auto industry experience to oversee the dismantling of GM. Though he is incredibly

incompetent and has no experience, our president asked
him to oversee the remaking of the U.S. auto industry.

Can we confirm any "unusual keenness or alertness" through
these policies? With the aforementioned facts, how should we
assess our leader? Again, there is no doubt he is a brilliant cam-
paigner and politician, but with these revelations, should we
continue to describe him as a brilliant person in general? Based
on actions and policy, we should see that we have hired an obvious ideologue, committed to pursuing his agenda regardless of
whether it demonstrates competence or complete insanity.

We have an administration that comfortably promote policies that dramatically expand government spending and influence into the private sector while irresponsibly increasing deficits and spending without restraint; seemingly removed from
possible consequences. These policies reward loyalists and are
arguably Marxist in nature. At best, they confirm a leadership
that is mismanaged, inexperienced, and incompetent. At worst,
these policies confirm our leader's foundations and core beliefs
are the "Chicago way;" it's all about power and politics, and
logic, competence, and experience take the back seat.

Perhaps we have been too encouraging. We have bestowed
our president with overwhelming adorations while disregarding logic and accountability. Because of our good will, Obama
has performed according to his foundations. Without accountability through checks and balances, and our deference to blind
faith in his leadership, we will receive the motivations of his
heart—not ours. We must not forget that he works for us, and it
is our responsibility to make sure that his entire leadership team
knows what we want and expect. We can choose to enable him
through additional ungrounded accolades, or we can confront
this new era of instanity by giving input and guidance to help
our leaders understand our collective vision and our focus.

Seeing Is Believing: The Necessity of Vision and Focus

"We are five days away from fundamentally transforming the United States of America."
  —Then-senator Barack Obama, Columbia, Missouri

What we have discovered thus far is that we have hired a leadership team committed to a complete and aggressive transformation of America … overnight! As noble as their desire and efforts may be, without proper strategic vision and intentional focus, we will likely become miserable failures.

Every president is chartered with building the vision and focus that will ensure success for the organization. Good leaders are those who have the uncanny ability to formulate a strategic vision, usually through collaboration with leaders and board members. They must get buy-in from all constituencies and provide the appropriate amount of focus to ensure the vision is accomplished with maximum efficiency. Establishing a realistic vision, and then harnessing the energies of the enterprise to execute proper focus, is a primary factor that separates winning businesses from those that are unsuccessful. In his book *The Marketing Imagination,* Theodore Levitt—author, economist, and professor at Harvard Business School—wrote, "No organization can achieve greatness without a vigorous leader who is driven onward by his own pulsating will to succeed. He has to have a vision of grandeur, a vision that can produce eager followers in vast numbers…He has to know precisely where he himself wants to go and to make sure the whole organization is enthusiastically aware of where that is … This is a first requisite of leadership, for unless he knows where he is going, any road will take him there."

After recognizing the patterns, background, and competence level of our leadership, it would be insane to think that our leaders can muster the appropriate amount of vision and focus needed to ensure success. As fully-vested board members, we must be willing to again stave off instanity and actually provide our leaders with our expectations. The onus is on us! Since we now know we cannot blindly rely on our leadership, which is woefully lacking in experience and readiness, we must help!

With the overwhelming adulation and adoration, coupled with the historical significance of the moment, there is a tendency toward overconfidence. Allowing our leaders to develop a false sense of overconfidence at this juncture is a huge risk, since there is no evidence our leadership is capable of delivering success. There is nothing inherently wrong with having a confident leadership team, but shouldn't their confidence be grounded in reality? Shouldn't confident leaders feel that way because they know what is possible, based on experience? Common sense tells us that confidence is derived from experience, knowledge, and competence. If there is no experience, proven competency, or history of success, we have nothing short of irrational exuberance and a state of baseless overconfidence.

We have been in a state of instant and selective insanity when it comes to trusting the capabilities of our leadership. If we were really inclined to believe in our leadership's ability to deliver, common sense dictates numerous people in our leadership team should possess backgrounds and lengthy track records indicative of accomplishing success at this level. Unfortunately, the grim reality is that everyone in and around our leader has scant experience and no proven track record of success! While we may have a confident leadership team, we have people with no real experience.

Though they are confident, they are incapable of accurately assessing where they need help. This attitude undermines the ability to be truly visionary and leads to an unhealthy state of overconfidence and arrogance.

In Proverbs 29:1, the Bible provides perfect wisdom through a well-known truism, which states, "Where there is no vision, the people perish."

As mentioned, since our leadership enjoys adulation, very favorable media attention, and accolades of all kinds, they tend to hold a higher level of confidence in themselves than what is deserved. Their confidence is somewhat understandable, since we have been silent during the implementation of this dramatic new era. Our leaders have mistakenly interpreted our silence as agreement with their policies and actions. While we have good intentions with our outpouring of adulation and optimism, we have created an unhealthy atmosphere, wherein the leadership begins to believe the hype, which breeds overconfidence. This ultimately leads to a state of unchecked arrogance.

So what? we may ask. *What's so bad about being confident, or even a little arrogant?* In our case, unchecked arrogance doesn't allow for unified, collective, bipartisan leadership. We elected a new leader to work with our existing team, which was made up of individuals with various political viewpoints. If we have a leader who is arrogant, he will act strictly on his political party's input, which significantly limits the vision and focus—and therefore, success—of our enterprise. Arrogance puts extreme limits on the ability to execute because instead of getting a leadership team that is truly reflective of our varied interests and committed to collaboration, we get a very narrow-minded approach to policy and government with disjointed and inefficient execution.

Though he is a novice, our new leader cannot claim ignorance; he knows the pitfalls of overconfidence and arrogance quite well. While he was vying for the job of president, he made clear promises about a new era of bipartisanship and promised "an end to petty grievances and false promises, the recriminations and worn-out dogmas, that for too long have strangled our politics." Even during his inaugural address, he promised to "usher in a transformational age". A new era where hope would replace fear, unity would overtake partisanship, and change would sweep aside the status quo. Only days later, however, his rhetoric rang hollow when, during a healthy discussion with Republicans and hearing their concerns about overspending on the stimulus, he flippantly retorted, "I won."

He effectively sent a loud and clear message that shut down any hope of bipartisan collaboration. As a result, there were no Republican recommendations on the stimulus bill, and it didn't garner a single House Republican vote. What happened to the promise of our new era of bipartisanship? Is this what the kind of collective brain trust we expect from our leaders? It is unfortunate, but arrogance reduces people we would normally classify as intelligent into petty adolescents.

At this juncture, arrogance within our leadership poses significant risk for us. It removes the incentive to take measured steps before implementing bold actions. This causes lethargy and a lack of attention to the finer details of running an enterprise. In our case, it prevents leadership from adhering to some of the basic principles and best practices. Again, producing a strategic vision and implementing focus are basic first steps required for running *any* enterprise. In his book *The Age of*

Unreason, Charles Handy—world renowned author and business consultant—confirms that every good leader must have a vision. He further confirms that the vision must be different, the vision must make sense to others, the vision must be understandable, the leader must "live" the vision, and the leader must remember that it is the work of others—the vision remains a dream without the work of others.

Since our leadership is running the largest and most complex enterprise in the world, isn't it a little odd to not have been properly advised as to the specific vision and focus that will drive their decisions? This is especially troubling and precarious since there is no unity or collaboration taking place before these new decisions are enacted.

The lack of an articulated strategic vision, attention to detail, and an intense focus, provides evidence that our leadership is at the very least overconfident, or more likely arrogant about their abilities. Consider this: Overconfident leadership has no incentive to collaborate, develop, or build a consensus for a plan that outlines a strategic vision and focus.

The 3000- year-old truism, "Where there is no vision, the people perish," becomes a cliché to the overconfident! Overconfidence and arrogance have brought us to the point where, if there is no apparent accountability, and a nebulous chaotic future, leaders have free reign to make up whatever irrational policies they wish … as they go. This creates an environment of crisis-driven management, whereby crises create justification for irrational policies. At the end of the day, policies are justified based on reaction to a crisis instead of the real culprit—incompetence or instanity.

It's no wonder that some journalists have commented about our leaders appearing giddy and punch-drunk as they make lofty and important decisions about the future of our enterprise. Evidence suggests they're sincerely arrogant and completely out of touch about what is required to deliver success to our enterprise. Though they have no experience, no proven competency at this level, no track record of success, and no desire to collaborate with other political parties, they actually believe they can deliver. The question is this: If they haven't outlined a vision, what will they actually deliver? What will our enterprise look like in ten years? What are our leaders' strategic vision and focus for us?

In the book *Leaders,* Bennis and Nanus state, "With a vision, the leader provides the all-important bridge from the present to the future of the organization." Visionary leadership succeeds because it provides a road map and path toward success. It is also a style of leadership that is willing and enthusiastic about being held fully accountable to the achievement of that vision. It is marked determination toward achieving the vision that provides the impetus for an intense focus. Focus is what then prevents the vision from being undermined and going off track. There is a dance of purpose and accountability created between vision and focus. It has been documented that when these two principles work together, even the most fragmented, mismanaged mess can be quickly fixed to perform efficiently while achieving success! The point is that these foundational principles must be put to work in order to benefit from them.

To be fair, our leaders are only executing what they know, though this is scary, since we know there is a foundation of Marxist and socialist tendencies. They are being completely driven by their own experience. Since they, for the most part, haven't worked in the private sector or held positions that demanded accountability in leadership, they are clueless about the importance of having vision and focus. Again, if they understood its importance, as David's proverb confirms in the aforementioned verse, why do we experience a state of bewilderment when it comes to analyzing their respective policy decisions? If we knew the vision and direction, we would have no need to question the logic of policies. If we knew what path we were on, we wouldn't question why it seems that our leaders are unfocused, or the seemingly schizophrenic pace at which budgets are passed, spending is authorized, and new policies are implemented.

The chaotic pace of incoherent policy decisions changes is a classic sign of a lack of vision and focus. We should ask: Why, during this leadership, is there a consistent pattern of crisis and emergency? Why is everything an emergency—emergency stimulus, emergency spending bills, emergency new powers to be granted, etc.? Further, why do we have to spend money at such a frenzied pace? What kind of planning takes place when there is a constant need to try and fix a cycle of chaotic messes? The truth is, if we're always in reactionary mode, it is impossible to plan and strategize, and therefore to build vision. Again, with no vision, it is certainly impossible to maintain focus and deliver success. We are encountering one of the most traumatic times in our history, and we have no plan, because there is no strategy. There is no strategy because there is no vision, and there is no vision because there is no time—only crisis management... wow!

"A business short on capital can borrow money, and one with a poor location can move. But a business short on leadership has little chance for survival... Organizations must be led to overcome their trained incapacity" (*Leaders*).

Though we have clearly uncovered a huge hole in our leadership, both in style and substance and in our need for strategic vision and focus, no doubt some will remain convinced otherwise. Instead of being caught in a state of instanity, whereby we simply defer to the assertions of others, we should be prepared to ask the following:

- What is the stated and confirmed strategic vision for our domestic economy—fixing unemployment, deficits, spending, bloated government, etc.?

- What is the strategic vision for our foreign policy? What are our goals for enemies and allies? How do we influence positive change in North Korea and Iran?

- What is the strategic vision for our social policy—
immigration, health care, education, and energy? With
all the new proposed spending in these arenas, how will
America look in five years?

It is painful to realize, but we have leadership pushing a
lot of new and radical ideas that will remake our society—but
there is no plan. This realization denotes a shocking level of
incompetence, but it's true! When we put approximately $640
billion aside in the 2010 budget for the government-run health
care plan, Obama was asked if this amount was sufficient. He
admitted that he didn't know. He went on to say that the plan
hadn't been written, so he had no idea whether it was too much,
too little, or just right. This is also true of most of the money
in the stimulus plan. It was almost a complete shot in the dark,
how much to put where, and when, and how. This is why—even
though we were told the stimulus spending would have immediate impact and forestall increased unemployment—we still
see unemployment steadily growing. It's now at 10%, and only
approximately 5% of stimulus funds were spent in the first five
months! Again, these obvious mistakes are to be expected when
you have no strategy, no plan, and no focus—just spending.

I am astonished to find that when I ask people about the
new era vision, they confess they don't know. Ironically, when I
ask the same people about the prior administration's vision, they
say it was to keep us safe. This aspect of the vision resonated
with people—even people who despised it—and from it, people
understood the intense focus surrounding the policies and decisions that allowed us to succeed. I ask simple questions: Where
are the current spending policies taking us? How will America
look in ten years? Amazingly, no one has answers, including our
leaders, who are pushing the plans.

Based on what we know and understand about our leadership, do we really think they have an actual vision of where they
are taking us in the next four to eight years, let alone the next

ten or twenty? Do we think they have *any* clue about the almost incalculable consequences of taking over private companies and industries while incurring insurmountable increased deficits? At some point, we will have to come to the realization that we have promoted people into leadership who are ideologically rigid and focused on pursuing their own agendas. They believe, with good reason, that we are complacent and lethargic about policy and governance in general.

Based on our citizens' track record, our leaders will expect continued complacency as they remake our enterprise into something more reflective of their backgrounds and foundations—progressivism, Marxism, and socialism. Now is not the time to remake America using new era rhetoric to expand government. We are at a critical point that requires our leaders to exercise intense focus on real problems like irresponsible spending and mounting deficits.

Not only are we going through a period in history when we are experiencing the trauma of spending and budget deficits, we are also experiencing our leadership's attention deficit. It's sad to say, but the patterns seem to indicate that we actually have a leadership that exhibits signs of attention deficit disorder! Since it is collective, it may not be an exactly clinical diagnosis, but the symptoms and outcome are similar. As I understand it, some of the symptoms of those diagnosed with ADD are acting impulsively and difficulty focusing. We certainly see similarities. Our leadership is impulsive, and they certainly exhibit a lack of focus. Going forward, we need focus from our leadership—not ADD moments!

Focus delivers success! If you've ever experienced being in an organization that recently hired a new CEO, you know that when the new executive comes on board, he brings strategies and ideas that revolve around how to focus the organization, moving forward. One of the first primary strategies every new executive employs revolves around trying to focus resources in order to maximize efficiency from existing deliverables—

products or services—in order to immediately become more profitable. From the first day, a new executive will stress the importance of having a unified and collective focus, as it is the primary factor that drives intent in all areas. Having intent in business transactions helps reinforce the collective vision of the organization; it also helps to immediately reduce costs, while increasing efficiency and the likelihood of success. Conversely, a lack of focus is the antithesis of the aforementioned. Needless to say, if there is little or no focus, inefficiency and costs skyrocket; this negates any chance of operational improvements or profitability.

A new leader who lacks vision and focus will sometimes resort to just trying to do something—anything, regardless of how irrational—in an effort to demonstrate the ability to take initiative. In these cases, when a leader just wants to demonstrate initiative, ideas about expansion and other costly ideas are typical. These initiatives ultimately prove irrational, as they tend to be too costly in light of the business goals; they don't fine tune, or promote reduction. Instead, they add additional burden to an already crippled enterprise; this allows a complete neglect of the existing systemic issues surrounding waste and inefficiencies, while pursuing expansion initiatives that do nothing more than add unnecessary costs and complexity, while compounding the problems. This is a dramatic summary of where we find ourselves today with our new administration. Unfortunately, we are in a situation with out-of-touch leaders taking actions leading to even more out-of-control policies.

> Without leadership … it is hard to see how we can shape a more desirable future for this nation or the world. The absence or ineffectiveness of leadership implies the absence of vision, a dreamless society, and this will result, at best, in the maintenance of the status quo or, at worst, in the disintegration of our society because of lack of purpose and cohesion. We must raise the search for new leadership to a national priority.
>
> Bennis and Nanus, *Leadership*

CHAPTER SEVEN

Making Money Count: The Balancing Act of Budget and Finance

> "We can't reduce taxes until we reduce government spending, and I have to point out that government does not tax to get the money it needs; government always needs the money it gets."
>
> —Ronald Reagan

There is one word we can use to sum up our current state, and that word is "lack." We seem to be in a perpetual cycle of lack, and we are slow to produce *any* remedies or effective actions to help us overcome this. Since we have reviewed backgrounds and experience, we can now see there is a huge lack of leadership, lack of experience, and tremendous lack in proven competence. These factors are not the overwhelming issues that result in a lack of success; many enterprises have these issues and continue to survive. What complicates our ability to achieve future success is embracing aggressive policies that, when taken into consideration with our depressed economy, exacerbate our lack of revenues, which offsets our lack of a balanced budget. All the issues of lack are incongruent with logic, reason, and any prudent model for success. For instance, what logic or reason can we use to explain a desire to expand budgets, expand deficits, and expand spending without any accompanying plans, strategies or focus? Or, how is it logical to desire to spend or invest money without any expectation of payback period, exit strategy, or some type of analysis to determine Return on Investment (ROI)?

An analysis that confirms a reasonable expectation of a payback is what characterizes a sound investment. When this analysis is not present, you just have spending. It is reasonable and prudent for a business or investor to perform analysis, but for some reason, our leaders have decided that this is unnecessary. Our leadership acts as though our government has unlimited resources—and through taxation, perhaps they do. They are seemingly unmoved and unconcerned about our plight or consequences. This provides clear indication that many of the new era policies being adopted by our leaders are out of touch with our thinking, and therefore reflect leadership that is out of control.

According to the U.S. debt clock, it is estimated that the U.S. government is obligated to over $100 trillion (or over $347,000 per citizen) in currently unfunded liabilities. This amount, combined with an existing budget deficit of approximately $2 trillion and a new budget of an additional approximate $4 trillion, means we are in a financial mess that could actually bankrupt us.

Admittedly, a trillion dollars is a huge number to fathom. Because it is so large, our leaders may actually view it as funny money, as it is out of the realm that most of us can even fully comprehend. Since a trillion dollars is quite unfathomable, perhaps we can better grasp it if it were put into more simplistic terms. Jack Uldrich, at jumpthecurve.net, gives good, tangible examples of the difference between one million, one billion, and one trillion by using seconds and going backwards. For instance, he confirms:

- 1 million seconds ago is equivalent to twelve days ago
- 1 billion seconds ago = thirty years ago
- 1 trillion seconds ago = 30,000 BC!

Wow! As compared to numbers we are used to comprehending, one trillion is a number that is clearly unfathomable. Our leadership acts as though this number is just another number, but clearly this number—especially in multiples—poses enormous risk for us. As evidence of the casual disregard our leaders have for trillions of dollars, in August 2009 they were told their budget deficit projections were off by approximately $2 trillion; they reacted as though $2 trillion was just a rounding error. They said they "underestimated the degree of economic crisis." A $2 trillion underestimate—and we act as if it's no big deal. This provides another good example of inexperience, incompetence, and our own instanity!

Common sense tells us that we need to focus our efforts and attention on how to fix the mess. Unfortunately, a state of instanity prevails, so our leaders attempt to remedy our fiscal mess by actually trying to justify that now is the time for more spending. The unfortunate fact is that there is no precedent that demonstrates even a remote possibility of success via a business strategy that relies on increased, unfunded spending as the method to prosperity.

> "Public servants say, always with the best of intentions, 'What greater service we could render if only we had a little more money and a little more power.' But the truth is that outside of its legitimate function, government does nothing as well or as economically as the private sector."
>
> —Ronald Reagan

As evidenced by VP Joe Biden's statements that we need

"to spend money to keep from going bankrupt," our leaders are "experimenting" by rewriting basic business principles about how to succeed. The grim fact is that even though conventional wisdom and common sense say otherwise, our leadership believes aggressive government spending campaigns while in the midst of massive budget deficits are a viable and prudent strategy that will lead to success. Instanity!

What contributes to the distress of wanton spending is the lack of strict oversight and accountability; our leaders actually desire to spend with no checks and balances or accountability! As evidence, they have admitted to approval of various spending bills and legislation without even reading them. Additionally, there have been mandatory oversight meetings to update representatives on the status of spending initiatives. These should have had at least twelve to fifteen attendees, and only two or three of our representatives have shown up. Instanity!

Now, let's review what we've observed and uncovered thus far:

- We have an enterprise with new leadership.
- Leaders are still trying to learn and build good leadership, expertise, and competence.
- Our leaders are taking us down a path without a purposeful vision, strategy, focus, or plan.
- Though our enterprise is still functioning, it is grossly mismanaged due to lack of focus and inefficiencies.
- As a result, we are losing trillions of dollars every year, with no plan for how to pay for the accruing debt.
- Our new era of leadership actually believes that instead of focusing on and fixing existing problems, they can just ignore them while spending even more money— four times more—and accumulating more debt.
- Since our leaders have no strategic plans, there will be

no accountability, no exit strategies, no payback periods, nor any expected ROI.

• We are expected to just defer our rationality and common sense to them—just trust them as they completely remake our enterprise into ...

... into what? Where are we going? What are we doing? Since managing our employees is our responsibility, why are we settling for this perpetual state of instanity? Some fundamental characteristics of good leaders are the ability to strategize, implement, and manage budgets and finance. Essentially, most good leaders are so deemed because they possess expertise at quickly identifying areas of waste and making immediate improvements by trimming budgets. The management of revenues and all transactions surrounding money matters are what is desperately needed in our leadership; this creates a cycle of ongoing efficiencies and improvements. If the aforementioned characteristics are demonstration of good leadership, what kind of leaders do we have? Shouldn't we at least trust that at some point they will begin to manage our enterprise like they would manage their personal finances?

When we experience personal money problems, we immediately curb spending and begin to look intently at all our obligations to determine where we can reduce costs. We begin to budget, strategize, and cut spending so we can find ways to realistically meet our minimum obligations. This is not rocket science; this is what any logical, thinking person would do. Shouldn't we expect that our logical, prudent leaders do the same? Before becoming president, Obama said, "There is no doubt that we've been living beyond our means, and we're going to have to make some adjustments."

Shouldn't we interpret this as a sign that he planned to reign in spending? Well, after he was hired, our president went on a spending spree, initiating a new round of stimulus spending, bailouts, fiscal budget increases, and massive deficit spending.

Later, our president said, "I've personally asked the leadership in Congress to pass into law rules that follow the simple principle—you pay for what you spend—so that government acts the same way any responsible family does."

This again sounded good and reasonable, but our leaders have continued to spend with reckless abandon by pushing a trillion-dollar health care and a trillion-dollar energy plan, and there is no apparent end in sight. It seems incredibly hypocritical and ironic that Obama harshly criticized Bush for running up a $3 trillion deficit during his eight years in office, especially since he will eclipse this number in less than two years. Current estimates confirm he will run up more debt over eight years than *all* other presidents in American history—from George Washington through George W. Bush—combined. Furthermore, as a result of these deficits, net interest spending would reach $840 billion in 2020. Think about this, almost a trillion dollars per year in interest alone! After committing American taxpayers to irrational spending and policies, our leader admitted that "our current spending is unsustainable." Even after this admission, we resumed irrational spending.

It is maddening and quite frightening to realize that our leaders are enjoying their new rise to iconic superstardom while our enterprise undergoes desperate financial conditions. Our leaders have become idols with adorable personalities, accepting only accolades, and feeling they are beyond reproach. This, at best, breeds overconfidence. At worst, it spawns out-of-touch and out-of-control arrogance. There is no doubt our leaders have interpreted our wishes and high hopes as a blank check, allowing them to implement whatever new policies and new spending initiatives they want. Fundamentally, though, they have become reckless with the power and authority we loaned them to act on our behalf.

We have dealt with some level of beginners' incompetence and a little arrogance, but it would be an act of pure instanity for us to willingly tolerate a reckless disregard for our best interests and well-being, and the well-being of future generations.

It is not patriotic to embrace policies and spending that will result in generational theft. Our leadership has not only proposed policies that will greatly increase the tax burden on the top wage earners in America, but they will also increase unemployment and additional tax burden on every household for many generations to come. This includes our children, grandchildren, and our great-grandchildren, and beyond. A significant percentage of their income will be spent in order to pay off or pay down the trillions of dollars in deficits we ushered in during this new era of instanity!

Summary

In this section, we have delved into the management of America—our enterprise. We took a focused look at leadership, vision and focus, and budget and finance, since these factors are the foundations upon which any enterprise expecting success will be built. In the end, we came to realize that at the moment, we are failing in all these critical areas. Though our findings are troubling, they have helped us realize how we have been complicit—due to our deference—with the insane policies and politics that now dominate our leadership in Washington. We have realized that our leaders do not inherently believe that their first priority is to serve "we, the people." We understand that our leaders have patterns that seem to indicate they seek to fulfill their own dreams and serve their own personal agendas, regardless of the consequences we will suffer. We cannot escape the fact, however, that it is our own relative state of instanity that has created our current climate. The way we overcome is to become vigilant in observation and grounded in logic and rationality.

In the end, this was an important analysis, as now we can confirm that we have summarily uncovered the following patterns:

- We have been swayed by the cult of personality to the point that we hired a president who touted a rhetorical mantra of hope and change, but who has limited or no leadership ability, no management or private sector experience, and no track record of success.

- He has broken the majority of his major campaign promises.

- He is prone to literally bow to, appease, and apologize to our enemies and allies rather than extol our virtues.

- He has risen from the ranks of community organizer and, by his own admission, has been strongly influenced as a disciple and teacher of Marxist and socialist ideology.

- He has used his rigid ideology to pursue policies with the zeal and arrogance that seem to permeate his administration.

- The Obama administration has demonstrated a defiant pattern of trying to rapidly implement policies that include a four-fold increase in new spending, a quadruple increase in budget deficit, bailouts for major private companies and industries, and government expansion into trillion-dollar health care and energy plans, all of which are incongruent with our majority goals and initiatives.

- Leadership needs to outline a vision and provide focus toward balancing budgets and controlling spending while maneuvering through this period of worldwide economic collapse.

- Consistent patterns and our new reality confirms that, we have out-of-touch and out-of-control leadership that we have enabled and been complicit with, as they have fallen into a perpetual embrace with the state of instanity

PART TWO

Preserving Our Country

"Democracy is always temporary in nature; it simply cannot exist as a permanent form of government. A democracy will continue to exist up until the time that voters discover that they can vote themselves generous gifts from the public treasury. From that moment on, the majority always votes for the candidates who promise the most benefits from the public treasury, with the result that every democracy will finally collapse due to loose fiscal policy, which is always followed by a dictatorship. The average age of the world's greatest civilizations from the beginning of history has been about 200 years. During those 200 years, these nations always progressed through the following sequence:

- From bondage to spiritual faith;
- From spiritual faith to great courage;
- *From courage to liberty;*
- *From liberty to abundance;*

- *From abundance to complacency;*
- From complacency to apathy;
- From apathy to dependence;
- From dependence back into bond

Preserving Our Country: Analysis of Our Founding Principles in an Era of Instanity

Coming together is a beginning;
keeping together is progress;
working together is success.
                    —Henry Ford

My Country, 'Tis of Thee

Through purposeful observation of various vantage points, we have provided new data. It should be very clear that America has been living in the state of instanity. Mindless participation in the insane policies that undermine our collective best interests is the epitome of instanity. Our country was built upon a foundation of appropriate checks and balances over which we have collective influence. Fundamentally, it is our responsibility to ensure the country continues its rich heritage of freedom and liberty for all. To that end, when we refrain from holding our government accountable at all times, it is simply un-American! Why do we do allow it? The answer emanates from popular culture, media mania, and the proliferation of ideologues who—through their collective adoration—have helped create a cult of personality.

Our country needs leadership of ideas, not personality. We have made critical decisions and countless excuses based on the cult of personality that surrounds Obama. It is clear we did not hire based on facts, credentials, or proven competencies; we hired based on a new and refreshing personality with immeasurable charisma. This has clouded our view. It's not surprising, then, that much of our motivation and desire for the current administration can be attributed to personality.

> In his book *The New Realities*, Peter Drucker—known as "the founding father of the science of modern management"—states, "The political motto for the new political realities has to be 'Beware charisma!' ... The desire for charisma is a political death wish. No century has seen more leaders with more charisma than our twentieth century, and never have political leaders done greater damage than our four giant charismatic leaders of this century: Stalin, Mussolini, Hitler and Mao." He adds further, "what matters is not charisma. What matters is whether the leader leads in the right direction or misleads." He waxed prophetic when he asserted, "And under present conditions charismatic leadership could not be anything but misleadership. It would lead toward yesterday rather than toward the new realities."

Wow! This was written over twenty years ago. Charisma, charm, and intellect are certainly endearing personal qualities, and they figure well when we subconsciously assess based on first impressions. However, with these qualities constantly touted and reinforced by the media and other outlets, we can easily fall into the trap of being swayed to believe in a manufactured image—an image that has little bearing in reality. This is how the cult of personality emerges and is reinforced.

On its own merit, the cult of personality is not harmful. Actually, most people we would characterize as powerful and charismatic are likely people who possess some degree of a manufactured presence. The problem arises when, due to personality, we decline to make critical assessments and instead excuse people for their actions. If we are unwilling to make common sense assessments because we are blindly following personality, we increase our risk of disappointment and failure—especially when much is at stake. Leaders will then fully leverage our extension of good will to escape criticism and accountability.

What's so bad about exercising good, old-fashioned common sense? It forces us to look beyond a pretty package and fancy marketing, to intently quantify and evaluate based on reasonable and objective criteria. It is perfectly reasonable and responsible to encourage the use of common sense in this matter. Unless we can regain a commitment to practice common sense, the cult of personality will become our reality and allow our leaders to push for their personal agendas while escaping any objective scrutiny and accountability.

At this point, it is important to acknowledge how the issue of personality may have impacted our voting decisions and how it may cloud our thinking—not allowing us to make rational and objective assessments. Throughout history we have not only seen benign public figures benefit, but we also have seen the rise of dictators, tyrants, and cult leaders, who have effectively benefited from this phenomenon. Unfortunately, there have been many victims of disastrous consequences as a result of the actions propagated by individuals who, through their personas, escaped public scrutiny. With that said, it is important for us to seriously scrutinize government motivation, initiatives, and policies without regard to like or dislike of current leadership. Our assessment should be grounded in objectivity and only focused on what transpires in relation to alignment with the U.S. Constitution and associated articles and declarations.

As noted, there are many radical changes that, if left unchecked, will dramatically alter the way we live now and in the future. America's rich history, its liberties, and its constitutional foundations are in the process of being permanently altered, and we are seemingly silent. Does this mean we are perfectly fine with the proposed changes? Are we fully complicit in the remaking of America and rewriting of our constitutional foundations? Or, as is likely the case, are we just stuck in a stupor of instanity?

Would you consider it insane for our government to conjure up budgets and spend our money with no oversight or specific plan? Think about it. Would it make sense for any business to be managed in such a manner? Isn't it insane to think that it's okay to undermine our Constitution by reducing liberties and freedoms in order to increase the dependence on government? What about the agenda for our government to expand in private markets, where our government has no background or proven competence? How about our desire to spend trillions more dollars, in addition to our unfunded liabilities that total well in excess of $100 trillion? How does it make any logical sense to increase spending, cripple our economy, and saddle future generations with debt, all in the name of stimulus spending? All these issues deserve our careful scrutiny. We can choose to take collective responsibility by telling our employees what kind of policies and changes we want, or we can choose to defer to blind trust and hope for the best. The latter will, of course, further perpetuate the pattern of instant and selective insanity—instanity!

In order to remain objective, it is important to continue our observation of the government from multiple vantage points. An additional vantage point that deserves consideration is to view current societal direction in relation to the historical policies, precedents, traditions, and historical foundations that have kept us successful and secure for the past 200 years.

A new era of government is being implemented, and our leaders have mentioned their intent is to not simply remodel, but to actually completely remake/transform America. Since taking office, our president has made several proclamations during interviews and public meetings that his intent is to remake America—completely transform America.

A remake of America sounds ominous and quite scary with our current leadership in charge. Before we take on this ambitious endeavor, we must first consider: Has our government and leadership successfully remade anything? Did our leaders remake the IRS, the Post Office, Social Security or Medicaid/Medicare? There are a large number of government departments that could use a remake, but instead they want to start by remaking the entire country. Does this make sense for a young and inexperienced administration? How will a remake impact our Constitution and Declaration?

The father of modern management, Peter Drucker, stated, "There is no place any more for political 'Revolutions,' for 'New Deals,' or 'Fair Deals,' or 'New Societies.' They do not even work as campaign slogans. Nor do the ideologies of salvation by society or the organization of power around interest blocs fit either the tasks to be done or the constituencies."

Mr. Drucker continues, "Neither can support leadership. They can only result in misleadership." Needless to say, there are a variety of issues we will need to confront and challenge during this new era of government. The issues facing America are urgent and require that we become engaged thinkers.

By understanding the risks and consequences of inaction, we should be unwilling to accept deference of our freedom and democratic Republic to others while our country is at such a critical stage. America is awaiting collective conscious to steer her in a sound, appropriate direction. The following memo is provided in the spirit of one concerned board member to another. It offers an overview of issues we, as Americans, should be aware of as we attempt to counteract the current state of instanity and eliminate its proliferation throughout our country and our leadership.

MEMO

To: Board Members
From: Fellow Board member
Subject: This land is your land; this land is my land.

Our great nation is under attack! This attack, however, is not as obvious and wanton as the terrorist attacks perpetrated on 9/11, but the fact that it is subtle doesn't diminish the potential threats, major impact, and irreversible damage. If we are not very careful, the damage from this attack can permanently alter our way of life, our liberty, and our pursuit of happiness.

We know the Declaration of Independence promises life, liberty, and the pursuit of happiness. If we undermine our founding principles and associated declarations, we will undermine our success in fulfilling the promises of these precious documents. For the most part, we have thrived for over 200 years with the Constitution as a promise of what we can expect from our government. This promise alone provided us with the perfect measure of hope and the possibility of change that has brought us this far. There is no doubt the Constitution has brought us unparalleled success and freedoms. Ironically, we seem indifferent, even though we see a subtle cultural shift away from it. We seem to have replaced the hope and change provided based on our founding principles, with hope and change promised by an individual. This is unfathomable! How can we set aside the actions of our forefathers and the promises guaranteed in our most precious historical documents; in an instant, how can we put our complete trust and faith in one person and in his administration? Instanity!

The evidence overwhelmingly confirms that, through our general lack of concern and our silence, we have somehow come to trust our unproven employee more than our collective common sense. A good example of this is when our government decided to spend our tax dollars to bail out private companies; we remained silent. When they decided to greatly expand in historically private markets by committing our tax dollars to buy major banks and financial institutions, insurance companies, and car manufacturers, we remained silent. If we were in tune with common sense and understood the limits of powers within our Constitution, we would've asked, "Where does our Constitution provide that our government can spend our money, to buy, manage, and oversee these various markets and industries?"

The answer is absolutely nowhere! How is it, then, that we can somehow remain silent while subtle policies that erode the foundations of our Constitution are enacted as a matter of policy? Where is our free market system of capitalism and our commitment to our democratic Republic? When will we again hold our government accountable to strict adherence to the very foundations that made us successful? We cannot remain indifferent; our Constitution depends on our immediate collective action.

Make no mistake—a new era of government has emerged. We are beginning to see a rapid shift in policy that will reshape our understanding of our Constitution. Very subtly, our Constitution seems to be losing its importance and distinction as a timeless document used to help direct our country. Instead, we seem open to the idea of progressive governance, which acknowledges the Constitution as a historical document and sees it as only partially relevant to our new era. Obviously, this is a slippery slope, and if left unchecked, we will enter a new era of governance without a solid foundation of principles and beliefs. Without hearkening to the wisdom and guidance of our founding fathers and the original framers, America will begin to look unfamiliar to us. Ultimately, she will begin to look like many European countries—one that can be easily folded into a world government.

Are our Constitution and Declaration to be used as critical pillars for our foundations, or are they to be used as doormats? If they are the foundation of America, we cannot risk them becoming undone. It is vitally important that we are diligent in making sure these critical foundations are not undermined at all costs. If, however, we begin view them as just doormats—basically reduced to being historical entry points—then we can just plan on these foundations being superseded by progressive laws and policies. Either way, we are at a point where we must choose! In choosing, we should be aware that the consequences of removing our foundations in order to make way for progressive new eras will bring down our house. Without proper foundations, failure is imminent.

If we love this country and want to continue to perpetuate success, we have only one choice—to stand up for the principles in our historical documents. This may mean we will have to be willing to disagree with our popular president sometimes if we are committed to preserving our greatness and success. Conversely, choosing to undermine our own consciousness in this matter will only mean one thing: We are choosing to live in a state of instanity.

God bless us all,
Fellow board member

CHAPTER NINE

The U.S. Constitution and Freedom: "The American Way"

Freedom is the recognition that no single person, no single authority or government has a monopoly on the truth, but that every individual life is infinitely precious, that every one of us put in this world has been put there for a reason and has something to offer. It's so hard for government planners, no matter how sophisticated, to ever substitute for millions of individuals working night and day to make their dreams come true. The fact is, bureaucracies are a problem around the world.

—Ronald Reagan

Based on political coverage of our leader and his administration, popular culture and most major media outlets would have us believe that we are beholden to the dreams, whims, and agendas of our superstar leaders. We should know that this is purely deception. The reality is that our politicians, even though we may have esteemed them to iconic levels, are completely beholden to us. The U.S. Constitution clearly confirms that the majority power lies with "we, the people," and with the states.

Popular deception would have us perceive we are powerless and stupid, and therefore in desperate need of brilliant leaders who look out for our best interests. Most times, there is a huge gap between what our leaders deem to be in our best interest, and what we would have them pursue in our best interest. The gap exists because we believe in the promises and commitments provided by our Constitution, while new leadership believes in a more progressive style of governance, which many times undermines our Constitution and its associated freedoms.

Fundamentally, our government is bound to serve us within the confines, framework, and foundation of the U.S. Constitution. The Constitution should be enforced and esteemed as the supreme law of the land, as it is the governing document that provides structure for how the country is to be run. Needless to say, this document is vitally important, especially now since we have begun to experience tumultuous economic periods and radical leadership. Excitement about new era regime and policy changes have a tendency to muddy our ability to think clearly about who we are, what rights we have, and where we are going as a country. Reliance on the foundation of the Constitution provides guidance for keeping our bearings straight.

Due to its significance, and in light of some of the major changes currently being implemented throughout our country, it may be useful to review the rights and liberties that have been secured for us by way of the Constitution. The U.S. Constitution and related components can be summarized as follows.

The Constitution consists of four major components. The first major component is the Preamble, which serves as an opening overture and prelude. The Preamble sets the appropriate context and provides vision and direction for the subsequent constitutional components.

The next components are the seven original articles. These articles provide the structure and framework for our government; they allow us to appropriately set fences around the government hierarchy, and around the power and authority we would grant to the federal and state governments.

Then, there are the twenty-seven amendments. These specific amendments provide the outline for our rights, laws, governmental limits, and protections extended to each American.

Finally, there is a paragraph that certifies the enactment of the Constitution by the states during the Constitutional Convention. That said, we cannot ignore the gravity and depth of this document, which commences with its primary focus on us: "We the people."

> We the People of the United States, in Order to form a more perfect Union, establish Justice, ensure domestic Tranquility, provide for the common defence, promote the general Welfare, and secure the Blessings of Liberty to ourselves and our Posterity, do ordain and establish this Constitution for the United States of America.

> "The [U.S.] Constitution is a limitation on the government, not on private individuals ... It does not prescribe the conduct of private individuals, only the conduct of the government ... It is not a charter for government power, but a charter of the citizen's protection against the government."
> —Philosopher and novelist Ayn Rand (1905–1982)

It is important to note that "We the people" is one of the most quoted phrases in the Constitution. It is clear that it was established by us, for us, and *to* us, surviving in perpetuity throughout all future generations. It is also interesting that the Preamble confirms a vision and direction for the country without granting any particular authority to the federal government. It begins to establish and confirm that this document is for "the people," and that the federal government will have no authority outside of what would be agreed upon in the articles and amendments to follow. It is important now to look at how the structure of our government has evolved with various powers and limits to facilitate the people in forming a more perfect union.

The articles can be summarized as follows:

- Article One: Describes and confirms the structure of legislative power (i.e. Congress and the legislative branch of the federal government). This article clarifies Congress as a bicameral body, consisting of the lower House of Representatives and the Senate as the upper house. The article also confirms the manner of election and the qualifications of members of each body.

- Article Two: Executive power—describes the presidency (the executive branch) by clarifying procedures for election and qualifications, the oath to be affirmed, and the powers and duties of the office.

- Article Three: Judicial power—describes the court system (the judicial branch), including the Supreme Court. This article requires establishment of the Supreme Court, and allows Congress to create lower courts, whose judgments and orders would be reviewable by the Supreme Court.

- Article Four: This article provides appropriate boundaries and structure to the relationship between the states and the federal government. For instance, it requires cooperation between states, and it also provides for the creation and admission of new states. It goes further to establish that the U.S. guarantees that each state adopts the form of a Republic—a state or country that is not led by a monarch, but in which the people have an impact on the government. The supreme power of a Republic rests in the body of collective citizenry.

- Article Five: Article V gives Congress the option of requiring ratification by state legislatures or by special convention. It also is the article that provides equal representation by confirming that no amendment can deprive a state of its equal representation in the Senate without that state's consent.

- Article Six: Federal power—Article VI establishes that the Constitution and the laws and treaties of the United States made in accordance with it are to be the supreme law of the land. It goes further to state that "the judges in every state shall be bound thereby, anything in the laws or Constitutions of any state notwithstanding." It also validates national debt created under the Articles of Confederation and requires that all federal and state legislators, officers, and judges take oaths or affirmations to support the Constitution. This is translated to mean that state Constitutions and laws should not conflict with the laws of the federal Constitution. If there is conflict, state judges are legally bound to honor the federal laws and Constitution over those of any state.

- Article Seven: This article establishes requirements for ratification of the Constitution. The Constitution would not take effect until at least nine states had ratified it in state conventions specially convened for that purpose, and it would only apply to those states that ratified it.

The articles provide other critical elements of the Constitution. With the Preamble as a launch pad, the articles go further to begin to more narrowly refine the scope and degree of appropriate government influence—or, in today's terms, government intrusion. While there may be people, many of whom are our elected leaders, who think progressivism, Marxism, and socialism are viable new variations that can be neatly tucked into a remake, the U.S. Constitution is the supreme law of the United States, and unless the people and their respective states say so, it cannot be usurped or undermined.

Make no mistake—the U.S. Constitution is fundamental to U.S. law, and to our entire political process. It provides the source of the legal authority that enables the existence of the United States of America and the federal government. In its entirety, it provides the framework for the organization of the government, as it clearly defines the three main branches: The legislative branch with a bicameral Congress, an executive branch led by the president, and a judicial branch headed by the Supreme Court.

In addition to providing the structure and organization of these branches, the Constitution very clearly outlines the powers and limitations of powers available to each branch. It also reserves numerous rights for the individual states, thereby establishing the federal system of government. The Constitution should be understood and respected as an unshakable foundation that, regardless of pressures placed on it, will not crack as it supports dreams upon which each American can build.

The next major component of the Constitution is the amendments, which can be summarized as follows:

- First Amendment: Provides the rights of freedom of religion, prohibiting Congressional establishment of a religion over another religion through law and protecting the right to free exercise of religion; freedom of speech; freedom of the press; freedom of assembly; and freedom of petition.

- Second Amendment: Guarantees the right of individuals to possess firearms.

- Third Amendment: Prohibits the government from using private homes as quarters for soldiers during peacetime without the consent of the owners.

- Fourth Amendment: Guards against searches, arrests, and seizures of property without a specific warrant or probable cause to believe a crime has been committed.

- Fifth Amendment: Forbids trial for a major crime except after indictment by a grand jury; prohibits double jeopardy, except in certain very limited circumstances; forbids punishment without due process of law; and provides that an accused person may not be compelled to testify against himself. This is regarded as the "rights of the accused" amendment, otherwise known as the "Miranda rights" after the Supreme Court case. It also prohibits government from taking private property for public use without just compensation—the basis of eminent domain in the United States.

- Sixth Amendment: Guarantees a speedy public trial for criminal offenses. It requires trial by a jury, guarantees the right to legal counsel for the accused, and guarantees that the accused may require witnesses to attend the trial and testify in the presence of the accused. It also guarantees the accused a right to know the charges against him. In 1966, the Supreme Court ruled that the Fifth Amendment prohibition on forced self-incrimination and the Sixth Amendment clause on right to counsel were to be made known to all persons placed under arrest; these clauses have become known as the "Miranda rights."

- Seventh Amendment: Assures trial by jury in civil cases.

- Eighth Amendment: Forbids excessive bail or fines and cruel and unusual punishment.

- Ninth Amendment: Declares that the listing of individual rights in the Constitution and Bill of Rights are not meant to be comprehensive, and that other rights not specifically mentioned are retained by the people.

- Tenth Amendment: Provides the powers not delegated to the United States by the Constitution, nor prohibited by it to the States, are reserved to the States respectively, or to the people.

It is important to note that these first ten amendments constitute the Bill of Rights, and that these amendments were ratified simultaneously. The remaining seventeen amendments had a separate ratification process. These rights established the basic American civil liberties that the government cannot violate. They define freedoms and institute a framework that ensures our democratic Republic system of governance. The Bill of Rights is also vitally important in providing further restrictions on the limits of government powers.

> "The whole of that Bill [of Rights] is a declaration of the right of the people at large or considered as individuals ... [I]t establishes some rights of the individual as unalienable and which consequently, no majority has a right to deprive them of."
> —Albert Gallatin, letter to Alexander Addison, 1789

The Bill of Rights has a preamble, which is a particularly illuminating and important document, as it clearly and succinctly defines government limits. The intent and spirit of these important amendments are best understood in the context of the preamble: "The Conventions of a number of the States, having at the time of their adopting the Constitution, expressed a desire, in order to prevent misconstruction or abuse of its powers, that further declaratory and restrictive clauses should be added."

The preamble states that the sole purpose of the amendments was to prevent the federal government from "misconstruing or abusing its powers." Therefore, further declaratory and restrictive clauses were recommended. When adopted, they placed additional restraints on the powers of the federal government. We should think of the Constitution as an extension of a system of limited government, denying the federal government the ability to encroach upon any rights that are not specifically enumerated. The fundamental question we should ask when we see the federal government initiate bailouts, mandate spending programs to the states, and expand powers is: By what authority? There is absolutely no power unless it is specifically enumerated in the Constitution.

The remaining seventeen amendments are summarized as follows:

- Eleventh Amendment: Clarifies judicial power over foreign nationals and limits ability of citizens to sue states in federal courts and under federal law.

- Twelfth Amendment: Changes the method of presidential elections so that members of the Electoral College cast separate ballots for president and vice presiden-Thirteenth Amendment: Abolishes slavery and authorizes Congress to enforce abolition.

- Fourteenth Amendment: Defines a set of guarantees for United States citizenship; prohibits states from abridging citizens' liberties or immunities and rights to due process and the equal protection of the law; repeals the Three-Fifths compromise; prohibits repudiation of the federal debt caused by the Civil War.

- Fifteenth Amendment: Forbids the federal government and the states from using a citizen's race, color, or previous status as a slave as a qualification for voting.

- Sixteenth Amendment: Authorizes unapportioned federal taxes on income.

- Seventeenth Amendment: Establishes direct election of senators.

- Eighteenth Amendment: Prohibited the manufacturing, importing, and exporting of alcoholic beverages.

- Nineteenth Amendment: Prohibits the federal government and the states from forbidding any citizen to vote due to their sex.

- Twentieth Amendment: Changes details of Congressional and presidential terms and of presidential succession.

- Twenty-first Amendment: Repeals Eighteenth Amendment; Permits states to prohibit the importation of alcoholic beverages.

- Twenty-second Amendment: Limits president to two terms.

- Twenty-third Amendment: Grants presidential electors to the District of Columbia.

- Twenty-fourth Amendment: Prohibits the federal government and the states from requiring the payment of a tax as a qualification for voting for federal officials.

- Twenty-fifth Amendment: Changes details of presidential succession, provides for temporary removal of president, and provides for replacement of the vice president.

- Twenty-sixth Amendment: Prohibits the federal government and the states from forbidding any citizen of age eighteen or greater to vote on account of their age.

- Twenty-seventh Amendment: Limits congressional pay raises.

The Constitution makes it abundantly clear that we have given our government certain powers and responsibilities with strict limitations. The government, in turn, has provided certain guarantees, rights, and liberties that correlate to the wishes of the people. Though some would argue we are entering into new era of government, we must be clear that if this supposed progressive era in any way undermines our Constitution, it cannot be taken seriously and must be thwarted at all costs.

> The [U.S.] Constitution is a limitation on the government, not on private individuals ... It does not prescribe the conduct of private individuals, only the conduct of the government ... It is not a charter for government power, but a charter of the citizen's protection against the government."
> —Philosopher and novelist Ayn Rand

The U.S. Constitution is a contract that provides protected rights and guarantees of freedom to American citizens; it is the supreme law of the land, which means it is foundational to our way of life. By reviewing the Constitution, we can see that this document was intended as a doorway to freedom, while providing a new world filled with unlimited possibilities. It was never intended to be viewed as a door*mat* to be tread upon as part of a process for entry.

An appropriate analogy is to view the Constitution as the framework for a house. The solid and unmovable rock foundation has been laid, and the frame has been set via the Constitution. Now, using our imaginations, we can begin to build our dream house, which is analogous to our future, filled with endless possibilities.

It is important to note that, again, the Constitution was specifically designed to be our foundation. By providing all citizens with context for freedoms and powers, there is a clear understanding of boundaries for all parties—citizens and all levels of government. Other forms of governance like progressivism, Marxism, and socialism do not provide consistent guarantees for all parties, and therefore represent unstable foundations. Using the analogy of building a house, these other forms of governance would be like trying to build a house on sand. With sand, which constantly moves and settles, no good foundation can be set.

Sand poses insurmountable challenges when trying to erect a building; there is difficulty at every step, since no good design, architecture, or foundation can be effectively built on sand. No building able to withstand changes in nature can survive over time if built upon sand. It would be a clear act of insanity to build a dream home upon sand when there is good, stress-tested, solid rock available.

This analogy was provided to illustrate a very important point. We are now at a pivotal time in history, where our leadership is smitten by the ideals of progressivism, or worse. Many of our leaders seem to believe that, though our Constitution exists, it should be viewed as a document that merely denotes an entry point into a way of life that can potentially change into whatever progressive form of government they wish. Patterns and behavior indicate they believe the Constitution is an evolving document. But, if this is the case, what happens to our guarantees of certain freedoms? Guarantees can't exist if we allow them to evolve into something nebulous, without a proper foundation. Likewise, when we include the issue of accountability, how can we even begin an attempt to hold our leaders accountable to an ever-changing and evolving constitutional framework afforded by progressivism? Progressivism provides our leaders with a convenient "back door" that excuses their obvious usurpation of the Constitution! Now, since we expect our Constitution to serve as a strategic weapon to combat oppression and tyranny, why would we allow our protected guarantees to be undermined by a progressive mind-set? One word—instanity!

Before going further, we should understand what the current era of progressivism means and what it entails. Fundamentally, new era of progressivism refers to ideology that believes our historical documents (like the Constitution and Declaration of Independence) are supposed to change and evolve over time as our society progresses (without due process of Constitutional conventions!); ultimately this mindset condones progressive initiatives that favor or advocate reforms that extend governmental control. These controls would influence power over the citizens, including the realms of economic and social policy. Progressive leaders ideally want disciplined government that pushes forward with egalitarian economic policies—distribution of wealth and classless societies—with government providing the oversight, regulation, and management of these policies. In short, progressivism is not at all equivalent to capitalism; it is the antithesis of it. As Americans, we have the right to live as capitalists, and our Constitution provides the appropriate framework for free market capitalism characterized by limited government. Since progressivism is a move toward bigger government influence and control, it is the exact opposite of the free market capitalist mind-set.

Generally speaking, people who are of the progressive mind-set can also be deemed statists. Statists believe citizenry and business exist only to enhance the power of the state; further, this ideology frowns upon individualism and looks to promote the government as the collective, unifying entity. Ideally, statists want the concentration and collection of all powers to be unified under the state.

Based on what we understand about our Constitution and progressive and statist ideologies, it should be offensive and appalling that our president and most members of his leadership team proudly identify themselves as progressives! To be sure, during a presidential debate, candidate Hillary Clinton proudly identified herself as a "modern progressive." Further, our president has also been affectionately identified by his peers as a social democrat.

As you can probably guess, a social democrat embraces strong Marxist roots. This is essentially a variation of the same theme of the need for state control in order to bring about a more egalitarian society. Actually, prior to becoming president, our leader confirmed his embrace of progressive ideology and mindset when he wrote, "I have to side with Justice Breyer's view of the constitution- that it is not a static but rather a living document and must be read in the context of an ever-changing world" (Barack Obama, *Audacity of Hope*). This is a surprising statement from a Constitutional scholar, as this mindset does not at all jibe with what historical Supreme Court Justice Joseph Story who wrote, "No man can well doubt the propriety of placing a president of the United States under the most solemn obligations to preserve, protect, and defend the constitution." Justice Story went further to proclaim, "The duty imposed upon him to take care, that the laws be faithfully executed, follows out the strong injunctions of his oath of office, that he will 'preserve, protect, and defend the constitution.' The great object of the executive department is to accomplish this purpose; and without it, be the form of government whatever it may, it will be utterly worthless for offence, or defence; for the redress of grievances, or the protection of rights; for the happiness, or good order, or safety of the people." Sound the alarms; there is a clear and troubling pattern emerging that, if left unchecked, could result in an impotent Constitution and regression to a pre-Constitution society.

The revelations about our leaders' foundations and leanings should not actually be surprising in light of the many policies currently being implemented. Without any thought about the wishes of the people, and without consideration of guarantees provided by our Constitution, our leadership has not only acted aggressively and boldly, but also irrationally. Our leader and his entire administration have been granted only limited enumerated powers; they took oaths to uphold our Constitution, and they must act consistently. This means we cannot lose our freedoms and guarantees outright. On the other hand, if we are not careful to inspect the personalities, language, and character of our leaders, we could cede our constitutional liberties and protections to the point of obsolescence.

The cultural popularity of a brilliant politician with a twist of historical fate is a recipe for how we have come to a point in history where we can allow an erosion of our Constitution. If we allow ourselves to be in a state of perpetual adulation, we can come to a point of feeling it safe to exercise blind trust and choose to simply defer. The unwise and ungrounded extension of trust, especially to those who do not share our vision, can be used to gradually undermine our foundations to the point that we become a country that is no longer recognizable. If we intend to appropriately intervene, we must learn to take full advantage of our collective powers. This will take diligence and fortitude, and since time is of the essence, we must start intervening now. Philospher Ayn Rand wrote, "We can evade reality, but we cannot evade the consequences of evading reality."

The fundamental elements of our Constitution pertain to power. Clearly articulated power, and the limits thereof, are reflective of the roots and foundations that have made our country a great success. Historically, America has been viewed as a model of what's possible by limiting government powers, while encouraging individual power and possibilities through innovation and through encouragement of entrepreneurship via free market capitalism.

In a similar fashion, other movements like progressivism, Marxism, and socialism are also motivated by power. The power from these ideologies, however, doesn't come from individuals, but instead comes from the government. These ideologies see state power as the primary tool to shape thinking and control what's possible at all levels—social, economic, foreign policy, etc. An obvious example of this is when government puts limits on income, wealth distribution, and on a number of other facets of life that we would classify as personal freedoms.

The subtle undermining of our Constitution is not just for consolidation of power to the state; it also has to do with an embrace and embodiment of ideology. Due to the aggressive path our leadership has taken for quickly implementing new policies and initiatives relating to all aspects of our lives, it seems clear that ideological motivations resonate at deep, personal levels of conviction. The arena of the soul is generally where we will find core beliefs. With better understanding of Obama's foundations, the actions and ideas pursued seem fully consistent with his background. Due to his personal charisma, charm, and popularity, his ideas have resonated with most of our other leaders; they now seem willing to embrace radical policies under the guise of progressivism.

What we should understand is that our leaders are brilliant speakers and politicians. They rely on personal influence and rhetoric to cover their intentional desire to undermine constitutional provisions. Our leadership has a tendency to want to forcefully engage in an intellectually dishonest diatribe about their full commitment to constitutional freedoms, while at the same time taking actions that confirm otherwise, through implementation of policies that undermine the Constitution. Gratuitous intellectual dishonesty is a consistent tactic that characterizes this era of governance.

To progressives, statists, and other radical ideologues, fulfilling commitments and promises in spoken words are not important; it is the fulfillment of the agenda that is primary. It should be understood that our current leadership possesses a zeal for power and ideology. As already noted, they are ideologically rigid, and if left unchecked, will leave us powerless to defend against unnecessary government intrusion.

By using the earlier analogy of the Constitution as the solid foundation for building a house, we should consider that it doesn't make sense to allow a new era of builders—who have absolutely no experience in architecture or construction—to tear down the foundation of a still-functioning house to make something they can only hope will function. It is absolutely insane for us to trust people who have no contractor's license and no architect's license to experiment with speculations—with the hope of building a better house.

Today, we are presented with leaders who are novices at reshaping government. Is it logical to completely trust them with our precious freedoms? Fundamentally, they are experimenting and hoping it all works out, but they have no strategic plan, no blueprint for success, no proven skills, or even a successful model for where they want to take us—for instance, other nations that have undergone similar changes and have been successful. A reliance on blind trust in this new era can only be conscribed as pure *instanity*.

CHAPTER TEN

The Dawn of a New Awakening

It does not take a majority to prevail ... but an irate, tireless minority, keen on setting brushfires of freedom in the minds of men.

—Samuel Adams

Contrary to what many of our leaders believe, we may have temporarily fallen asleep, but we are not wholly complicit with the agendas or the belief that we are in need of a larger degree of government intervention. Many leaders have made the absurd statement that we actually want *more* government. Recent polls show, however, widespread opposition to anything that resembles expanded government—government reliance, or government with the power to control and provide for us. If there is a large opposition to more government intervention and control, what is the apparent urgency for implementing these policies? Fundamentally, there seems to be an attempt to whittle away constitutionally defined limits of powers in order to consolidate into a more powerful government entity. If this process can be done quickly and expeditiously, we will lose personal power and freedoms without even noticing. Then, the Constitution will be deemed a doormat, providing only nebulous guidelines for citizenry instead of guarantees; our foundations will be forever shattered under the guise of a new, progressive era …

We should again understand that our government leaders have limited powers for very good reasons. Those who laid our constitutional foundation were very clear in their thinking and resolve about putting limits on government. Concerning the government's authority, our forefather Thomas Jefferson asserted: "[G]iving [Congress] a distinct and independent power to do any act they please which may be good for the Union, would render all the preceding and subsequent enumerations of power completely useless. It would reduce the whole [Constitution] to a single phrase, that of instituting a Congress with power to do whatever would be for the good of the United States; and as sole judges of the good or evil, it would be also a power to do whatever evil they please. Certainly, no such universal power was meant to be given them. [The Constitution] was intended to lace them up straightly within the enumerated powers and those without which, as means, these powers could not be carried into effect."

Some may believe that allowing government control is a worthy and just cause; some people are willing to give up personal liberties in order to pursue a more perfect union. On the surface, this may have some appeal, but even though this form of governance may seem somewhat noble, based on the backgrounds and patterns of our leaders, we should know this power grab is mostly self-serving. It will produce disastrous outcomes for us. We should understand that, for government leaders, more power obviously translates into having more control, money, influence, and unlimited favors granted them over the span of their political careers.

For we, the people, additional government power and control will force increased government dependence. As we know, dependence on the government is synonymous with poverty. Poverty is a form of oppression and bondage as it is the exact opposite of freedom and liberty guaranteed under the Constitution. If we allow the evolutionary drift of progressivism to take root, our vital protections will be forever lost.

We have seen many instances throughout history that evidence imbalance of power between individuals and government, where government domination produced disastrous results. As a matter of fact, there is not one example where this model has been proven successful for all involved. It doesn't make sense to even consider straying from our proven model of governance founded upon constitutional freedoms—to begin experimenting with other forms of governance. Most of those have been consistently proven unsuccessful, if not outright disasters.

Too much governmental power increases limitations on citizens. It puts excessive limitations on our ability to earn to our maximum potential, prevents us from thinking courageously in the pursuit of entrepreneurial innovations, and it limits our ability to succeed, as a individual and as nation. It also allows the state to design and control all available choices, which fundamentally undermines our freedom to make choices and live with our own consequences. This is especially poignant since we already have the perfect balance of power via the Constitution. Actually, it would make more sense for us to put more limitations on our leaders since, as we have already confirmed, most of our leaders have no experience in the private sector, very limited leadership experience, and limited competence at any level.

Our government poses the biggest impediment to our success. Again, their track record confirms all of their existing ventures and departments are woefully inefficient and mismanaged. They're the ones who need tweaking!

In all, there is still hope. The good news is that the people have the majority power. Though our leader has been called a "messiah" and "the anointed one,"—he's even been called God by Newsweek editor Evan Thomas—he is not omnipotent or omniscient and has no legitimate claim to these powers. We possess the ability to produce change. Our Constitution provides that we are a Republic and exist within a system of democracy, not a dictatorship. Therefore, regardless of our leaders' personal motivations, they are seriously limited by us.

The Constitution provides that our leaders must serve us within strict confines and boundaries as outlined, and all of our leaders have taken an oath to this effect. Our leaders should confirm that their service to us is being carried out in a spirit of humility, and with a depth of care and of gravity—consistent with the feeling of fear and trembling—while meeting our concerns.

Since we are the ones with the power, it is insane for us to settle for allowing our elected leaders to treat us with a sense of cavalier disdain. This is unchecked arrogance, and it serves as another confirmation of the current state of perpetual instanity.

When our leaders arrogantly pass legislation and spending bills without specifically understanding what's in them, they demonstrate a complete lack of will and desire to serve the people. With the rights and freedoms and guaranteed to us by way of the Constitution, we have also inherited responsibilities and obligations that are critical to our system of checks and balances. Our responsibility is to make sure that the people we hired actually fulfill their obligations to us by doing the work we hired them to do.

When we betray our responsibility to hold our leaders accountable for the job they do or don't do, we undermine our system of checks and balances. This creates a vacuum of power and provides an opportunity for our leaders to pursue their personal agendas without taking care of the people's business. It also conveniently whittles away at the powers provided in the Constitution.

Though the incredible logic outlined in our Constitution is evident, some may still feel a little intimidated to confront leaders and to hold them fully accountable. Just in case we are still a little reluctant, we should know that our founders created another valuable document to help make this point. It goes beyond standing up for our rights and responsibility; it actually goes further to confirm that it is our duty to do so. It reaffirms our rights and liberties, while further preventing government dominance and intrusion. It is our Declaration of Independence.

The Declaration of Independence is a perfect document to help understand the determination of our forefathers to rid themselves of what they perceived as tyranny inflicted upon them by King George and the British. They wanted to experience freedom, and they wanted to chart and control their own destinies without being beholden to an oppressive British government.

Against the backdrop of oppression and tyranny, our forefathers' drive, determination, and vision toward independence prompted the drafting of the Declaration of Independence. The Declaration reads as follows:

> When in the Course of human events, it becomes necessary for one people to dissolve the political bands which have connected them with another, and to assume among the powers of the earth, the separate and equal station to which the Laws of Nature and of Nature's God entitle them, a decent respect to the opinions of mankind requires that they should declare the causes which impel them to the separation.

This first section makes the case that, as a matter of natural law, people have the right to assume political independence. It goes further to acknowledge that the grounds for independence should be reasonable, logical, and fairly objective to the point that they can be explained. Wow! If we compare and contrast this thinking against our current political climate, we cannot deny we have wholeheartedly forsaken this wisdom. There is no doubt that we have become so politically polarized that we have allowed our zealous political affiliations to reduce our perspectives to a point of complete irrationality ... instanity!

The next section continues:

> We hold these truths to be self-evident, that all men are cre-
> ated equal, that they are endowed by their Creator with certain
> unalienable Rights, that among these are Life, Liberty and the
> pursuit of Happiness. That to secure these rights, Govern-
> ments are instituted among Men, deriving their just powers
> from the consent of the governed, That whenever any Form
> of Government becomes destructive of these ends, it is the
> Right of the People to alter or to abolish it, and to institute
> new Government, laying its foundation on such principles and
> organizing its powers in such form, as to them shall seem most
> likely to effect their Safety and Happiness. Prudence, will dic-
> tate that Governments long established should not be changed
> for light and transient causes; and accordingly all experience
> hath shewn, that mankind are more disposed to suffer, while
> evils are sufferable, than to right themselves by abolishing the
> forms to which they are accustomed. But when a long train of
> abuses and usurpations, pursuing invariably the same object
> evinces a design to reduce them under absolute despotism, it is
> their right, it is their duty, to throw off such Government, and
> to provide new Guards for their future.

This section provides us with some of the basic principles that should be used as a guide to our rights, as far as maintaining our freedom. The Declaration of Independence confirms, and we should understand, that freedom is not a gift from government—it is a right given to us by God. Every human being is endowed with certain "unalienable rights," including "Life, Liberty, and the Pursuit of Happiness." A new system of government was initiated and designed to form a more perfect union. From this union, we are guaranteed liberty and freedom.

It is also goes further to confirm that we are to hold our government fully accountable for not violating our rights and usurping it's powers. When rights are infringed upon, and when our government begins to expand to the point of intrusion, "we the people" have the right to "alter or abolish" that government.

Today, this right is carried out by voting out those not serving our interests. Declining to take a stand against federal government expansion, allowing excessive spending, and declining to thoroughly read the contents of every bill before voting are good examples of not serving our interests. Our forefathers also dealt with some of these issues, as they were duly noted in subsequent sections of the Declaration.

The next section summarizes charges against King George and demonstrates that he infringed upon rights of colonists to the point of tyranny. He was therefore declared unfit to rule.

> Such has been the patient sufferance of these Colonies; and such is now the necessity which constrains them to alter their former Systems of Government. The history of the present King of Great Britain is a history of repeated injuries and usurpations, all having in direct object the establishment of an absolute Tyranny over these States. To prove this, let Facts be submitted to a candid world.
>
> He has refused his Assent to Laws, the most wholesome and necessary for the public good. He has forbidden his Governors to pass Laws of immediate and pressing importance, unless suspended in their operation till his Assent should be obtained; and when so suspended, he has utterly neglected to attend to them.
>
> He has refused to pass other Laws for the accommodation of large districts of people, unless those people would relinquish the right of Representation in the Legislature, a right inestimable to them and formidable to tyrants only.
>
> He has called together legislative bodies at places unusual, uncomfortable, and distant from the depository of their public Records, for the sole purpose of fatiguing them into compliance with his measures.
>
> He has dissolved Representative Houses repeatedly, for opposing with manly firmness his invasions on the rights of the people.

He has refused for a long time, after such dissolutions, to cause others to be elected; whereby the Legislative powers, incapable of Annihilation, have returned to the People at large for their exercise; the State remaining in the mean time exposed to all the dangers of invasion from without, and convulsions within.

He has endeavored to prevent the population of these States; for that purpose obstructing the Laws for Naturalization of Foreigners; refusing to pass others to encourage their migrations hither, and raising the conditions of new Appropriations of Lands.

He has obstructed the Administration of Justice, by refusing his Assent to Laws for establishing Judiciary powers.

He has made Judges dependent on his Will alone, for the tenure of their offices, and the amount and payment of their salaries.

He has erected a multitude of New Offices, and sent hither swarms of Officers to harass our people, and eat out their substance.

He has kept among us, in times of peace, Standing Armies without the Consent of our legislatures.

He has affected to render the Military independent of and superior to the Civil power.

He has combined with others to subject us to a jurisdiction foreign to our Constitution, and unacknowledged by our laws; giving his Assent to their Acts of pretended Legislation:

For Quartering large bodies of armed troops among us:

For protecting them, by a mock Trial, from punishment for any Murders which they should commit on the Inhabitants of these States:

For cutting off our Trade with all parts of the world:

For imposing Taxes on us without our Consent:

For depriving us in many cases, of the benefits of Trial by Jury:

For transporting us beyond Seas to be tried for pretended offences

For abolishing the free System of English Laws in a neighbouring Province, establishing therein an Arbitrary government, and enlarging its Boundaries so as to render it at once an example and fit instrument for introducing the same absolute rule into these Colonies:

For taking away our Charters, abolishing our most valuable Laws, and altering fundamentally the Forms of our Governments:

For suspending our own Legislatures, and declaring themselves invested with power to legislate for us in all cases whatsoever.

He has abdicated Government here, by declaring us out of his Protection and waging War against us.

He has plundered our seas, ravaged our Coasts, burnt our towns, and destroyed the lives of our people.

He is at this time transporting large Armies of foreign Mercenaries to compleat the works of death, desolation and tyranny, already begun with circumstances of Cruelty & perfidy scarcely paralleled in the most barbarous ages, and totally unworthy the Head of a civilized nation.

He has constrained our fellow Citizens taken Captive on the high Seas to bear Arms against their Country, to become the executioners of their friends and Brethren, or to fall themselves by their Hands.

He has excited domestic insurrections amongst us, and has endeavoured to bring on the inhabitants of our frontiers, the merciless Indian Savages, whose known rule of warfare, is an undistinguished destruction of all ages, sexes and conditions.

It goes further to demonstrate attempts were made to find resolution to the issues.

In every stage of these Oppressions We have Petitioned for Redress in the most humble terms: Our repeated Petitions have been answered only by repeated injury. A Prince whose character is thus marked by every act which may define a Tyrant, is unfit to be the ruler of a free people.

The next section shows there was disappointment that these attempts had been unsuccessful.

Nor have We been wanting in attentions to our British brethren. We have warned them from time to time of attempts by their legislature to extend an unwarrantable jurisdiction over us. We have reminded them of the circumstances of our emigration and settlement here. We have appealed to their native justice and magnanimity, and we have conjured them by the ties of our common kindred to disavow these usurpations, which, would inevitably interrupt our connections and correspondence. They too have been deaf to the voice of justice and of consanguinity. We must, therefore, acquiesce in the necessity, which denounces our Separation, and hold them, as we hold the rest of mankind, Enemies in War, in Peace Friends.

The final section confirms that the only viable solution and remedy is for the people to change their government. It confirms that as a result the breech of trust, the colonies are compelled eliminate political ties with the British and become independent states.

We, therefore, the Representatives of the united States of America, in General Congress, Assembled, appealing to the Supreme Judge of the world for the rectitude of our intentions, do, in the Name, and by Authority of the good People of these Colonies, solemnly publish and declare, That these United Colonies are, and of Right ought to be Free and Independent States; that they are Absolved from all Allegiance to the British Crown, and that all political connection between them and the State of Great Britain, is and ought to be totally dissolved; and that as Free and Independent States, they have full Power to levy War, conclude Peace, contract Alliances, establish Commerce, and to do all other Acts and Things which Independent States may of right do. And for the support of this Declaration, with a firm reliance on the protection of divine Providence, we mutually pledge to each other our Lives, our Fortunes and our sacred Honor.

What incredible bravery! The founders who initiated and signed the Declaration of Independence are a perfect example of people taking a personal stand with fortitude and conviction. They were intent on providing a pathway and vision for America; their vision has already spanned many generations, over hundreds of years. If we exercise common sense, we can continue the fulfillment of their vision. Consider this: How many of us have the fortitude to take such a stand today? According to the Constitution and the Declaration, we have a right and responsibility to stand up to any of the leaders we've hired if they take actions that undermine their *strict* responsibility to uphold the powers and limits of our Constitution. We should understand that the act of expanding government by adding additional spending and liabilities into the private sector and into added social services can be an affront to our freedoms—unnecessary government expansion and intrusion.

Exceeding the limits placed on government powers and government ownership and control undermines our collective powers. Our powers become unbalanced with the majority power ceded to our government if we decline to exercise our rights and responsibilities by providing the appropriate checks and balances through close scrutiny of governmental actions.

Passing legislation without the appropriate diligence demonstrates that our system of checks and balances has failed. Essentially, these failures demonstrate a lack of integrity and ethics. We are being underserved and misrepresented. When leaders decline to perform the job they were hired to do—reading, understanding, considering ramifications, and voting on bills are just some of their duties—they perpetrate an arrogant affront to the people.

Every decision our leaders make on our behalf should be done with caution and circumspection in humility and with gut-wrenching significance, to the extent of fear and trembling.

We have passed stimulus, omnibus, tarps, and budgets without our leaders even reading and fully understanding the contents of these major initiatives. Most of these bills were passed hurriedly and contained hundreds of pages of major amendments that were added only hours before the vote. If we were fully inclined to provide appropriate checks and balances to our government, we would exercise our rights and responsibilities by voting out of office anyone who voted on something they didn't read and understand. This is the American way! This is an example of being free from tyranny.

Due to renewed public insistence that our leaders read legislation before voting, Democratic California representative Henry Waxman hired a speed reader to read a proposed bill as a way to mock the people; ironically, the speed reader didn't even finish, as there were over 1,000 pages. Where is our collective outrage? Why will we put up with such a blatantly arrogant disregard of our interests? With this one act, our common sense should tell us Mr. Waxman does not take us or his job seriously, and is certainly not concerned with our best interests. Common sense might also say that if a speed reader can't finish it, how could Waxman or his congressional colleagues be expected to read all proposed legislation in its entirety before voting?

With proper checks and balances, his career as politician should be finished! Unfortunately, the state of instanity blinds us from common sense. Therefore, Mr. Waxman will be able to enjoy a long political career, rife with even more outrageous acts that confirm annoyance and disdain toward us—unless we act!

The leaders we have hired should be burdened to serve us with the "full weight and conviction" of our Constitution.

Our Constitution and Declaration have provided us majority powers to chart a successful path for our country. These documents clearly demonstrate that we are fundamental to providing appropriate checks and balances for our government; checks and balances that are fundamental elements to freedom and our Republic. As confirmation of our duties to the Constitution, we should hearken the profound wisdom of Thomas Jefferson when he said, "the two enemies of the people are criminals and government, so let us tie the second down with the chains of the Constitution so the second will not become the legalized version of the first." It's the dangerous—yet subtle—pattern of complacency and silence that creates a convenient environment for more government control. Increased government control reduces the power of the people. Less power in the citizenry ultimately leads to oppression, and, as we have seen, oppression opens the door for many forms of tyranny.

We should have learned something from the sacrifices of our forefathers as they stood against incredible odds for their principles. Their sacrifices paved the way for us to experience hundreds of years of freedom and a well-formed democratic Republic. At this juncture in our history, we can lose many of the powers they provided us by simply deferring our responsibility. If we allow ourselves to become complacent and lethargic while absconding responsibility, we become fully complicit with our leaders and cede our powers to them. Our silence allows the subtle erosion of our powers and provides a blank check for our leadership to spend the country into oblivion.

The State of the State Is the State: Statism ... the New State of the Union

"It is to me a new and consolatory proof that wherever the people are well-informed they can be trusted with their own government; that whenever things get so far wrong as to attract their notice, they may be relied on to set them to rights."

—Thomas Jefferson

The only price we must pay in order to maintain our collective power, freedoms, and a democratic union, is to hold our leaders fully accountable. Notably, this is a more than fair tradeoff, as it's a small price for such a huge benefit. Current U.S. leadership also knows what's at stake and counts on our continued lethargy to pave the way for the new era—a new America with expanded government and expanded governmental power. Control is now in sight!

A new state is forming right under our feet. The new state is designed to expand their constitutionally-authorized limited powers into a state without limits that is more reflective of unlimited powers. Of course, we are making this trek in a very subtle way; it is happening under the guise of the government needing to provide more "services" for its citizenry during what many consider the worst economic crisis since the Depression. When our leaders are allowed to gain more control over additional aspects of our lives by re-authoring and rebuilding social and economic policy, we will defer our interests, and by default, cede our powers to the state. We see good examples of this when we observe patterns in current policy that allow government to spend our tax dollars on industry bailouts, intervene on executive compensation, and assume management input and oversight of private companies. Further examples are when we see new era policies for government-run universal health care and new energy policies for cap and trade. All these policies lead to expanded governmental power and control.

When we inquire about the obviously intrusive level of government intervention, our leaders continue intellectually dishonest dialogue. It is filled with excuses about the necessity of this level of government intervention because this is the worst economic climate of our lifetime, and there is urgent need to prevent extreme crisis and calamity. In the end, we're left with feeling that perhaps government has the answers, but make no mistake—our deference leads to a serious breach of powers, and if left unchecked, will cost us dearly.

The practice or doctrine of giving a centralized government control over economic planning and policy is defined as *statism.* As we allow the undermining of our powers and defer to our leaders without appropriately holding them responsible and accountable, we promote statism. Based on patterns, policies, and goals of our leaders, we have elected people who are wholly vested in this approach to governance, without regard to our constitutional provisions! Once we cede power and control, we lose our ability to have choices and make independent decisions. Furthermore, our leadership won't easily give up power or give some of it back once it has been ceded through deference. We are in a very tenuous spot, and we must recognize that liberties and freedoms lost now will result in a permanent loss for generations to come.

The current administration—the president and the entire Congress—is the best example of pure statism we've ever had in office. We are observing a masterful and seemingly calculated progression toward rendering our collective powers obsolete through dependence.

As noted, government dependence is the antithesis of freedom and liberty. After reading and considering our precious documents, which confirm our collective powers and the established boundaries of government intrusion, it is clear that our founders understood that government expansion is always at the expense of personal freedoms. The Constitution confirms the understanding that less government translates into more personal freedoms. Some of our government may have noble intentions for intrusion, but the reality is that when government infuses itself into a process, it only begets more government. A bigger, more complex government doesn't work. History confirms that personal liberty and freedom work. On the other side, it is also abundantly clear and indisputable that big government doesn't.

There are obviously expansive cost structures required to run expanding governments, and statism is only realistic if the state controls the majority of revenues and services. Since our leader already proclaimed that we are on a path that is unsustainable, how is this new era agenda going to be implemented? The unfortunate answer is taxes—new, unrestrained, and more comprehensive taxes.

Don't Tax Me, Bro!: The New Weapon for Government Power and Control

The pace and direction of the many changes impacting our country make it vitally important that every American make a concerted effort to periodically review the Constitution and Declaration of Independence. After reviewing these documents, we should have an extreme love and respect for these vital foundations that have secured our guarantees to freedom and established our way of life.

A fundamental characteristic of our founding documents is that they provide citizenry with a level set of criteria that allow for making assessments about how we are to be served by our government and leadership. We are provided a reasonable expectation for what our leaders will and won't—or shouldn't—do. The bottom line is that all our leaders have taken an oath of office and have sworn that they will—at all costs—uphold our Constitution and the entirety of its framework and provisions. Likewise, the oath confirms they won't—or shouldn't—do anything that erodes or undermines the foundation and framework of the U.S. Constitution. How is it possible, then, that our leadership is accelerating into new era policies that don't align with our constitutional framework? If we see our leaders taking directions inconsistent with Constitution, shouldn't we immediately vote them out of office? How do we remain lethargic and in a relative stupor while dramatic changes are being implemented?

Some actually believe alternate government models like progressivism, Marxism, or socialism, can work and may offer improvements to our governance. Though history confirms otherwise, some allow irrational dreams of the remake of a new America to overrule prudence and logic...instanity! These models cannot work within the confines of a democratic Republic and democracy because they cannot provide maximum freedom and liberty while also allowing government control.

When we compare and contrast a model of freedom and liberty to models that involve government control, we see they are on opposite ends of a paradigm; they mutually exclude one another! On the end where liberty and freedom reside, we have hundreds of years of historic evidence that we can consistently achieve more wealth and success (individually and collectively) under this model. On the end where government control is consolidated, we have consistent evidence of tyranny that promotes oppression and extreme poverty. We need to ask, "Why are our leaders so determined to pursue radical ideologies that only deliver bigger, more complex, inefficient, and more expansive government?" We should also ask how this irrational transformation will be implemented.

We have already noted that our leadership seems more driven by radical ideology than to maintain a commitment to their spoken word—commitment to fulfilling their constitutional oaths, and to the many promises and commitments made to citizenry. This drive cannot be fully explained. It is illogical and irrational and devoid of explanation, as there is no historical precedence that confirms any of these ideologies produce a viable path to successful governance.

For now, it is easier to try to explain the pursuit of new era policies as being driven by motives that provide our leadership with a sense of accomplishment at a purely emotional level, as opposed to logic and reason. It seems our leadership sincerely believes, embraces, and embodies ideology that thrives on money, power, and control. It's a fact that if the unifying government controls all the money and resources, it will garner all the power, willingly ceded from citizenry due to a nanny state; this leadership will effectively control all social, economic, and foreign policies through tightly-controlled levers designed to regulate all revenues and services. In this case, all choices and decisions will also be controlled—even down to the minute details of life and death—by the state. To get full compliance to such a radical power shift, there must be a general state of lethargy and complacency, fear, and intimidation, and a healthy dose of intellectual dishonesty served through melodic political rhetoric. Ironically, this epitomizes our current political climate, so watch out!

The primary tool that can be used as a method to control, immobilize, and dictate the actions of the citizenry, is taxes. While paying our fair share of taxes is honorable, overtaxing entire classes of individuals and businesses can be unfair and dishonorable. Dishonorable tax policies can precipitate resentment and produce class warfare, not unity and patriotism. This means ideas for promoting an egalitarian society should be only brought about through responsible governance—lowering taxes and by limiting government—and by actively promoting ideas that confirm the many possibilities for success that can be achieved through innovation and entrepreneurship.

Ultimate control of most, if not all, aspects of life can be produced through irresponsible manipulation of the tax system. Socialized governments are notorious for using seemingly ever-increasing taxes to enforce control mechanisms on all industries and businesses; citizens are also heavily taxed as a way to control wealth within the population. The bottom line is that tax policy is heavily used to promote government control. In the U.S., however, policies that undermine freedoms and liberty through unequal and unfair targeted taxing will be met with negative consequences that will cause more harm than collective good.

Unfair and disproportionate levying of taxes causes even more tensions and resentment between the people. When one class of people or entire segments of society are pitted against others, everyone loses. The government will lose because new era tax policies will be met with increased rampant fraud and corruption, as tax cheats at all levels will take full advantage of loopholes in order to evade—just ask current Treasury Secretary Timothy Geithner. Many will perceive these new era tax policies as a form of targeted abuse against those who have played by the rules, according to our laws and constitutional guarantees, while motivating themselves, working hard, and persevering. They are targeted and punished because of their accrued accomplishments and success. This is when tax policy can cross the line from being perceived as a patriotic duty to help our country achieve success to being a weapon unfairly and unequally applied as a means to control, immobilize, and dictate the actions of the citizenry.

Taxes that are laser-targeted as a method of control can be likened to a taser—in this case, a tax laser. This is an apt analogy, since ironically, a law enforcement officer's use of a taser provides equivalent results. For instance, law enforcement uses tasers to immobilize, control, and dictate the actions of suspects who show signs of resistance. In the end, it is demoralizing and ultimately produces a sense of resignation within the offending suspects. Likewise, unfair and unequal tax policies produce these exact outcomes, especially since these policies will produce limits on freedoms and choices, restrictions on spending behavior, and allow for new means of revenue enforcement. In the end, we will have similar feelings as those who have been tasered by law enforcement; we will be left feeling demoralized and resigned to the fact that we must relent our old way of life to a life dictated by new era governance. This imminent possibility should lead us to raise our collective voices and cry, "Don't tase me, bro!"

Following the taser analogy further, imagine someone with whom you are enamored running for sheriff in your town and campaigning on a platform of fairness. Let's say he also advocated the use of tasers as the ideal nonlethal weaponry for suspects who show signs of resistance. Since he stood for fairness, you respected and admired this individual, and you campaigned for him and fully supported his candidacy. After he won the office as sheriff, imagine driving down the road and obeying all laws that govern the road. Imagine he targets you and pulls you over for no apparent reason. When you simply inquire about why you have been pulled over, he becomes aggressive and proceeds to taser you. Again, this is the person you campaigned for and wholeheartedly supported. Would you be outraged by this brazen act? Of course you would!

Though tasers are a tool law enforcement officers can use to help with unruly people, they can also be used as a tool for abuse; like any other weapon, they can be overused or applied inappropriately. Unfortunately, this is the exactly analogous to the scenario we're faced with today with our new era government! Tax policies are being overused and inappropriately applied to "We the People."

During the presidential campaign, we were fully entranced by our leader as he passionately promised with absolute conviction that he would not raise taxes of any kind, even that he would reduce them for 95% of Americans. There were many instances during the campaigning and respective debates when we saw our now-president rebuke, mock, and belittle his opponents by labeling them out-of–touch and unrealistic because of their tax policies, most of which called for little or no tax increase but also no tax decrease. Though we were warned by other candidates, and our leader was rebuked repeatedly for proposing tax plans that could not work, our leader defiantly asserted that his plan for cutting taxes for 95% of Americans—while also pursuing massive health care, energy, and education reforms—would work. Well, our leader was wrong, and almost immediately after winning the election, he began proposing VAT (value-added taxes) and cigarette, health care, and energy tax policies that if implemented would cause a tax increase for all Americans! You may say, "But, he promised … How could this be?" The answer is one word: *Instanity!*

Broken promises and flip-flops are key indicators of incompetence; when hiring people to do a job that is clearly over their head because of their lack of prior experience, these signs of gross incompetence are predictable. Since our leader and his entire leadership team have no executive management experience, they cannot know with certainty the complications of managing complex budgets and finance while balancing aggressive new policy initiatives. The fact is, as was confirmed earlier, the commitment to fulfilling spoken word is not important to someone emotionally driven by an agenda; our leader was just saying what he felt he needed to say to get hired. We now know that this is another example of our leader being intellectually dishonest, but his overconfidence swayed us. Irrationally and illogically hiring new leadership without consideration of proven background and experience makes us wholly complicit with the current state of instanity.

New era policies being proposed under the guise of social improvements amount to tax increases and will have a profound impact on *all* Americans. There is no doubt that mounting budget deficits that, according to *The Wall Street Journal* , hit $1.1 trillion in June of 2009, have had an impact on new proposals on taxes. Should we overlook and excuse gross miscalculations as a reason for not delivering on the promises of cutting taxes for 95% of Americans? Now, among other new tax initiatives, Congress is considering implementing a value-added tax similar to that of the French and adding additional taxes on employees and employers for health care plans. New cigarette taxes have already been implemented under the Obama administration, and while I am not a defender of cigarettes, the fact is that new cigarette taxes disproportionately affect the poor. Demographic statistics confirm the underemployed, poor, and non-college educated are the highest percentage users of cigarettes and will be the ones who bear the brunt of these new taxes. While some may be provoked to quit by this new tax, many smokers will remain heavily dependent on cigarettes. With costs up to seven dollars a pack, this new tax will definitely disproportionately affect and penalize those who are already struggling for survival in this economy.

New and expansive tax policies demonstrate an unruly and inequitable expansion of government and government control. We should keep in mind what our forefather James Madison, had to say about these tactics that fundamentally undermine the limited constructs afforded by the Constitution. Madison said, "If Congress can do whatever in their discretion can be done by money, and will promote the General Welfare, the Government is no longer a limited one, possessing enumerated powers, but an indefinite one, subject to particular exceptions."

The biggest and most expansive tax increase affecting *all* Americans is the proposed new era energy policy encompassing cap and trade. This initiative has also been labeled as "cap and tax," since according to *The Wall Street Journal,* the Heritage Foundation, and many others, it represents the single biggest tax increase in U.S. history. If implemented, this new era energy policy will impact every individual in every household in America. No one will be exempt from the increased taxation impact of this heavily-veiled tax policy. The ironic and unfortunate reality is, the very demographic that our leadership has expressed a commitment and desire to help—the poor—will be hit hardest and have increased difficulty surviving. The poor will bear the brunt of these taxes since they are most susceptible to having even minimal increases in utility bills and cost of goods and services take them over the brink. They will be forced to pay a disproportionately higher percentage of income without receiving *any* value. Our government will produce an environment that will force us to spend more without providing *any* value for the citizenry ... instanity!

Many say that any new spending and subsequent taxes are justified based on the many inherent threats of global warming and our need to take care of the planet. This argument would be absolutely justified if it could be defended based on facts. We need to see a clear and undeniable correlation, which would need to be combated with purposeful worldwide strategies. It would need to be implemented based on genuine, committed determination reflective of purely altruistic motives. Unfortunately, none of these factors are driving the current new era energy policy.

In order to thoroughly examine and assess proposed energy policies, we should first understand the meaning and significance behind cap and trade. The proposed cap and trade system should first and foremost be thought of as a charade. When looking at the underlying factors of this new system, "charade"—cap and trade = charade!—is the most appropriate term to properly characterize it. It is a system that is being made up out of nothing tangible and that is designed to give government the ability to enforce taxes based upon factors that are made out of thin air … literally. To be specific, the idea is to make up a system that can be used to indiscriminately tax all aspects of living, starting with consideration of how much CO_2—ozone-depleting carbons—emission we create through ordinary activities like breathing, eating, and driving, to more complex business factors that monitor industry/ business use of energy, their various manufacturing processes, use of "environmentally safe" materials, etc.

Needless to say, this kind of tax system will invade every aspect of our daily living, and the biggest benefactors of this new taxation will be the U.S. government and big business.

To explain further, cap and trade can be summarized as a taxation policy that will be used to monitor, control, and penalize for anything the government deems as causing CO_2—since every human breathes CO_2, even breathing will be factored in this equation. The "cap" part of this new policy can be summarized as when our government determines a baseline of what they think should an appropriate carbon footprint, or baseline of allowable carbon, for all individuals, industries, and businesses. The government will "cap" that baseline as an allowable amount of carbon to be used.

The "trade" part of this energy policy charade comes in when government allowances for carbon limits are exceeded. In this case, "We the People" will be forced to buy, sell, and trade for additional energy credits, using brokers who will sell "allowances" to us to help bring us back under the government-mandated allowable limits. Obviously, this will lead to a significant amount of government intrusion into every area of our lives, but the intent is to wield the "tax laser" as a deterrent to help curb and control excess energy consumption while also providing a method of monitoring and controlling U.S.-generated CO_2 levels.

One of the biggest problems with this charade is that there is no undeniable correlation and consensus between scientists and governing bodies. When you consider there are still many scientists who are unconvinced as to whether rising CO_2 levels are man-made or just reflective of the earth's normal cyclical patterns of running hot and cold during prolonged periods. In the seventies, many scientists sounded the alarm for man-made global *cooling* and the resulting catastrophic events that would ensue if we didn't do something. Well, we did nothing, and now, approximately twenty-five to thirty years later, scientists are again sounding the alarm of immediate disaster due to man-made global warming. While there are surely well-intended scientists and scholars on both sides of the global warming debate, Al Gore notwithstanding, the facts do not undeniably confirm whether our climate patterns are cyclical and God-made or man-made. Additionally, even if we achieved a unified consensus of "warming" and its causes as being man-made, we still wouldn't know if any effort to regulate and control CO_2 levels would have any appreciable impact that would help save the planet. We should ask ourselves, if there are so many differing hypotheses and unknowns, why are we so aggressively pursuing this new taxation policy? Why do we allow our government— with its history of mismanagement and gross inefficiency—to force us into new policies of taxation and government control? Have we gone insane? Instanity.

European Union Parliament member Godfrey Bloom from the UK made a speech during a debate on the outcome of the Copenhagen Climate Change Summit. He blasted, "Global Warming" as a "Scam, Scam, Scam!" Godfrey called Al Gore a "snake oil salesman" and a "crook." He asked his fellow members, "When are you all going to wake up?"

No doubt, some blindly trust the many global warming claims and side with our government's belief that science unequivocally confirms there is man-made warming, and it results from consumption, thus leading to rising CO_2 levels. Based on current estimates from the EPA (Environmental Protection Agency) however, our government should be concerned about conflicting evidence.

The EPA has closely monitored warming trends and conducted detailed scientific studies over the years, and their newest studies confirm that while CO_2 levels have risen—manmade or not—over the past several years, global warming has actually decreased, and there is actual global cooling that has occurred over the past decade! This report directly contradicts our government assertions and hypotheses that posit that with a decrease in CO_2 emissions through strict regulation and control, we can cause a decrease in warming. In summary, this new data confirms there is apparently is *no* correlation between rising CO_2 levels and global warming! The charade continues.

The EPA report was delivered to our leadership prior to their push for votes on the proposed "cap and tax" bill. Though they were briefed and updated, they willfully suppressed this vital new evidence and did not inform the people about conflicting evidence. What? Is the suppression of vital information that would enable the people to make informed and unbiased decisions "change we can believe in?"

New "cap and tax" legislation is being touted as legislation vital for helping preserve the planet, now and in the future. Scientists confirm, however, that if there is a viable and purposeful strategy that will help curb global warming—it if exists—it would require new energy policies to be implemented and collaborated upon worldwide. This means that if the U.S. implements new energy policies without help from other countries with large populations and manufacturing, like China, India,

Mexico, and parts of South America, the strategy will likely have *no effect* on the very issues we are purporting trying to solve. China, India, Mexico, and countries in South America have already told our government they will not agree to implement any new energy policies consistent with our proposals. Even with news that other countries are unwilling to participate in our energy charade, and after also recognizing that our energy policies will have no effect unless universally accepted, our leadership remains undeterred. They are still aggressively launching headlong toward implementing new energy restrictions. In light of the contradicting scientific evidence and lack of support from other countries, our leaders are acting completely irrational and illogical. They are not only willfully and purposefully deciding to ignore reality and embrace sham "science", but they are also willing to perpetuate massive fraud and deception as a means to justify their respective ends which is to keep "we the people" in a perpetual state of instant insanity.

Recently, a purported "hacker" has discovered thousands of private e-mails and correspondence between some of the biggest scientific bodies and their respective individual contributors in the global warming debate. The messages confirm how prominent global warming scientists hid information about recent declines in global temperatures, tampered with data, and purposely deleted correspondence and data that conflicted with their global claims. In the end, we can confirm the *Intergovernmental Panel on Climate Change (IPCC)* and many of their foremost scientists used various tricks and schemes to thwart any kind of oversight as they fundamentally colluded to keep all dissenting voices and skeptics silent. Haven't we heard Al Gore and others castigate dissenters by saying "the debate is over" global warming is a scientific reality? Why then would we discover overwhelming evidence confirming hidden truths behind their global warming tactics of alarmism which includes deleted e-mails, hidden declines, inaccurate data, destroyed research and the redefinition of peer-reviews for their own uses? According to Investors Business Daily, "... 2007 report helped the IPCC win a share of the Nobel Prize. But its work is looking less credible by the day. Can any of its claims be trusted? Its authors—who merely compiled others' work and did no research of their own—sure haven't inspired confidence in their work. In fact, their blunders are quickly pushing the global warming farce toward a grand collapse."

Implementing fraudulent new energy policies at this time would force many new restrictions that would severely limit not only individual freedoms, but also freedoms and guarantees for manufacturing and businesses. This would open the door for businesses and entire industries to move operations to less-restrictive areas like China, India, Mexico, and South America. In short, this charade would produce all hype and would come at a very high cost. It represents meaningless symbolism that will ultimately result in a complete waste of time, resources, and unnecessary pain inflicted upon the American people. Make no mistake—cap and trade will do nothing more than cap our incomes while forcing us to trade in our freedom. "We the People" will be the biggest losers; big business and the U.S. government, however, will be the big winners.

The "cap and tax" charade is being aggressively pushed because of, as noted earlier, the need for more money, power, and control; these are the key elements that resonate at the heart of this matter. We will never hear our leaders actually admit their intellectually dishonest motivation, but by looking closely at the pattern of actions and intentions, we can begin to surmise what is behind these aggressive new energy policies.

Our leadership would like us believe they have purely altruistic motivation, designed to help the planet, create jobs, and to help the U.S. become a leader and model for environmental responsibility. They have touted new energy policies that will help the planet by ushering in wind, solar, and other CO_2-reducing energy innovations without mentioning the much higher costs we must endure due to the necessarily higher cost of doing business.

Our leadership has touted that these energy initiatives will bring millions of new "green" jobs without mentioning the millions of job losses that would necessarily occur due to business moving overseas. They have touted a new era of being environmentally responsible without mentioning the fact that these policies will make us *more* dependent on imports from the Middle East and elsewhere, while our radical efforts will have *no effect* on warming, unless, at the very least, all other large countries jointly implement.

When it comes to cap and trade, the consistent pattern of intellectual dishonesty reaches new lows. Consider this: Our president defiantly defends these new era energy policies as not being new forms of taxation, while at the same time he says, "Under my plan, electricity rates will necessarily skyrocket." Huh? Also, consider the fact that Al Gore and many members of Congress have personal investments in "green" companies and stand to personally gain from the new energy policy. The fact is that the proposed new layer of energy taxes represents the U.S. government's most significant revenue generator of all time! It will allow enforcement of monitoring and controlling revenues, and by virtue of its comprehensive reach, citizens cede their powers guaranteed under the Constitution. By default, the government gains complete control of all aspects of life in the U.S.

C.S Lewis wrote, "What we call man's power over nature turns out to be a power exercised by some men over other men with nature as its instrument." This quote is quite poignant and prophetic, especially after considering the facts surrounding proposed new era energy policies. It is seems clear that the lofty new energy policies are designed in an attempt to exert man's power over nature—Earth's natural cycles of warming and cooling—and while engaging in this seemingly benign and altruistic pursuit, we now see men being supremely motivated by accumulating more power, using nature as the instrument. Logically speaking, it is ludicrous and insane to believe the president and Congress can control the climate, which is natural and controllable by God alone. Obviously, they have proven they can't even control monetary policy, budgets, and spending—fully tangible factors that are definitely under human control. Instanity!

In summary, issues surrounding global warming are still being debated. Regardless of what is asserted, there is no universally accepted conclusion on this issue. As noted, other large industrialized countries will not join the U.S. in implementing these new era energy policies and actually look to use our restrictive new polices to attract more U.S. businesses and investments. The result will actually produce catastrophic consequences, as these policies will cause accelerated job losses—some estimates say over two million jobs will be lost by 2012, loss in GDP—some estimates project lost GDP at $9.4 trillion through 2035, and force an oppressive new tax on the poor—some estimates predict the average American family will have an increased energy cost of $1,241 to $3,000 per year. More expensive U.S. goods and services will also naturally result, further complicating our trade imbalance and economic recovery. Fundamentally, our rights, liberties, and freedoms will be significantly reduced if we allow implementation of the "charade"; we will encounter a natural restriction of choices, which will lead to a less hopeful and less dignified existence.

Cap and trade policies provide another point that further confirms a consistent pattern indicating a lack of leadership. In this matter, our leader has failed to clearly articulate a plan for success, he provides no vision using an existing successful model, and he has failed to provide undeniable facts that support his assertions of projected outcomes or consequences. With that said, there is little doubt the proposed new era energy policies are being driven by self-serving politicians and powerful businesses already vested in "green," like GE, Goldman Sachs, and others, who stand to earn hundreds of billions! For the people, implementation of the cap and trade charade means all pain and no gain—instanity.

The Spread of CZARS: The New Washington Epidemic

"[N]either the wisest constitution nor the wisest laws will secure the liberty and happiness of a people whose manners are universally corrupt."
—Samuel Adams, essay in The Public Advertiser, 1749

A few years ago, a new virus was discovered called SARS—severe acute respiratory syndrome. This disease was highly contagious and spread rapidly, mostly in parts of Asia. As it began to spread around the globe, the SARS epidemic had immediate and destructive effects, significantly impacting daily activities in the lives of everyone in the affected regions. Chaos and uncertainty ensued, with severe impact to major industries, manufacturing, travel and tourism, and all other aspects of social and economic existence. Though the fight against SARS is still being fought in some areas, the final outcome will note that the SARS epidemic delivered a devastatingly traumatic impact worldwide.

SARS, and its ultimate impact, provides a good analogy for the current epidemic sweeping Washington—the emerging czar epidemic. While the epidemic in Washington by no means, delivers the deadly results that SARS has, its ultimate impact is similar in name, pattern, and behavior.

The use of czars is not a new phenomenon; it has evolved over multiple presidential administrations. Actually, FDR seems to have started the trend when he had executive positions he referred to as dictators; these people were appointed to oversee and control prices within specific industries like lumber and steel in order to maintain price stability. This trend was continued in Richard Nixon's administration, but instead of calling his appointees "dictators," he called them "czars." Ultimately, the use of czars became an accepted practice. President Ronald Regan had a drug czar, President George H.W. Bush also had a drug czar, and President Clinton had three czars: health, drug, and AIDS. President George W. Bush had four czars: cybersecurity, national intelligence, drug, and AIDS. By comparison, some reports indicate President Obama has hired nearly forty czars, and counting. Under our new president, czars have grown into epic proportions. Our new president is "czar-struck!"

People who support and encourage the use of czars say these positions help manage specific and important initiatives that presidents themselves cannot manage and oversee on a daily basis. In principle, this seems to be reasonable justification and is somewhat plausible. However, if the use of czars is overused, it can grow into a destructive force of epidemic proportions.

A reasonable question to ask is, "What's the problem with czars?" Since they can be used to help streamline the efforts of our president, "What's the big deal?" First, we should recognize that anything can be abused if it's overused or incorrectly applied. This logic is especially true when it comes to the use of czars. Czars are unelected federal government executive officers with broad powers and responsibilities. To uphold the sanctity of the Constitution, people with this degree of authority are typically elected and confirmed through Congress. Czardom is not constitutional, and if overused can be used to undermine our system of checks and balances. The potential for revolt and outrage from the states has helped limit use of czars in prior presidential administrations.

It is interesting to note that prior presidents showed judicious restraint by limiting their czar appointments from one, on the low end, to four; our current president, however, has appointed almost forty within his first year of presidency. Why the dramatic shift in czar usage? Have the issues confronting the federal government grown ten times more complicated while transitioning from one administration to another? As noted, other presidents have used czars for specific, strategic purposes, to provide the president with manageable oversight over initiatives. Does having forty czars as direct-reports seem even remotely manageable or strategic? Our president has elevated his presidency to "super czar-dom." The overuse of czars is symptomatic of incompetence, which, based on background, is predictable, but the larger issue is that this blatant overuse of czars poses significant risk to checks and balances extended through our Constitution.

There are several articles of the Constitution that could be undermined by the use of czars—notably one, two, and four—as our federal government has been extended enumerated powers and structure. The use of czars is not specifically enumerated as an extension of some type of special discretionary presidential authority. To confirm, the preamble to the Bill of Rights states, "The conventions of a number of the States, having at the time of their adopting the Constitution, expressed a desire, in order to prevent misconstruction or abuse of its powers, that further declaratory and restrictive clauses should be added."

This confirms our system of checks and balances was designed to protect our liberty and freedoms by limiting federal governmental powers, while at the same time preserving the majority powers to the states by way of the citizenry. This ensured that power could never be consolidated by an overreaching federal government. The overuse of the privilege to appoint czars can undermine this constitutionally-mandated system of governance.

We should understand that czars are appointed positions; they are handpicked and specially appointed to serve the president alone. Czars are appointed without having to be confirmed by the Senate, and they are not accountable to *anyone* except the president. This means that if they were to undertake a special project on behalf of the president and were called to testify before Congress for some reason, they could claim executive privilege, making these unelected and unconfirmed people somewhat untouchable—to a degree, elevating them above the law.

Though they represent an affront to our Constitution, our tolerance for czars of past administrations has to do with the fact a few czars can be effectively managed by a president. Further, due to such a small number, they would not likely create any consequences that could fundamentally undermine our system of governance. Forty czars, on the other hand, are a direct and arrogant assault to our system of governance, and can produce destructive consequences. There is no defensible logic to having forty czars as direct reports in addition to the entire White House staff and cabinet—an estimated one hundred people. One hundred direct reports? This is not only illogical, it is a good example of unchecked and unhinged insanity! It is documented that even the best managers can only effectively manage twelve to fifteen people; one hundred is completely out of the realm of what is humanly possible. People touting our leaders' brilliance will still, no doubt, make excuses for this gross mismanagement, but remember that even Jesus Christ limited himself to only twelve disciples.

The czar of czar's, Czar Obama, will not likely consider any of the facts for effective management as a way to implement effective governance since he has arrogantly graded his first year in office as a B+; narcissism notwithstanding, by all objective measurement, Czar Obama is on track to be the worst president in American history and he will only have himself to blame for our dismal state of affairs wrought with duplication, waste and incredible inefficiency.

Since we already have federal government offices and departments headed by elected and nominated individuals, there will be significant overlap and ridiculously higher costs associated with the additional layer of czars. This overlap will lead to turf fights and power struggles, further complicating an already inept and grossly inefficient government. When problems between authorities and departments ensue, czars will prevail, as they have been appointed by, have direct access to, and report directly to the president. The czar debacle not only poses a high cost to the people, due to the loss of our checks and balances afforded by the Constitution, but it also has an extremely high cost to taxpayers, since redundant people need duplicate personnel, offices, expenses, and overhead. We should ask ourselves, with our current economic crisis, are czars a justifiable expenditure and good use of our tax dollars? Better yet, why are czars being so vigorously pursued and implemented as standard policy in this administration?

Our system of governance, with its powers and limits, is established to provide the people, by way of our states, complete transparency and accountability. This means everyone in our executive and legislative branches of government is accountable to us in some way. The only way to get around the lengthy process of nominations, confirmations, and subsequent appointments, is to use self-determined power and authority to appoint people. For people looking to cover up a pattern of making bad nominations and subvert the process of constitutional provisions, czars are the perfect antidote. Czars can effectively provide an avenue for implementing another form of government that is not limited or restricted by those pesky background checks and confirmation hearings. They are not limited to act in accordance with and fully accountable to the people. To the contrary, czars are completely unaccountable; their accountability and allegiance is strictly to the president.

Our other branches of government do not answer directly to the president; they answer to us. The czars don't. If the czar epidemic continues, we will lose the ability to hold our federal government fully accountable. Meanwhile, the unelected, unvetted, and unaccountable czars, many of whom may have nefarious intentions, grab power and authority from our president.

There have already been reports of a few czars that would likely not have passed a full Senate confirmation because of their backgrounds. For instance, science czar John P. Holdren has advocated (in his book Ecoscience) that governments use methods like forced abortions, the implantation of birth control capsules in all women, use of sterilization substances in drinking water, and other eugenicist policies to control populations. He has stated, "Individual rights must be balanced against the power of the government to control human reproduction ... some people, respected legislators, judges and lawyers included, have viewed the right to have children as a fundamental and inalienable right, yet neither the Declaration of Independence, nor the Constitution mentions a right to reproduce." By these statements, we can see Holdren is a strong advocate of population control, even to the extent of government force.

Our president's pick for regulation czar, Cass Sunstein, is a personal friend of Obama from Chicago. He believes animals (livestock, pets, and other animals) have the right to sue humans in the American courts. He also is on record calling for the need to determine the value of each human by formulas that take into consideration age and usefulness. What's puzzling about Mr. Sunstein's views is, while he seems to highly regard the life and livelihood of all animals, he is callous with human life. He is a primary advocate of limiting investment in humans based on some formula for determining "usefulness", but he advocates preserving the life of animals at all costs even if it means allowing them to argue their case before a court judge. Insane!

The green czar, Van Jones, is just as controversial. He is an ex-con and self-proclaimed communist! Van has proudly identified himself as a communist and a black nationalist. With this background and these foundations, is it likely he would have passed our confirmation hearings? Of course not! Press reports suggested that the White House failed to properly vet Jones (again, this is to be expected when incompetence prevails). Since he was so controversial, Van Jones resigned after a couple of months on the job. Van Jones is simply another good example that further confirms the new president sorely lacks wisdom and leadership and needs guidance from the people. Unfortunately, a pattern of unchecked arrogance may prevent any attempts for intervention, and this will lead to more irresponsible actions.

Mark Lloyd is another controversial appointment by our president. He is Chief Diversity Officer at the Federal Communications Commission. He is someone who believes "our freedom of speech rights are exaggerated." He is on record for saying that he felt the Fairness Doctrine, which required broadcasters to present contrasting points of view on controversial matters, didn't go far enough. It should be no surprise that someone of this mindset would praise Hugo Chavez's' revolution of Venezuela as "really incredible"! This helps explain why Lloyd has casually asserted that there is a need to replace current radio management and talent " ... with people of color, gays and other people ... " According to Lloyd, "We're in a position where you have to say who is going to step down so someone else can have power." Hmm ... sounds Marxist; sounds insane!

With our current president and administration, there are so many bad or just outright dangerous appointments that a book could be written on this topic alone. That said, there is one more appointment that does require special attention and our extreme vigilance. This Obama appointment is especially troublesome because it involves our children. President Obama has appointed homosexual activist Kevin Jennings as our "safe schools czar" at the U.S. department of Education. Jennings founded the Gay, Lesbian, and Straight Education Network (GLSEN) and this organization promotes the acceptance of homosexuality in public schools. Not withstanding the fact that GLSEN co-sponsored a youth workshop where it helped guide students through the mechanics of sex acts, oral sodomy, and lesbian sex, but according to numerous new outlets, Jennings seems to encourage child sex with older men.

According to the Washington Times, a teacher was told by a 15-year-old high school sophomore that he was having homosexual sex with an "older man." At the very least, statutory rape occurred. Mr. Jennings had a real chance to protect a young boy from a sexual predator; he not only failed to do what the law required (reporting child rape and abuse) but actually encouraged the relationship. Let's get this straight; our president has hired someone who kept quiet while having full knowledge of a sexual predator committing statutory rape and child abuse on one of his students, as a "safe schools czar?" Absolutely insane!

Radicals with clear Marxist and communist mindsets seem to flourish in the Obama administration. Ron Bloom, a manufacturing czar, is on video proudly proclaiming that he "kind of agrees with Mao" and that he believes "that the free market system is nonsense." Another appointee is Anita Dunn who proudly proclaimed to students that "Chairman Mao is one of the two people" she turns to most. Then there's Carol Browner, who was appointed to the cabinet, and is a member of the International Socialist Organization. Do we see a pattern here? Our president has surrounded himself with people who admire radical models of government and rouge regimes of political figures responsible for horrible suffering and, with the killing of tens of millions of their own people, inflicted the most devastating atrocities in human history!

As a direct affront to established provisions for properly vetting nominees, our president chooses to subvert our processes. In doing so, he undermines our systems of checks and balances. Our leader appears to be building his own, self-serving government, accountable to no one but him.

What are we doing? Is this America? We are now seeing disconcerting results stemming from allowance of decades-old practices. The only explanation for sitting passively while our president appoints radicals leaders, usurp Constitutional protections, and extend to them extraordinary powers to transform America, is we have gone instantly and selectively insane. We have allowed this to fester; now it has thrown us into a state of pure instanity!

There is no doubt our president is "czar-struck". He seems to have grandiose visions for remaking America with or without our constitutional checks and balances. Thus far, approximately forty czar positions have been appointed. The ever-growing field of czars is as follows:

Afghanistan czar	Mideast peace czar
AIDS czar	Mideast policy czar

Border czar	Pay czar
California water czar	Regulatory czar
Car czar	Science czar
Climate czar	Stimulus accountability czar
Domestic violence czar	Sudan czar
Drug czar	TARP czar
Economic czar	TARP oversight czar
Energy czar	Technology czar
Faith-based czar	Terrorism czar
Great Lakes czar	Urban affairs czar
Green jobs czar	Weapons czar
Guantanamo closure czar	WMD/Terrorism czar
Health czar	Copyright czar
Information czar	Cyberspace czar
Intelligence czar	

We can no longer tolerate or sugarcoat the facts. We are losing control of our Republic through czars. Remember, all these czars have large budgets, personnel that overlap with existing personnel, and the power and authority that come from working directly for the president and with full backing of the presidential seal. There is a pattern of a growing and very powerful shadow government, and this government will give our president and his entire administration unprecedented power with virtually no oversight from the people. Czars can be used to bypass Congress and aggregate control to the president. Just as with our most dangerous viruses and diseases, our "czar-struck" leadership has implemented something that may have seemed relatively innocent at first but has rapidly transformed into something stronger, more resistant, and capable of delivering more destructive results to all those who are affected.

While aspiring for more influence, power, and control, our president has attained the infamous distinction of being a "super-czar" president. "Super-czardom" has reached the level of being classified as an epidemic characterized as having great momentum and power behind it; if we do not neutralize it, it will consume us. Like SARS, czars are an imminent threat that we must not take lightly.

We need to ask ourselves by what authority our leaders take these radical steps. The Constitution certainly doesn't provide for this manner of governance. We are forced to come to grips with the fact that we cannot wholeheartedly embrace the foundations of the Constitution and Declaration of Independence while also fully supporting the new era politics of our leadership. These actions rest on opposite ends of the spectrum and mutually exclude one another.

It hurts to realize that we, the people, are the primary culprits who have precipitated this dangerous juncture in our history. Our lethargy in holding our leaders accountable and lack of intervention in the election cycle can be attributed to the same old culprit that robs us of logic, rationality, and common sense—the rise of a state of unchecked instanity.

They Call Me MISTER Fibs!

"The same prudence which in private life would forbid our paying our own money for unexplained projects, forbids it in the dispensation of the public moneys."
—Thomas Jefferson

Undoing the primary foundations of our Constitution doesn't happen overnight; it requires very methodical and persistent steps to be taken by a trusted and popular president. Placing a high degree of trust in any U.S. president is insanity, since we have a history of hiring presidents who left their respective offices with less than honorable track records. There is no doubt

175

this will continue to happen. The larger question is, though, don't all presidents get sworn into office by taking an oath to uphold the Constitution at all costs? If upholding the Constitution is a primary duty, how have we arrived at a point in history that inarguably confirms presidential policies and patterns that directly undermine the very Constitution they were sworn to uphold? Are we that gullible and illogical? We must assume there is a high degree of intellectual dishonesty.

There is a great Sidney Poitier movie from 1967 called In The Heat Of The Night. In one scene, Mr. Poitier introduces himself with an air of sophisticated, yet defiant, eloquence, saying, "They call me *Mister* Tibbs!"

When I see our president speaking with a similar air of sophisticated, yet defiant, eloquence, I am reminded of Mr. Tibbs, but with one small twist. In my silly imagination, I envision our president saying, "They call me Mr. Fibs!" While watching Obama host a seemingly endless schedule of press conferences, meetings, and preemptive special infomercials, my Mr. Fibs analogy, helps me get through the barrage of baseless promises, hyperbole, and obvious incompetence with laughter and humor.

Our leadership made many promises during the presidential campaign and during the first six months in office. By my count, very few (if any) of these promises have been kept. What does this mean? It means that we have been entranced by the many assertions delivered with eloquence and style, without interrogating the substance—delivery or manifestation of outcomes. Perhaps a review of some of the many promises made will help provide more clarity and confirmation.

Promises, Promises

Stimulus

Promise: We were promised that the passage of stimulus package would immediately save or create three to four million new jobs, preventing the jobless rate from climbing over eight percent. We were warned that if the stimulus was not passed, the unemployment rate would climb to nine percent, and imminent disaster would ensue. Several months after passing the stimulus, our president and members of his administration asserted that the stimulus was working as expected.

Fact: The stimulus plan was passed, but the jobless rate continued to climb. The unemployment rate easily surpassed the eight percent threshold and is now over ten percent; it is at its highest rate since 1983—10%. Many expect it to rise further still. Some economists assert that we likely could have saved the almost trillion-dollar stimulus expenditure and arrived at the same jobless rate. Was this money wasted? When confronted with the results of the stimulus fiasco and facts about the promises for jobs not being met, Vice President Joe Biden offered as an excuse, "Everyone guessed wrong." What? Guessed wrong? Instanity!

. . .

Transparency

Promise: While campaigning in Manchester N.H, our president said, "When there is a bill that ends up on my desk as a president, you the public will have five days to look online and find out what's in it before I sign it, so that you know what your government's doing."

Fact: Our president has signed many bills, but only six have been posted on the White House website, and not one of those was posted for a full five days after presentation from Congress.

. . .

Tax Cut for 95% of Americans

Promise: While campaigning, President Obama promised with conviction that he would cut taxes for 95% of all Americans. His confident assertions were particularly poignant in the midst of

McCain's counterargument that this was unrealistic and impossible. Obama, of course, resorted to name-calling and depicted McCain as being out of touch.

Fact: There have been far-reaching new taxes proposed for *all* Americans. A cigarette tax has already been implemented, and based on demographics of cigarette smokers, this tax has a hugely disproportional impact on the poorest Americans and on middle income earners, as it will severely cripple their budget for daily living expenses. Additionally, the proposed cap and trade charade and new proposals for health care will have increased tax implications for all.

· · ·

Energy Independence

Promise: During the presidential campaign, Obama was being confronted about his purported "no drilling" stance. During a debate with John McCain, he vigorously defended that he was a candidate who supported pursuing all methods of energy exploration and confirmed that we need to pursue more drilling, clean coal, wind, solar, and even nuclear power. He strongly asserted that his plans would quickly move the U.S. away from dependence on foreign oil.

Fact: Since taking office, our president has aggressively moved to cancel oil drilling leases, but he has not undertaken any new initiatives for the use of clean coal or nuclear energy. Additionally, his policies aggressively pursue taxation of the air we breathe via cap and trade, which will increase and elongate our dependence on foreign oil. Our leadership should have prompted initiatives that take full advantage of the country's hundreds of millions of barrels of crude oil—offshore and underground—and a virtually unlimited supply of natural gas underground. If our leaders were truthful and sincere, we would be pursuing the use of our own resources instead of spending eight times more on foreign energy resources.

. . .

Earmarks

Promise: Our president was critical of pork barrel spending in the form of earmarks, urging changes in the way that Congress adopts the spending proposals.

Fact: After winning the presidency, our president signed spending bills containing nearly 9,000 earmarks, many of which were put in by members of his own staff when they were still members of Congress. In culmination of the insidious level of intellectual dishonesty, while signing the bill, Obama said, "Let there be no doubt, this piece of legislation must mark an end to the old way of doing business, and the beginning of a new era of responsibility and accountability."

. . .

Lobbyists

Promise: While campaigning, our president assertively and defiantly promised he wouldn't have lobbyists in his administration.

Fact: In his first two weeks in office, President Obama made seventeen exceptions.

. . .

New Era of Bipartisanship

Promise: During the campaign, and even after the election, our president made a hopeful promise and appeal for a new era of political bipartisanship. During the inaugural address, he even promised an end to the "petty grievances and false promises, the recriminations and worn-out dogmas, that for far too long have strangled our politics."

Fact: We probably have the most polarized and resentful Congress in history. The venom spewed by ideologues in both parties is vile and extremely ineffective. The bottom line is that it took only three days after the inauguration before discussions between the parties produced no common ground, and each party again began to staunchly pursue its respective agenda. Our president's promise to unify parties and produce bipartisanship rings hollow.

. . .

Darfur

Promise: In 2008, Obama castigated President Bush for considering normalizing relations with Sudan, calling the idea "a reckless and cynical initiative." Obama went further to add, "We cannot stand down." While campaigning, Obama stated, "I will make ending the genocide in Darfur a priority from day one."

Fact: After seven months, the Obama administration has not provided a definitive strategy or policy position for Darfur. There have been requests for helicopters and other aid from the people in the region, but our leader and his entire administration remain quiet on Darfur. Contrary to his rhetoric and condemnation of others, our president hasn't renewed calls for sanctions or provided any other means to help the very people he said would be a priority from day one.

. . .

Automobile and Financial Institutions

Promise: When asked about the federal government's expansion and oversight of private industries like the auto and banking businesses, our president emphatically stated, "I do not want to run auto companies ... I have more than enough to do." President Obama has taken a similar position when asked about financial institutions.

Fact: Our president has taken a stake in these two struggling industries. In a gross example of government intervention, our president not only thought it okay to invest on our behalf into these struggling industries but took it upon himself to hire and fire executives and place federal government oversight into both the automobile and banking industries. Also, many banks were pressured into taking government money. Some banks that tried to decline or immediately pay the government money back were not allowed to do so.

. . .

Budget

Promise: While campaigning and participating in heated debates about mounting budget deficits, presidential candidate Barack Obama promised to rein in the federal budget. Obama emphatically pledged that he would enforce strict adherence to pay-as-you-go (PAYGO) rules mandating that any tax cuts and new entitlement expansions be fully offset. He went on to say, "There is no doubt that we've been living beyond our means, and we're going to have to make some adjustments." President Obama also stated, "I've personally asked the leadership in Congress to pass into law rules that follow the simple principle: You pay for what you spend, so that government acts the same way any responsible family does."

Fact: Our president has signed spending plans for stimulus, omnibus, and tarp and is looking to add a new budget and government-run health care *without* the offsetting PAYGO rules he promised. The CBO (Congressional Budget Office) predicts the Obama budget will create $9.3 trillion in national debt over the next ten years; this year's budget deficit is approximately $1.5 trillion. Over the next four years, the deficit will nearly quadruple under Obama. Of course, Obama provided appropriate spin on his penchant for spending by saying that current spending is "what lays the foundation for a secure and lasting prosperity." He is obviously of the same mind-set as Biden, who indicated that there is a viable and prudent strategy that supports massive spending as a way out of our severe economic crisis. Instanity!

• • •

Enhanced Interrogation Techniques (EITs)

Promise: Our president has strongly asserted that EITs absolutely do not work. He has promised the American people that these techniques have not provided any "actionable intelligence" and that he would prove his assertion.

Fact: At least four U.S generals, and a number of high-ranking people in the CIA, have confirmed that EITs did provide "actionable intelligence" and did save tens of thousands of lives during the War on Terror. Our president has been encouraged and admonished to provide memos or any other documents to prove his assertions that these techniques are ineffective and without merit. To date, our president maintains his assertion without providing any evidence to the people, as he promised.

• • •

National Security

Promise: President Obama has repeatedly stated he would be tough on our enemies and a hawk on issues involving our national security. Obama says he is firmly committed to keeping America safe. Per the U.S. Constitution, a strong national defense is a minimum mandate for a competent Commander in Chief.

Fact: Obama's national security policies have failed. Coddling captured terrorists, bowing to rouge regimes and Islamic states that harbor terrorists, politicizing terrorist interrogation methods, and providing the U.S. justice system and all it's accoutrements (including U.S. taxpayer funding) to the very people who want to kill us is nonsense. These policies are not only idiotic and incoherent, but they actually put America at an even greater risk to our life and liberty. The national WMD commission established by Congress has given the Obama administration an "F" for failing to protect America from nuclear, chemical, and biological attacks. Former Sen. Bob Graham, D-Fla., chairman of the bipartisan Commission states, "Nearly a decade after 9/11, one year after our original report, and one month after the Christmas Day bombing attempt, the United States is failing to address several urgent threats, especially bioterrorism. The report charges the administration "is simply not paying consistent and urgent attention to the means of responding quickly and effectively so that [WMD attacks] no longer constitute a threat of mass destruction." Incredibly, the Commission concludes there still exists "no national plan to coordinate federal, state, and local efforts following a bioterror attack, and the United States lacks the technical and operational capabilities required for an adequate response."

While castigating the president's policies, that can only be objectively considered illogical and incoherent for protecting America, the Commission gave the administration an *F* for not improving the nation's ability to respond rapidly to a biological attack inflicting mass casualties, and an *F* for poor implementation of the education and training programs needed to train national-security experts. Another *F* was given to Congress for poor oversight. Three F's have been rendered from an objective and bi-partisan commission; this is three devastating strikes on our systems of national security, one of the most important issues impacting America … Clear insanity!

. . .

There should be little doubt that the "Mr. Fib" analogy actually has merit. A pattern of brilliant rhetoric and masterful deception has emerged; this requires that we practice extra vigilance to ensure adherence to our constitutional liberties. Some will, no doubt, make excuses by saying that all politicians stretch the truth and have played a part in undermining our constitutional framework, and this is absolutely true! In comparison, however, we have never been so insanely entranced by and enamored of an extremely popular president and administration. This means that if we remain complacent by extending blind trust for this new era of governance, the risks to our freedom and liberties are exponentially higher. The new era government and leadership have aggressively pursued radical policy agendas. Most of these new policies are completely incoherent and insane. With close interrogation, we can mitigate most of the new era instanity.

Oxymoronic Idiocies Pursued During Economic Crisis

A power over a man's subsistence amounts to a power over his will.

—Alexander Hamilton

No Stimuli Stimulus

"[A] wise and frugal government … shall restrain men from injuring one another, shall leave them otherwise free to regulate their own pursuits of industry and improvement, and shall not take from the mouth of labor the bread it has earned. This is the sum of good government."

—Thomas Jefferson

Our new leadership has a very aggressive agenda. We have seen more "urgent" initiatives and policy changes in the first six months of this administration than we have seen over the entire tenure of some other administrations. We have seen more press conferences in the first seven months of the Obama administration than we had over the entire eight years of the Bush administration. Our president's personal ambition and determination are driving change, and change is definitely happening at a dizzying, and sometimes blinding, speed. Many times, when things happen so quickly, we are completely blind to what happened or to its consequences.

During times of rapid change, we need the president and Congress to provide answers while speaking in a straightforward and methodical way about what we are doing, why we're doing it, and where these changes are taking us. With all our challenges, we do not need melodic, teleprompter-led speeches, as though in continual campaign mode. We need facts, figures, and projected outcomes—not a barrage of continued nonsensical rhetoric and innuendo.

Immediately after coming into office, our new president embarked on trying to provide America with a stimulus package designed to combat and cure one of the worst economic crises ever. Our leaders were in unanimous agreement with this initiative as unemployment rates began to climb to the highest levels in decades. We knew that if unemployment rates continued to rise each month, there would be no realistic hope or expectation for a recovery in the short-term. Our leadership unanimously agreed to shore up job losses in order to add confidence and stabilize the various markets—stocks, currency, etc.

Common sense dictates that the key to implementing any new initiative designed to effectively alter or change outcomes requires providing incentives for the desired behavior. Most times, behavior modification and the ability to alter or change perceptions begin by providing effective incentives. For example, when we want to change our children's behaviors and perceptions while encouraging them to do their chores, we use allowance, or other incentives, to encourage the development of the desired behavior. If the desired behavior doesn't develop, we intuitively know we have not provided proper incentive and must look for other incentives to bring about the desired outcomes. Generally speaking, when provided with the right incentives, we see an immediate change in perception and behavior. This concept directly correlates to all facets of life, including business, management, sales, and even animal training.

The fundamental idea behind Obama's economic recovery plan, which passed in February 2009, was to immediately change the perceptions of the markets from pessimism to optimism while changing the behavior of employers from contraction through multiple rounds of layoffs to growth through hiring, promoting, and expanding. In other words, just as we use incentives to fundamentally change the perceptions and behavior of our loved ones, our government leaders hoped to use the stimulus plan to provide incentives that would result in a change in perception and behavior of the markets and business in general.

The Wall Street Journal estimates that, over the past decade, small businesses created approximately seventy percent of new jobs. Only an estimated two percent of the stimulus spending went to small businesses—just two percent! If the intent was to sincerely create jobs, at least a proportional percentage of the stimulus money should have been allocated to small businesses for job creation. Small businesses should have been the primary stimuli for generating stimulus. Allocating stimulus spending that is designed to help immediate job creation with no stimulus investment provided to the primary job creation vehicle is just not reflective of common sense policy. If the stimulus spending was sincere and designed to take immediate effect, shouldn't significant portions have been allocated for helping small businesses?

Unfortunately, almost a trillion dollars were allocated for stimulus spending with very little or no results. Now that our leadership has committed our tax dollars to fund an over $800 billion stimulus, where are the promised outcomes from the stimulus money? Why hasn't it provided the positive impact on unemployment as promised? Early data now suggests that the stimulus plan has failed miserably at providing the projected economic stimulus. Our leadership has essentially failed because they provided no stimuli for the stimulus! Without providing the appropriate stimuli, it is insane to expect results from a large and complex economy such as ours.

I am definitely no economist, but I am a businessperson and a successful sales professional. From the inception of this stimulus scheme, my common sense indicated this spending program would fail to immediately stimulate the economy as promised. Failure to deliver was predictable because there was no specific plan, vision, or focus. The stimulus "plan" was not focused or targeted, and history has taught us that the implementation of expansive government programs without strategy usually translates to failure.

"Mr. Obama believes he can conjure jobs and a durable expansion from the private sector while waging political war on its animal spirits. It can't be done. This reflects a larger problem, which is his belief that economic growth springs mainly from the genius of government."—The Wall Street Journal. The fact is, government does not create jobs. Noted economist Thomas Sowell writes: "What does it take to create a job? It takes wealth to pay someone who is hired, not to mention additional wealth to buy the material that person will use. But government creates no wealth. Ignoring that plain and simple fact enables politicians to claim to be able to do all sorts of miraculous things that they cannot do in fact. Without creating wealth, how can they create jobs? By taking wealth from others, whether through taxation, selling bonds or imposing mandates. However it is done, transferring wealth is not creating wealth. When government uses transferred wealth to hire people, it is essentially transferring jobs from the private sector, not adding to the net number of jobs in the economy."

If our leaders desired increasing spending and new employment, providing immediate tax incentives would have helped! Likewise, if there was need to stabilize employment and reduce layoffs, encouraging lending institutions to free up capital markets and provide employers with additional financial choices would have provided an immediate impact. Fundamentally, a common sense approach to stabilizing markets, employment, and increasing consumer spending could have come by using tax and financial incentives as levers to calm the interests of both employers and employees, and therefore capital markets.

In the end, the stimulus package passed by Congress and signed by our president has fallen well short of expectations. The root of its lack of effectiveness is that it didn't address the fundamental issues facing America—capital market stabilization and employment. While it may have calmed dread and fear of the markets, it would not provide long-term outcomes as promised. The unfortunate reality is the almost one trillion dollars of taxpayer funds were used as a political power grab, providing our leaders with the ability to reward their constituents via payback for loyalty... under the guise of stimulus. It provided incentives for unethical political behavior instead of appropriately providing incentives for capital markets and businesses that could have been used to help the people.

As evidence, consider that more than $200 billion in stimulus money went directly to states and cities, nearly seventy percent went to education and health care spending, and only twenty-four percent went to infrastructure spending. We should recall that infrastructure spending was the primary arena touted as creating the much-needed and immediate jobs. If jobs were the targeted incentive, why would the overwhelming percentage of new spending go to states, health care, etc. and such a small percentage be allocated to the needed infrastructure jobs?

Many ideologues will try to assert that the stimulus package—as passed—was absolutely the correct remedy for America. Instead of trying to convince otherwise, we should just look at the facts about stimulus expenditures and try to make logical, prudent, and coherent conclusions about whether it was the right remedy at the right time.

- We were warned that we were in a major crisis and told the stimulus bill had to immediately be passed or the U.S. would suffer devastating consequences. Specifically, we were promised that if the stimulus bill was passed, the unemployment rate would not go above eight percent until at least 2014. Our leaders said that if we didn't pass the proposed stimulus bill, unemployment would increase to nine percent. Well, we passed it, and the unemployment rate continued to climb and has already risen to approximately ten percent.

- We were promised that there were "shovel-ready" infrastructure projects that would create an immediate job impact on unemployment. Key Obama administration officials pledged that the stimulus measure would save or create from three million to four million jobs. After more than six months, however, only approximately five percent of stimulus funds were spent, with the majority of infrastructure spending now projected to take place sometime in late 2010 or beyond. How was this supposed to provide the immediate job relief? How were these decisions supposed to calm the fears of capital markets?

- We heard our president use either very fuzzy "logic", or provide us with another good example of blatant intellectual dishonesty, when he said during a news conference, "we began by passing a Recovery Act that has already saved or created over 150,000 jobs." This statement is dubious and inaccurate, as the facts confirm the U.S. has lost more than approx. 4 million jobs since Mr. Obama took office, according to the Bureau of Labor Statistics. Even if the stimulus saved or created as many jobs as he asserts, that does not compare to the high number of recent job losses; the rate of unemployment has doubled in the last year. In July 2009, the Federal Reserve confirmed that based on new data and analysis, there will likely be no net new jobs for the next 5 years! Mark Twain famously quipped, "There are lies, there are damned lies, and then there are statistics."

The aforementioned facts confirm that the stimulus package has not caused the immediate generation of jobs or confidence throughout the markets. What will happen when unemployment rates continue to rise month by month and quarter by quarter? Will market correction reflect new lows? Through misuse of the nearly one trillion dollars in spending, we have entered into very treacherous and uncertain territory. At this juncture in our history, we need real solutions that deliver results. To get there, we need straight talk and real leadership. We now know our leader and his leadership team are novices, at best. We desperately need them to learn from their on-the-job training and translate that learning into definitive strategies that will create the kind of change we can believe in. There is no doubt our president has enormous political capital—high personal approval ratings confirm this fact—but he has not exercised leadership when it comes to moving our collective agenda forward.

Speaker of the House Nancy Pelosi and Senate Majority Leader Harry Reid have used their partisan agendas—by way of special interest groups, unions, and other partisan lobbies— to craft the vitally important stimulus spending legislation with seemingly minimal input from the White House or from Republicans. Our president's reliance on Pelosi and Reid for the stimulus spending plan again demonstrates lack of leadership and puts all associated entities at risk. Prolonged periods of economic bondage, mostly in the form of extreme taxation on future generations, will naturally result from these decisions, which were not targeted, were misaligned, and out of focus in relation to economic realities and stated priorities. Unfortunately, instanity prevails.

DOA Health Care

In 1961, Ronald Reagan waxed prophetic when he stated,

> "One of the traditional methods of imposing statism or socialism on a people has been by way of medicine. It's very easy to disguise a medical program as a humanitarian project. Most people are a little reluctant to oppose anything that suggests medical care for people who possibly can't afford it ... You and I can do a great deal. We can write to our congressmen, to our senators. We can say right now that we want no further encroachment on these individual liberties and freedoms, and at the moment the key issue is, we do not want socialized medicine. Write those letters now; call your friends and tell them to write them. If you don't, this program, I promise you, will pass just as surely as the sun will come up tomorrow, and behind it will come other federal programs that will invade every area of freedom as we have known it in this country until one day, as Norman Thomas said, 'We will awake to find that we have socialism,' and if you don't do this, and if I don't do it, one of these days, you and I are going to spend our sunset years telling our children and our children's children what it once was like in America when men were free."

There is little disagreement about the need for a dramatic improvement in American health care policies. According to *World Magazine,* U.S. spending for health care has grown from 7.2% of the GNP to 16.2% in 2007. Medicare and Medicaid accounted for nearly twenty percent of the federal budget and more than twenty-seven percent of total health care expenditures, and, approximately forty-seven million Americans are uninsured. Needless to say, many people are finding health care—especially preventive health care—too expensive. During these economic times, many employers have ceased providing coverage due to increased costs for medical plans, and therefore many people do not get appropriate preventive medical care until extreme illness or an accident prompts an emergency room visit. The costs for emergency care, medications, and all other aspects of medical attention are extremely high and completely out of reach for those who have no medical plan coverage.

Most of our leaders are committed to making a change in the way we provide coverage and oversight to all aspects of health care. Our leadership hopes to pass new health care legislation that will provide a comprehensive, government-run health care system covering everyone in America, including the approximately twelve to twenty million people who are here illegally. The pursuit of health care reforms that provide comprehensive coverage for all people in America is a very noble and a seemingly worthwhile cause. When we consider the massive over-billing, fraud, prescription price gouging, excessive litigation, and other factors that have resulted in hundreds of billions in losses and inefficiencies, there is little disagreement about the need to pursue strategic, logical, and prudent reforms.

Do we need reform or a complete remake? Our leadership seems bent on the idea of remaking everything. They have touted the desire to completely remake America—health care, financial industries, automobile industries, and energy policies. There is a vigorous pursuit to remake major, strategic, high-risk, trillion-dollar systems but absolutely no attempt to just *fix* what is already in place. Our leaders want a total remake, even though they have no experience, proven competence, or history of success in remaking *anything*. This is the epitome of arrogance and also smacks of irrational, irresponsible, and unrealistic expectations. Polls suggest that we don't trust government in this health care effort. Our hesitancy is due to the fact that our leaders have not yet earned the right to ask us to trust them as they embark on high-risk, costly remakes.

Common sense dictates that before embarking on elaborate and costly remakes of existing systems, we should at least look to fix what's broken before attempting to replace it. Additionally, we should only embark on these kinds of radical efforts *after* our leaders have earned the right to ask for our support, *after* they've proven themselves and have provided a realistic vision for success. Before implementing new government-run or government mandated health care, shouldn't we first fix the massive problems we have with Medicare and Medicaid? Shouldn't we ask our leaders to provide a map of an existing, successful, government-run health care model?

Recent polls confirm that the vast majority of Americans with coverage—over eighty percent—actually like their existing employer-sponsored medical plans and respective coverage. They like their doctors, their clinics or hospitals, and their access to services. The government-run health care model proposed by our leadership will be fashioned after government-run health care plans implemented in the state of Massachusetts and the governments of Canada, France, and the United Kingdom. These government-run health systems were implemented with the same zeal, justification, and premises—to control medical costs, and to provide health care for all the population— our leadership uses. Unfortunately, when comparing mortality rates, wait times, accessibility, and costs of these government-run systems, all these respective models are failing as compared to the existing U.S. health care. Is it logical, rational, or prudent for our leadership to insist on remaking an entire system after a model that has failed? Should we remake a health system that the vast majority (80+%) of Americans actually like for the ten percent who are not covered? When government forces all people to sacrifice for the benefit of a few, it is not representative of a democratic Republic; it is clearly more aligned with remnants of old, communistic approaches to governance.

Imposing an immediate remake of an entire system that appropriately serves ninety percent of the population is at best an imposition, and at worst a good example of the state of instanity.

> Imagine living in a community of one hundred households, with ten of them unkempt. In this community, everyone is quite happy with their homes; most homeowners consistently keep their areas clean and their lawns manicured. The ten unkempt homes, which are situated on smaller lots, are the exceptions.
>
> Now, let's imagine a homeowners' association learns of the ten exceptions. In their zeal for consistency, the association announces it will require all homeowners to pay association fees and will begin to enforce a new community standard. Even though your community has been autonomous for generations, you are told to submit to the control and enforcement of the homeowners' association so a new era of compassionate consistency can be implemented.

This is quite analogous to our current health care dilemma. It is widely accepted that something should be done to reform health care for the uninsured ten percent of the population, but the government is proposing a remake of a system with which the overwhelming majority are satisfied. Further, the majority will be unduly taxed—either through their employer, or directly—to pay for the ten percent, many of whom are illegal residents.

> As a major initiative, the housing association says it will impose and enforce mandatory association fees. They confirm the fees will be used to deliver new services targeted at providing consistency across the community. The added irony is that the homeowners' association has a history of losing money, being plagued by massive corruption and inefficiencies, and has not been successful by any measure at providing any services to any other community. Their record notwith-

standing, they press forward to impose significant new fees on ninety of the homes while exempting the ten homes; they justify this disparity by saying additional fees are unaffordable for these homeowners.

The fact that our leadership has not produced any success within any major department or government agency is cause for alarm. The major imposition of a new health system will not only require collection of more fees, but will also require surrender of rights of all medical records so inept government bureaucrats can monitor, manage, and oversee life-or-death decisions. Again, this remake and imposition on the ninety percent is for the benefit of only approximately ten percent. Instanity!

To further their goal toward compassionate consistency, the association demands immediate lot reductions on ninety homes and lot expansions on the ten homes that had smaller lots—universal land distribution for all parcels will be immediately implemented. Furthermore, the association institutes that heretofore, all services for lawn maintenance and cleanup will be directly provided by the association. They admit, however, that workers for the association also provide maintenance to other communities, so services will be rationed accordingly and take place every three to five weeks; garbage pickup and lawns that were on a weekly schedule will now be serviced every three to five weeks.

This, again, is an analogy, but it parallels quite closely with proposed government-run health care. Does is make any rational sense to willingly forfeit input and control of our health by putting it into the hands of people with incentive to ration health care services? To accommodate the ten percent, bureaucrats will be looking to provide consistency for the whole. In other words, we are being told to sacrifice a health care system liked by most for the opportunity to participate in a new system that will be equally disliked by all. Instanity!

As a final insult, the entire leadership of the homeowners' association is vehement in expressing their altruistic motives for consistency and compassion; as for their own households, none of them will subject themselves to participating in the programs they espouse. This is the ultimate hypocrisy!

We should know that though our leaders are steadfast in their agenda to enforce a new government-run health care plan for all of America, they will not participate in their health care initiative. Our leaders have approximately twelve top-of-the-line health plans from which they can choose, and they are not interested in sacrifice for the greater good. Our leaders believe that though their ideas are good enough for us, they want no part of them because they are not good enough for them. This is crazy! Last time I checked, our leaders worked for us. Aren't they sworn to serve the people?

Since our leaders have been granted certain power and authority to serve us, it is incumbent on us to not even consider their plan to remake our health care unless they subject themselves to it as well. We must demand that no serious consideration be given to a health care remake until we get total commitment from our leadership—president, congress, and all other branches of government—to enroll and participate. No plan should be implemented without our leadership doing what they are paid to do by leading the way and confidently subjecting themselves to their new health policies. If we see that it is good enough for them, maybe we will be inclined to consider it; we should render anything less DOA. If leadership declines participation, we will have another good example of out-of-control elitism and outright arrogance.

I think our politicians' reluctance to participate in their proposed model has less to do with the inconvenience than the fact that they have seen the incriminating data from countries who have already implemented this health care model. According to a May 27 report from the BBC, the UK health care wait times are:

- 8 months for cataract surgery
- 11 months for hip replacement
- 12 months for knee replacement
- 5 months for a slipped disk and hernia repair

Last year, approximately 4,000 women were forced to give birth in places such as elevators, cars, and restrooms due to rationing, wait times, and lack of midwives.

While these wait time statistics are alarming, it gets worse when looking at the prostate cancer survival rates between the U.S, Canada, and the UK. According to the American Cancer Society and the Canadian Cancer Society the U.S. five-year relative survival rate is 100%. For Canada the five-year survival rate is 95%, but for the UK, the five-year relative survival rate is only 77%—a 23% decrease in survival in the UK, for something that is 100% survivable in U.S.

Our leaders do not want to be a part of this model of health care because of their desire to live. Self-preservation is what rules the day for our leaders. The American people, on the other hand, will necessarily experience a large percentage of deaths due to wait time and rationing. Of course, our leaders have gone on record to say there will be no rationing of health care, especially for the elderly, but this is preposterous. Common sense easily confirms that with approximately fifty million more people coming into a free health system that will not undergo an exponential increase in doctors and nurses—commensurate with the number of new patients—some form of rationing will necessarily have to take place. There is no question about it; it's common sense!

While being scrutinized for one of the few times our president adamantly denied that abortions would be provided via government funding in his new health care proposal, Obama complained that people making this claim were "bearing false witness" about his plans. At the same time, however, he firmly declined to provide an addendum to the plan that specifically prevents government funding of the practice. Lawmakers say that if a specific addendum is not added to health care proposals, unrestricted government funding of abortions would ensue under the generic label of women's health. If our president is sincere about his stance on abortion (and about government funding for it), why not provide the specific and necessary addendum? Why should there be any lies or deception about this issue and the inevitable need to ration? Why not come clean with the daunting facts that confront us if we undertake this initiative? It is clear our government is motivated by personal agenda, no matter what it may cost.

During his September 2009 health care speech, President Obama strongly asserted the cost for his proposed health care initiative—$90 billion per year in the first ten years—would be completely covered by new taxes, cuts in Medicare and Medicaid, and a huge reduction in fraud, waste, and inefficiency. If we are aware of so much money spent on fraud, waste, and inefficiency, shouldn't it have been isolated and recovered already? How could such waste have been recognized but completely ignored until now? The truth is, President Obama has not quantified that his purported tens of billions of dollars per year in waste actually exist; this means he is likely not to find it. Without a track record of having recovered any significant fraud, waste, or inefficiency in any other government programs, coupled with a pattern of ineptitude and inefficiencies that exists within our government, this assertion is nothing but high hopes and wishful thinking. High costs and significant expansion are quite real and predictable, so we need an actual strategy and plan for health care, not wishful thinking.

Government expansion again rears its ugly head, as it seems to be a key motivation in the health care initiative. Any government-run health care policy automatically translates to the need for tremendous government expansion, huge and complex bureaucracy, and the unique consolidation of power and authority that comes from taking over all aspects of health for all of society. According to Daniel Hannon, a member of British Parliament, Britain's health system is currently the third-largest employer in the world, with over 1.4 million workers, of which the largest percentages are administrators—not doctors and professionals. Health care is the single largest budget item in Britain's budget.

Just imagine if we followed in the footsteps of other socialized countries with a similar health model; the U.S. health care system would require a tremendous amount of personnel. It could easily make the U.S. government the largest employer in the world, almost overnight. The monumental government expansion would be so enormous and complex that the waste, fraud, and abuse would be never-ending.

Uneducated Education

Education was mentioned as a high priority for our new leadership. There is no doubt our K-12 educational institutions, dedicated to providing our children a foundation for learning, achievement, and success, are now failing to produce consistent results. We should understand that when American educational institutions fail, we all fail.

The U.S. government has designed primary and secondary education school systems to help produce generations of people who are the best and the brightest among all other nations. The general idea is to develop consecutive generations of a highly intelligent and highly-motivated population, so that these new populations can perpetuate moving our country forward as they become the next generation of leaders and entrepreneurs.

Producing generations of leaders and entrepreneurs is one of the keys for maintaining our freedoms, as provided in the Constitution. As people become self-reliant and ambitious, they are more likely to develop new innovations and confidently start new business enterprises. This translates to fully embracing concepts of free market capitalism and mitigates the need for government intervention. This paradigm is the engine for maintaining a thriving society, free from the bondage of increased government oversight, control, and intrusion.

The paradigm shifts dramatically, however, if the U.S. is not successful in providing a solid educational foundation to American children. Fundamentally, a failure to provide a successful model for education means a reversal of the trend toward producing intelligent and innovative thinkers, committed to living lives of independence. Instead, we will produce generations of people who will have to heavily rely on the government for sustenance as they become dependents of the state. In this scenario, nobody wins. The government becomes overburdened by high costs and inefficiencies for programs and services designed to help the uneducated. Society then becomes polarized and insensitive to the plight of others because of bad choices. Individuals become bitter and resentful because their bad choices have limited their ability to thrive as part of the greater society.

The goal of the U.S. educational system is to produce people who are smart, confident, ambitious, and wholly self reliant. Recent studies comparing U.S. education to other nations confirm however, the U.S. educational system has significantly declined in meeting the aforementioned goals of education, as it is severely outranked by most developed nations. This means that we will predictably experience an imminent decline in competitiveness (on the world stage) unless there is an immediate and dramatic change to our educational system.

The U.S. has public school systems that are completely funded by our government (state and federal). Even with hundreds of billions spent on education, we experience high dropout rates, reduced budgets, bloated expenditures, and overbearing teachers unions and lobbies, as some of the issues preventing the delivering of consistently high standards in children's education. Statistics show other developed nations spend a fraction of what the U.S. spends on childhood education, and are getting far superior results! There is no debating the fact there is an urgent need for immediate reforms of our education system(s).

There has been a concerted effort to experiment with various types of reform. Through these efforts, we have confirmed that some educational reforms can be effectively remedied by the introduction of alternate and competing forms of schooling. With the help of alternative education models like charter schools, homeschooling, and private schools, it has been determined that children can be provided learning environments more conducive to their learning styles and behavior. Since a disproportionately large percentage of the poor, as well as African-American students and other minorities, suffer from ineffective or marginally-effective public schooling, the alternative learning environments have proven to be a real inspiration and foundation of renewed hope for these groups; these alternatives tend to produce higher test scores and produce a larger percentage of college-ready graduates. Unfortunately, even though these alternatives are far more cost-effective, our government has declined to fully embrace them. You heard correctly—even though our leadership spews glossy rhetoric about social justice, compassion, and empathy, they will not help fund proven and effective alternatives as viable methods of reform.

The facts confirm that, since 1965, eight of the top eleven cities with the highest levels of poverty and the lowest education results have been run by liberal Democrat social progressives. According to estimates, the Washington, DC, public schools graduate only sixty percent of the students, and of them, only nine percent complete college within five years. There is a tremendous amount of rhetoric and fantasy about Democrats being champions of educational reform and embracing high goals for better education. In reality, the facts confirm that since Democrats placate the powerful teachers' unions instead of putting kids first, they have produced more negative outcomes than positive, relegating generations of largely minority students to poverty and underemployment.

One good example of sheer instanity plaguing Obama and all Democratic leadership is their opposition to a quite successful school voucher program, the DC Opportunity Scholarship Program. This program was instituted in Washington, DC, and was visible to Congress and the president. The program was a landmark education program that provided opportunities to thousands of students by allowing them to attend private schools they would not otherwise have been able to afford, through the use of government-funded vouchers.

The program was heralded as a great new model for helping the underprivileged and for providing the government with a more cost-efficient alternative for educational reform. By all accounts, it was touted as a huge success, as it produced higher test scores, reduced dropout rates, and was cost-effective—the vouchers were fully funded at approximately half the per student cost of public schools. By all measures, the voucher program met or exceeded expectations. Most importantly, it helped provide additional school choices, including private school education, for children who would be otherwise relegated to substandard learning environments and education. Irrespective of all the many proven benefits, our new era leadership, who campaigned on these type of reforms and on leveling the playing field via social justice, voted to cancel the voucher program without offering *any* justification. This is another example of pure and unadulterated instanity!

> Rather than subjecting kids to rotting schools, vouchers have brought change to hundreds of families, who opted for private or parochial schools. If Barack Obama had fought for this program, it would be saved. But he refuses to help these low-income families. By supporting the teachers' union, he sadly has become the status quo candidate on education.
> —Brian Burch, President of Fidelis, a Catholic-based political, legal, research, and educational organization

The real insidious irony is that Barack Obama told the *Milwaukee Journal-Sentinel* in February 2009 that he was open to voucher programs; then, without justification, he later announced his intentions to squash the DC pilot program. Before being hired as our president, Obama told the *Milwaukee Journal-Sentinel*, "If there was any argument for vouchers, it was 'All right, let's see if this experiment works,' and if it does, then whatever my preconceptions, my attitude is you do what works for the kids," the senator said. "I will not allow my predispositions to stand in the way of making sure that our kids can learn. We're losing several generations of kids, and something has to be done."

By June 2009, the teachers' lobby convinced Obama to work against the voucher program. While trying to justify his relatively insane position, President Obama later told *ABC News*, "We don't have enough slots for every child to go into a parochial school or a private school. And what you would see is a huge drain of resources out of the public schools."

I thought the idea was to find educational models that work! Why would our leadership think it is wise, prudent, or justifiable to throw out cost-effective alternatives that provide quantifiable results, in favor of wasting taxpayer dollars on systems that are not working? What explanation, other than pure instanity, is there?

Joanne Jacobs, of *The Washington Post*, wrote, "For all the talk about putting children first, it's clear that the special interests that have long opposed vouchers are getting their way."

The sad fact is that, despite all the criticisms about Washington lobbyists and special interests, Barack Obama has again chosen to not exercise leadership and instead has continued his predictable pattern of caving to powerful unions and their respective lobbyists in Washington. This dreadful leadership lapse has unfortunately resulted in relegating thousands of the neediest children he promised to help to a future of continued poverty and underemployment. A demonstration of reckless disregard and condemnation of generations of underprivileged children, in order to adhere to the wishes of lobbyists groups and unions, is unforgivable. These actions do not reflect the change we were supposed to believe in. They reflect a selfish, cruel and arrogant disregard for the people.

Let us not again look to excuse our leaders' behavior. The dismantling of the voucher program is a blatant moral lapse with a twist of unpatriotic selfishness. This stance will definitely undermine our constitutional freedoms by ultimately forcing the government to enact more programs to help the uneducated. Our historical patterns confirm that the more we have to rely on government, the more power is ceded, which reduces our independence. The incredible irony in all this is that the very people who our president expressed his strongest desire and commitment to help—the poor and minorities—are the ones who are disproportionably affected by his new era oppressive policies; they will experience additional harm instead of good. Instanity!

We can see disturbing patterns as we again reflect on Alexander Hamilton, who gave us a powerful and prophetic quote: "Power over a man's sustenance results in a power over his will."

Fighting Fire with "Fired!": The Chicago Way

There is mounting evidence that confirms perhaps we made a huge mistake in hiring our new era of government leadership. The convergence of policies, proposals, and procedures are usually good indicators for assessing whether leaders are succeeding in delivering effective governance and leadership.

Thus far, we have looked at *outcomes* from new era policies implemented and some of the new era proposals representing desires of our new leader and of his administration. We have yet, however, to look at procedures surrounding this era of new leadership. If you are not yet convinced about our potential error in judgment, perhaps an intent look at *procedures* will provide more definitive confirmation.

The President of the United States, needless to say, has a very demanding job. His roles and responsibilities seem endless, as he is empowered to provide a clear pathway to success for our society, economy, and foreign policy. With the many demands and pressures placed on the office of the president, both domestically and abroad, there is no time to waste on the minutiae of governance, or micromanagement, of little details. He is wholly responsible for delivering the big vision for a successful America.

With that said, how is it our president feels it is his right and obligation to take it upon himself to fire the CEOs of private companies, like GM? Even though he has absolutely no experience in the auto industry, our president felt the need to intervene in the management of a private company, fully trampling the Constitution and clear limits to his power along the way, and fire a citizen working in a private industry. This is a completely unprecedented act for a sitting U.S. president. No doubt, many will side with Obama and say the firing was fully justified, but this sets a very dangerous precedent. As outrageous as this is, the real irony is that he didn't include members of the unions as culprits in the company's problems. Common sense would tell anyone who understands the severe issues confronting GM that, at the very least, union bosses shared significant blame in its troubles, and as such, deserved to share in suffering any appropriate consequences. How can our leader think it is in his purview to specifically meddle in the minutiae of personnel decisions outside of his direct responsibility?

The GM firing was just the beginning. According to *The Wall Street Journal* and several other media outlets, our president also decided to fire one of our highly-regarded U.S. inspector generals as well. In a similar fashion to the GM CEO firing, the firing of the inspector general fully demonstrated a malicious and brazen abuse of power, as it took place without valid justifi-

cation or adherence to proper protocol and procedures. According to reports, Inspector General Gerald Walpin was fired by
President Obama without cause. Reports confirm Walpin was
investigating the misuse of AmeriCorp funds by a nonprofit
agency in Sacramento headed by Obama friend and supporter
Kevin Johnson. During the course of his investigation, Walpin
discovered that Johnson had dispersed significant funds to individuals who were providing personal services for him: washing
his car, running errands, etc.—a clear misuse of taxpayer funds.
Since Walpin issued a report detailing the misuses of funds and
posed a direct threat to Kevin Johnson, evidence suggests Johnson called in a favor from our president and got Walpin fired.

Think about this: Inspector generals are a watchdog agency
over our government and are charted with making sure our tax
dollars are being spent the way they are supposed to be. These
people inspect all facets of government-funded projects and
are one of the very few balances in our system of government,
wholly charged with preventing fraud, misuse, and abuse of our
money. Now consider that a person actually got fired by our
president for doing a great job while looking out for us and
blowing the whistle on clear acts of misuse. He prevented continued waste, misuse, and corruption with taxpayer funds. For
our president to pay attention to this level of personnel while
holding an office responsible for the world is, in itself, astonish-
ing, but, if our president had any appropriate response for Mr.
Walpin's effort, it should have been in the form of a promotion
or achievement award, not a firing. To what system of government have we transitioned? Instant and insane politics.

Not only did our president fire Mr. Walpin to protect his
friend, but he fired our inspector general without cause. Even
after Obama co-sponsored a bill while he was in the Senate,
requiring that Congress be given thirty days' notice before the
president terminates any inspector general, he took actions
superseding his own bill. Additionally, the senate bill prohibits IGs from being fired without cause. The provisions of Mr.

Obama's bill were drafted to ensure the independence of the position and to prohibit the removal of any inspector general for purely political reasons. *What?* With this action, our president has demonstrated behavior indicative of someone who is unethical, hypocritical, and completely illogical—the epitome of instanity.

Overreaching to fire the GM president, combined with the inspector general fiasco, provides clear indication of the procedures our president is inclined to use. These procedures do not speak well of our leader, as they demonstrate he is still driven by the agendas of his foundations and beliefs—Marxist and socialist—and not constitutionally-mandated limits. The wisdom of Jesus' words again resonate volumes: "For the mouth speaks what the heart is full of. A good person brings good things out of a treasure of good things; a bad person brings bad things out of a treasure of bad things."

With these firings, we notice patterns rooted in community organizing and political thuggery. Our president's agendas and procedures seem to be driven more by nepotism, favoritism, cliques, and cahoots, instead of procedural discipline that comes with running the United States.

It is quite illuminating, yet disheartening, to realize our president has acted immorally and wholly consistent with the unmitigated gall of a tyrannical dictator instead of with logic and reason consistent with the office of the presidency. These actions should shame us all.

Other Policy Idiocies, and Their Impact on the U.S. Constitution

"There is not a more important and fundamental principle in legislation, than that the ways and means ought always to face the public engagements; that our appropriations should ever go hand in hand with our promises. To say that the United States should be answerable for twenty-five millions of dollars without knowing whether the ways and means can be provided, and without knowing whether those who are to succeed us will think with us on the subject, would be rash and unjustifiable. Sir, in my opinion, it would be hazarding the public faith in a manner contrary to every idea of prudence."

—James Madison, Speech in Congress, 1790

Numerous new policies and initiatives are being implemented at the speed of light. Most of these new initiatives pose significant constitutional as well as major social and economic implications. To facilitate understanding of some of the major new era issues embraced by our current leadership, I have provided a chart that summarizes the many changes of which we should be aware.

• • •

Policy/ Issue	Results in ...	Which produces ...	Economic/Outcome
Limits on Gun Rights	Undermining of 2nd Amendment and 9th amendments rights	Stricter gun laws; these laws reduce or eliminate Constitutional guarantees (right to keep and bear arms).	If enforce stricter gun laws, may mean MORE crime (England experience a 340% INCREASE in gun deaths and injuries after passing restrictive gun laws); with gun laws, criminals commit even more crimes with less deterrent! Reduces fundamental rights and freedoms breeding further distrust between government and citizenry

Policy/ Issue	Results in ...	Which produces ...	Economic/Outcome
Remake of healthcare (HR3200*)	Socialized medicine and health; undermines Constitutional limits. Limits democracy and capitalism. Allowing government to literally govern life and death decisions of its citizenry!	Statistics from governments with "universal health", confirm higher costs, death rates, rationing, and lower levels are outcomes. Plus, it adds bureaucracy, complexity, waste and inefficiency.	Estimates range from $1 Trillion-$1.5 Trillion (over 10 years). Additional burden adds to deficit while increasing accessibility to only approx. 10% more of population. Adds Significant new taxation. Increased deaths of elderly due to rationing, wait times and government bureaucracy. Small businesses suffer oppressive taxation; business closures and increased unemployment rates.

Policy/ Issue	Results in ...	Which produces ...	Economic/Outcome
New Energy "green" policies (HR2454*)	Largest tax increase in history of U.S. (via "Cap & Trade"). More tax schemes with no verifiable benefit or reasoning... The American way?	More government intrusion, control, oppression of the poor, more job losses, and undermining of Constitutional "limits".	Trillions of dollars are at stake, most of which goes to U.S. government and "big businesses" already invested in "green". "We the people" lose again to "bigger government". Unemployment increases and number of small businesses decreases.
Increased taxation policies	Oppressive mis-use/over use of taxation policies. Perpetuates cycle irresponsible government/overspending	Increased tax fraud, cheating and corruption. Doesn't encourage need for balanced budgets!	Multi-Trillions drained from GDP with no real improvement (in services). Increases and elongates deficits. Entrepreneurship, innovation and the "American dream" suffers.

Policy/ Issue	Results in ...	Which produces ...	Economic/Outcome
Expanded union influence Employee Free Choice Act (H.R. 1409, S. 560)	"Card check" and "Fast track" policies force "private" businesses to unionize. Unions gain more members, and government influence.	Unions gain more control of labor. More "special interest" groups (like ACORN, SEIU and others) gain power which will precipitate more fraud, corruption and influence in White House	Loss of incentive for entrepreneurs and small businesses. Encourages corruption. More Business closures/ job loses /unemployment. Decrease in entrepreneurship, innovation and competitiveness
Increased deficit spending	No Balanced budget. More borrowing from foreign countries. Loss of sovereignty. Currency fluctuations	Generations of excessive taxation. Loss of control over economic destiny. Inflation, recession, or depression can result from spending	Estimate put current un-funded liabilities between $50-100 Trillion; president confirms deficit is "unsustainable" and spending must be curbed. Current course means U.S. will lose sovereignty, or worse (go bankrupt) as a "debtor" nation.

Policy/ Issue	Results in ...	Which produces ...	Economic/Outcome
Captured terrorists (Non U.S. citizens) provided Miranda rights/ "Mirandize" POW's	Gives Terrorists rights and allows use of American courts. POW's now provided protections of U.S. Constitution (specifically designed for American citizens).... INSTANITY!	Reduces cooperation from terrorists. Shows weakness and appeasement. Lack of resolve and enforcement; no deterrence. Raise court costs (paid by U.S. taxpayers)	Courts will be clogged by terrorists awaiting trials. Can add hundreds of millions of U.S. taxpayers dollars to court costs/processes/procedures for people who want to harm us or have maimed or killed our heroes in military. May let some guilty terrorists go free, due to lack of proper protocol and "procedures"
Government regulation of salaries	Government "over-reach" and infringement on regulation of salaries (even in private sector) ; Sets up systems of "bullying" and intimidation of individuals & businesses	Exceeds governmental powers and limits. Expands government influence and control in private sectors. Undermines system of free-market capitalism	Reduces incomes and investment of high earners. Reduce new business start-ups, and investment. Establishes systems and tactics of fear, uncertainty and doubt perpetrated by the (supposedly) limited Federal government. A clear "breech of Constitutional provisions... Insta-nity!

Policy/ Issue	Results in ...	Which produces ...	Economic/Outcome
"Fairness doctrine" or other models to levy excessive fines on talk radio	Limits 1st amendment rights to free-speech of radio other media. Would allow government to monitor and control media by mandating alternate views	Much less, if any, talk radio. Loss of rights guaranteed via free speech. Cedes powers to government. Supersedes Constitutional limits.	Media will be come less objective and truthful as they become government controlled propaganda outlets. Distrust will be commonplace as listeners revolt. Lies and deception in media will become commonplace.
Appoint judges who "legislate from the bench"	Judges set new precedence for laws. Rewrite laws and rights without consideration of strict adherence to Constitution (or voters). Homosexual marriage and other issues will be overturned by whims of "activist" judges, not by wishes "we the people".	Permits instituting of "progressive" new laws. Constitution becomes less meaningful and important as "world" laws and courts take precedence over U.S. Loss of guarantees, privileges and provisions of Constitution.	Judges become the most powerful people in the land and they determine the course and paths for shaping society. Judges will use their personal discretion to re-write and re-interpret new laws, and the Constitution. "We the people" will lose power, as judges rule based on their ideology and individual preferences, not on strict Constitutional interpretations.

Policy/Issue	Results in ...	Which produces ...	Economic/Outcome
Amnesty/Illegal immigration	Reduction in national security. Ineffective border enforcement; no enforcement of immigration laws. Increases risk of terrorism. Ignores Constitutional provisions for security of citizenry.	Less secure America. Unfair and unequal for those who have waited their turn (for many years) to become citizens. Encourages more government dependency..	Huge cost to taxpayers. Increases drain on resources and dependence on government. Entitlements (Medicare, Medicaid, soc. Security etc..) will grow to over $2.6 Trillion, further increasing deficit/spending.
Transnationalist judges and court appointees	Obama's appointment of people who share "globalists" perspectives (like Harold Koh, Timothy Geithner, and Judge Sotomeyer) creates a transnational deference to world communities	Reliance on the "global community". No sanctity and sovereignty of rights, freedoms and guarantees of the Constitution; weakens Constitution.	Without strict Constitutionalists, government decision-making power becomes subservient to international bodies like the United Nations. Reduces sovereignty while allowing for establishment of New World Order. Supreme Court begins to defer to World Courts. Military and decisions about defense restrained by world authorities.

Policy/Issue	Results in ...	Which produces ...	Economic/Outcome
Reduction of States' Rights	Undermines and usurps 10th Amendments rights of the states. Federal government exceeds enumerated limits while states' majority powers become subservient	States become dependent on federal government. Individual states' rights/responsibilities to citizenry dictated by federal government	Dangerously unbalanced powers between states and federal government. "Bondage" to federal government (via programs and policies enacted and enforced by federal government). citizens as outlined in Constitution and Declaration
Government Bail-outs	Usurps "limited" powers granted by Constitution . Industry "winners and losers" determined by government.	Undermines free markets/capitalism; limits competition, and accountability. Rewards bad behavior, "penalizes" healthy businesses	Businesses adopt an unhealthy reliance on taxpayers and government; taxpayers get no benefit, but government get major influence and powers. Billions in taxpayer dollars spent without payback or exit strategy.

Policy/ Issue	Results in ...	Which produces ...	Economic/Outcome
Ever-powerful (and expanding) Federal Reserve	No checks and balances; no accountability. Allows un-checked and unregulated greed, corruption and market manipulation	No audit/oversight or accountability for the most powerful entity overseeing U.S. financial/markets	Tens of Trillions of unaccounted taxpayer dollars. Since Fed is exempt from congressional oversight/approvals, additional trillions will be printed, spent, lost, and unaccounted for; No ACCOUNTABILITY... Insane!!

*These legislative bills will no doubt undergo major changes and modifications before the vote. Regardless of their final outcome, the spirit and intent are what should be noted.

Note: It is important to note that that *all* of the aforementioned policies inherently undermine the U.S. Constitution, as they demonstrate an undisciplined and unrestrained federal government. This model of government far exceeds the enumerated limits and intent of the Constitution. Our forefathers specifically restricted our government to ensure preservation of liberties and freedoms of all U.S. citizens.

. . .

After considering the vast implications of enumerated powers and limits, as well as provisions and guarantees of the Constitution and Declaration of Independence, how are our new era policies helping preserve our freedoms and liberties? If we tried to overlay our Constitution onto the noted emerging policies, we would clearly see they are mutually exclusive. The only appropriate descriptions are incoherent and idiotic. They wholly supplant and undermine the foundation of our most precious democratic union. It seems our leadership is fully complicit in rewriting the Constitution via the remaking of America.

Certainly, some could argue that all past presidents bear some degree of blame, as the U.S. Constitution has experienced erosion and has been whittled at by most, if not all, past presidents and their respective administrations. With our current new era government, however, we see the mounting of an aggressive assault on the framework of what's left of our most precious documents. The real irony to our predicament is that the assault on the Constitution is being mounted by the very leaders who took oaths to protect it. Insane!

Characteristics of new era policies are not only insane, but they also demonstrate a pattern of governance that, instead of encouraging independence and freedom, encourages an unhealthy and unbalanced dependence on the federal government. We have seen throughout history that an increase in dependence on government leads to out-of-control government expansion, overzealous power grabs, and unnecessary government intrusion. This is not freedom. These actions are more indicative of socialist and tyrannical mind-sets that lead to oppression endured under the regimes of the past.

We should begin to sense that our freedoms and liberty are in grave danger. We must remember that the Declaration of Independence was made possible because our forefathers fought against tyranny and oppression rendered by the British Empire. The current cycle of expanded government and clear overreach of powers provide conditions that open the door for new levels of government encroachment through meddling, monitoring, control, and oppression—not freedom! If not corrected, we are entering a throwback to the pre-Constitution era. Through lethargy and complacency, we are allowing the revival of a type of government from which we declared ourselves free.

As noted, Albert Einstein's definition of insanity is "doing the same thing over and over again and expecting different results." Well, current new-era leadership seems absolutely bent on creating new government structures that have historically proven dangerous and oppressive. Our Constitution and Declaration of Independence were provided as safeguards and have been erected to prevent reverting back to policies of oppressive regimes. Yet, we have allowed erosion of many of our constitutional safeguards, and we are now completely nullifying the Constitution. By Einstein's definition, it is clear we are in a cycle of insanity!

Summary

> It does not take a majority to prevail, but an irate, tireless minority, keen on setting brushfires of freedom in the minds of men.
>
> —Samuel Adams

With the highest hopes and the best of intentions, we hired leadership in whom we thought we could trust and believe. As it turns out, we can only say it was all just hopeful, ungrounded optimism and wishful thinking.

Our emotions overruled logic and rationality, and now we see an emerging pattern of dire consequences, which we will endure unless once again we rise up and begin to act as guardians of truth, freedom, and liberty. If we don't do it, it will not be done, as it is obvious our leaders are looking to govern with selfish ambition. Our leaders are under a trance of greed and are aggressively driven by money, power, and control. This makes them incapable of performing the duties we hired them to perform on our behalf.

Our leaders have been derelict and irresponsible with the powers we have loaned them. Knowing that "power corrupts, and absolute power corrupts absolutely" is a truism, we expected our leaders would be able to appropriately limit themselves and use judicious discipline while conducting our business. We were wrong! In the end, we, the people, failed.

We have thus far failed to take full responsibility for our Constitution and Declaration. We have failed to oversee our employees and hold them fully accountable for any of their actions that went against the enumerated principles and values contained in our most precious historical documents. We have failed to exercise our own common sense by using logic, reason, and rationality to overcome bouts of instanity. We are not without blame, as all presidents have taken the trust and authority we extended to them to slowly but surely erode our foundations of freedom and liberty while we pine in a lethargic stupor of blind trust.

We have become our own worst enemies! Our founders passionately entrusted us to be the ultimate balance for our government's actions. The Declaration of Independence confirms that, by way of the states, we are empowered by right and duty to closely interrogate the actions of government and to throw off any usurpations of government in order to maintain our freedom and liberties. We have the sole obligation to enforce our contract with our government!

John Quincy Adams stated, "You will never know how much it has cost my generation to preserve your freedom. I hope you will make good use of it."

Have we made good use of it? Let's review.

- We have been provided by the U.S. Constitution and Declaration of Independence, an overwhelming number of provisions and guarantees to U.S citizens.

- Somehow, we have allowed our president and members of his administration to embrace and adopt "progressive" policies—they call themselves "social progressives"—which are used to justify controversial tax and spend programs like cap and trade and government-run health care.

- These policies are antithetical to the tenets of the U.S. Constitution as the supreme law of the land, since they erode constitutional limitations while ushering in a dominant government that is focused on policies that grow and expand government.

- This growth is indicative of a statist mind-set, in which policies are not motivated by the betterment of citizenry, but instead for the money, power, and the consolidation of control under the state.

- This creates dependence on the federal government and forces states and their respective citizenry into polices of excessive taxation and control.

- This control is enabled through the president's use of unelected, un-vetted, and unaccountable czars, who oversee all aspects of our lives while shadowing existing bureaucrats, so our president can have his own direct reports.

- This further enables the president's power and control to, at his discretion, take over private enterprises under the guise of "too big to fail" bailouts.

- These policies are unpopular, so our president uses rhetorical spin and intellectual dishonesty as a way to conceal an out-of-control government with a history of severe incompetence.

- Our leaders have not earned the right to embark on high-cost, high-risk remakes, especially since there is no apparent business plan or model for success.

- This confirms that our leadership aggressively pushes its selfish agendas to overwhelm the system with initiatives that are nothing more than oppressive new tax schemes to further help expand government while fully undermining constitutional provisions.

- This also causes blindly trusting citizens to cede power, when they are just trying to live free from tyranny and oppression provided by the enumerated rights and guarantees in the U.S. Constitution and Declaration of Independence.

- These documents confirm that we should expect the government to act within the specified limits and get out of the way of citizenry, as we live with the expectation of being able to freely pursue life, liberty, and the pursuit of happiness, which come as by-products of truth and freedom.

Oh, God—what have we done?

PART THREE

The Just Shall Live By Faith

"Democracy is always temporary in nature; it simply cannot exist as a permanent form of government. A democracy will continue to exist up until the time that voters discover that they can vote themselves generous gifts from the public treasury. From that moment on, the majority always votes for the candidates who promise the most benefits from the public treasury, with the result that every democracy will finally collapse due to loose fiscal policy, which is always followed by a dictatorship. The average age of the world's greatest civilizations from the beginning of history has been about 200 years. During those 200 years, these nations always progressed through the following sequence:

- *From bondage to spiritual faith;*
- *From spiritual faith to great courage;*
- *From courage to liberty;*
- From liberty to abundance;
- From abundance to complacency
- From complacency to apathy;
- From apathy to dependence;
- *From dependence back into bondag*

CHAPTER TWELVE

The Just Shall Live by Faith: Our Faith Foundations—the Pathway to Success

"The choice before us is plain, Christ or chaos, conviction or compromise, discipline or disintegration. I am rather tired of hearing about our rights and privileges as American citizens. The time is come, it now is, when we ought to hear about the duties and responsibilities of our citizenship. America's future depends upon her accepting and demonstrating God's government."

—Peter Marshall, The Rebirth of America

When one sees that the energies of the universe are aligning, one should pay attention and seize the moment, not by waiting for a desired result to happen, but by directing those energies with subtle pushes here and there.

—Albert Einstein

United by Faith, Entranced by Secularism

"It is the duty of all nations to acknowledge the providence of Almighty God, to obey His will, to be grateful for His mercy, to implore His protection and favor ... That great and beneficent author of all good that was, that is, or ever shall be, that we may then unite in rendering unto Him our sincere and humble thanks for His kind care and protection of the people."

—George Washington

By now, you may think this book reads more like a fantasy novel than a serious book filled with facts. Unfortunately, we cannot just pinch ourselves and wake up from this; we are not living in a dream. We are living in a time of stark reality. A very serious and strategic attack has been ignited to capture the soul of America. If we are not vigilant, we will lose our hearts and souls, along with the sense of significance of what it means to be American.

We should know that the fight for our nation's soul is not simply coming by way of battles waged between political parties. The fight is much more strategic and pervasive than simple party identification. It is s being waged at the highest levels and with the highest priorities through fervent ideology bent on accelerating the secular, progressive agenda. Secular progressives are a rising movement generally hostile toward issues of faith and traditional American values. Their agenda is to fundamentally transform life in America by purposefully undermining our country's faith foundations.

With the radical agenda being promulgated in America today, I am reminded of a scripture in Romans 12:2 where Apostle Paul writes, " ... be not conformed to this world: but be ye transformed by the renewing of your mind ... ". Note Paul's wisdom when he confirms that transformation of our "world" (our worldview, political views etc ...) takes place by a renewed (or changed) mind. This is noteworthy because as we observe the subtle changes in governance, erosion of ethics and principles and continued undermining of Constitutional freedoms and liberties without complaint, we are experiencing the complete transformation of America that President Obama promised. The new era of "change" has increased our tolerance for corruption and deceit and has begun the progressive transformation of our "world." In this way, Obama is on his way to keeping his promise of transforming America, and his scheme is proving "masterful!"

We have been unwittingly enlisted in the battle of a lifetime; this battle is for our collective soul. Battle lines have been clearly drawn between secular ideology and the ideology of faith. There is no denying that our country was founded upon faith in God, as our forefathers heavily depended on divine providence drawn from their individual and collective faith to create a vision for our country. Since secularism and faith are at opposite ends of the spectrum, we will need to choose, and I believe God is giving us the chance to "choose this day who we will serve." If we choose to reject secular progressivism and hold fast to our faith foundations, we will have to closely scrutinize policies and proposals and hold our leaders accountable. We will have to combat an out-of-control and out-of-touch government.

When we overlay our Constitution and our faith with current progressive policies, how are we doing? Are we staying true to the successful foundations our framers set for us, or have we already allowed implementation of radical, secular, and progressive agendas that have eroded our freedom and that undermine our faith?

In this section, we will see that when it comes to issues of faith, we willingly practice instant and selective insanity. Through multiple presidential administrations and court decisions, we have been quite silent while allowing our government to implement sweeping changes that are clearly contradictory to our principles and faith. How and why have we become a country that allows our government to implement policies that go against our personal beliefs and undermine our faith? Can we have become "a nation of cowards," as Attorney General Eric Holder asserts? Perhaps so, but I doubt it—I think it can be traced to something more subtle and quite a bit more pervasive. It's the prevalent state of instanity.

We cannot overlook the fact that our great nation has deep foundations in faith. Our Constitution, and most, if not all, of America's historical documents confirm America's commitment to and dependence on faith. America was founded upon principles of faith, and even after over 200 years of history, over ninety percent of Americans still overwhelmingly identity themselves as people of faith—Christian, Jewish, Muslim, Buddhist, Hindu, or others. It would be a huge disservice to simply overlook this important aspect of our lives and not pay attention to the possible consequences of current social trends and directions.

People of faith share many core beliefs. Regardless of religion, there are consistent threads, morals, values, and principles that cut across religious boundaries. As we reflect on our beliefs, we need to know how to respond when we realize that there is an emerging pattern in our new era leadership that intends to implement policies and positions that include:

- Government funding for killing of unborn
- Government control of life and death decisions for elderly
- Implementation of homosexual marriage policies
- Classification of people of faith as extremists or terrorist threats
- Government funding for embryonic stem cell research as opposed to adult stem cell strategies
- Funding and encouragement of killing of unborn babies around the world
- Further removal of anything related to God from public forum

Should any of the aforementioned issues require a response from people of faith? Should we take a position based on principles and core values, or should we simply defer to our leaders and hope they do the right thing? Have we become a purely secular country with no significant foundation of faith? As confirmed by his speech in Turkey, our president believes we are not a Christian nation—what do we say about that?

Again, analyzing faith as a key U.S. vantage point will provide clarity about what is truly at stake. The importance of observing Obama and his administration from multiple vantage points provides the ability to objectively analyze policies and decisions. The faith vantage point will summarize some of the major issues that confront people of faith during this new era of governance. There is no doubt that this administration will challenge us to either stand for our principles or defer to policies that may significantly undermine the foundations at the core of our beliefs. Before we know it, we could be a nation of secularists, with little or no moral foundations, faith, or spiritual beliefs. This would not only be insanely irresponsible of us, but it would also mean a complete collapse of the very foundations to which much of our success can be attributed.

To help orient our thinking about what confronts us, please review the following memo.

MEMO

To: Board Members
From: Fellow board member
Subject: By sight, not by faith?

He's awesome, brilliant, handsome, sexy, and in some circles he's even been characterized as a savior or messiah. No, I am not referring to Jesus Christ with these glowing terms of endearment; these are terms many people use in reference to President Obama.

What? Have we lost our minds? Oh yeah, it's that instanity thing again. Admittedly, against all odds, President Obama has ascended as the new CEO of our enterprise. In some ways, lofty accolades are to be expected. After all, our new employee looks the role and talks the talk of an effective executive. In reality, however, we have yet to see him walk on water, heal the sick, or make money manifest out of thin air. If he "walked on water" by building new bridges with our allies and enemies; "healed the sick" by enacting new, affordable health care reforms and alternatives—not government takeover; and manifested money to immediately reduce spending and eliminate our deficits, we would probably have some rationale for speaking about him with glowing, messianic characterizations. At present, however, we have seen nothing to indicate anything close to messianic anointing. We have allowed ourselves to be swayed by melodic orations, and our desperation has created these false images about our chief executive and his new administration.

The unfortunate reality is that we do not have the Messiah running our enterprise; we seem to have completely deferred our hopes to Barack Obama. Instead of ordaining our president as "the one," shouldn't we—people of faith—rely on the primary tenets of prayer and the core beliefs of our respective faiths to help make rational moral and ethical decisions about the direction of our enterprise? Of course! But, even though all faiths condemn idolatry, bondage, tyranny, and the taking of the most innocent of lives, we have failed to allow these principles to guide our decisions and current assessments about our leadership.

Regardless of how we practice faith, shouldn't we use the fundamental tenets of our beliefs as our moral base for making decisions? Since we are, by great majority, people of faith, we are to provide the input and direction to our president. We are vital to checks and balances; real hope and change must come from us. All U.S. leaders work for us. We are responsible for monitoring the actions of our leaders to confirm that new policies and initiatives conform to our collective moral standards and beliefs.

We cannot allow policy decisions to be made based on political expediency and the personal ideology of our leaders. We are at a point where it is no longer acceptable to rely on happy talk and nebulous characterizations of faith. We need to evaluate actions and outcomes. We are chartered to be "fruit" inspectors—"We will know them by their fruit." While there is no prerequisite or litmus test about one's faith, prior to electing our new leader, he openly discussed his Christian beliefs and their big influence on his life. This was, no doubt, comforting to us.

Now, since he has been managing the direction of our enterprise, we should begin to see the fruits of his labor and judge his motives; are they principled or purely political? What fruits have we seen come out of this administration? What are the patterns of policies and decisions representative of our president? Unfortunately, for people of faith, there are troubling and inconsistent patterns emerging.

When it comes to issues of faith, unfortunately our president is not a man who seems to act consistently with his conviction. While proclaiming to be a follower of Jesus, he is ardently pro-abortion, and as a matter of policy, has increased momentum toward killing of the unborn by funding and proliferating the practice around the world. There have also been a number of people appointed and new policies proposed that seem to encourage and condone euthanasia for the elderly. Does this align with the principles of anyone's faith? Are these zealous, life-ending policies based on principles or on political party ideology? There are new era policies that would classify people of faith as potential extremists or terrorists. Are these ideologies and policies reflective of the new era of government we thought we were getting when we voted?

Though the aforementioned issues are disturbing, it is unfair to put all the blame on the current administration. If we would have asked serious questions and listened intently during our vetting process, we would know that these actions are consistent with the administration's background. We neglected to ask specific questions about Obama's faith and whether it would impact his leadership, policies, and plans. Let's face it—there were many opportunities to ask probing questions, but we were completely enamored and decided it not necessary to inquire about his faith. It seems we have somehow become indifferent and waved off faith as irrelevant for choosing our leaders.

Faith, however, has been the critical foundation that helped build our rich and successful history. How is it logical or rational to now completely disregard the issue of faith when deciding on our new leadership?

Needless to say, we are seeing patterns of radical change that impact our faith foundations. Again, it seems we allowed ourselves to be swayed by the rhetoric of hope and change, and we selectively abandoned our core principles. In an instant, we willingly engaged in idolatry by worshipping and paying homage through trinkets, T-shirts, and pictures—almost anything reflecting this new era. Enthusiasm is one thing, but idol worship is clearly another; we were clearly engaged in wanton idolatry. Does *any* faith justify the worship of idols? We chose to sacrifice our core beliefs and principles, and by deferring, we now have an administration that is seemingly committed to progressive secularism. Secularism reduces the significance of faith. The bottom line is that we embraced instanity, and now there are consequences.

There is still opportunity for people of faith to have an impact. Let us not forget that our president is to use his power and authority to serve and act on our behalf. This point is critical! This means that as long as we commit to using our common sense in conjunction with our collective faith, we can help dictate social policies that will not undermine our principles. On the other hand, if we continue the recent trend of practicing selective deference and blind faith, this new era administration will be able to pursue whatever policies and plans they want. This, of course, will perpetuate the general state of instanity in America. The simple remedy is to provide guidance and direction to our leaders by demanding they not pursue policies incongruent with our beliefs. Then, we will be able to hold them accountable to implement only the directives that align with our principles.

Let's keep in mind that as we begin to replace instanity with common sense, we should not neglect our rich heritage of faith. We are people of faith, and we must stop undermining our principles by making excuses based on good looks, popularity, and charm. Let's stand for our collective faith and pursue a world view that appropriately reflects it. Further, let's begin again to hold our leaders accountable to *our* standards and principles. With this, we win, our leaders win, and our faith wins!

God bless us all,
Fellow board member

We Shall Live By Faith

Our Constitution was made for a moral and religious people; it is wholly inadequate to the government of any other.
—John Adams

After reviewing our rich history and understanding the many great sacrifices rendered to build the foundation of this country, it is easy to see why the United States is a great nation. It is a great nation not just because of its form of a Republic, freedoms, and liberties, but also because it was founded by principled people who were divinely and supernaturally inspired to establish this land as "one nation under God."

The incredible book, *The 5000 Year Leap*, chronicles how our founding fathers painstakingly looked at all of history beginning in biblical times, and all of the respective forms of government (carefully considering the ones that worked, and those that failed) since the "beginning" to formulate their idea of the best form of government for America; our Constitution came out of this incredible feat of awesome responsibility and reverence toward God. The book confirms that while we may be tempted to overlook, disregard, or consider our Constitution as outdated, it took almost 200 years to put it together. When finished, our forefathers considered the U.S. Constitution to be "a document written for the ages;" timeless, boundless, and never-changing. Our forefathers believed they were brought together by God's divine providence; after considering the miracle of the U.S. Constitution, I have no doubt they were!

Our founders were driven to establish this land as an independent country living under the divine authority of God. Founders and framers were so profoundly inspired and devoted that their commitment to God was inexorably in and through most—if not all—their writings and historical documents. Their commitment to God was not for show; it was so much a part of them that it seems they couldn't implement new policies for governance without clear acknowledgment of God's divine providence.

Throughout America's history, we have had clear evidence that faith in God has always played an integral role. All founding documents, including the U.S. Constitution and the Declaration of Independence, are full of acknowledgements toward God. The Washington Monument has a capstone inscribed with, "Praise be to God." "In God we trust" is not only written on all U.S. currency, but it is also written over the southern entrance of the U.S. Capitol. There is no doubt that our founding fathers were driven by a compulsion and responsibility to recognize God in their personal lives and in all major aspects of policy and direction for the country.

Since many of our early leaders seem to have had a personal belief in and respect for God, God was fused in their vision for the U.S., their government and policy making, and in the respective laws. Benjamin Franklin proposed that the Constitutional Convention of 1787 begin each day with a prayer. Thomas Jefferson admonished us that "Liberties are a gift from God," and our first president, George Washington, wrote that he felt all nations should "acknowledge the providence of Almighty

God and obey His will." These few examples confirm that faith in God fundamentally provided the lens through which our leaders viewed the world. They received morals, principals, and guidance through their faith in God. These were principled men who could not, even if they wanted, separate their governmental practices from their faith.

Over time, it seems we have evolved—or devolved—to the point where our leaders view faith as just a good belief system or characteristic. They do not see faith as something to be embodied as an intricate part of a lifestyle, and instead choose to see it as something to compartmentalize as completely separate from their daily lives and worldview. This means that instead of men inspired by God who rely on faith to inspire new policies, we have men purely inspired by men, relying primarily on their political parties and associated agendas to determine polices and governance practices.

There is no doubt that we have come this far by faith. Historical documents confirm that our forefathers trusted in God and looked to use the God "lens"—a purposeful look toward God—for guidance and divine provision for building the country. This way of thinking has eroded over time, to the point that our leadership now seems to be driven more by men than by God, as the primary characteristics of power and control are motivated by political ideology rather than any issues of faith in God. This is why we hear manufactured platitudes and clichés from candidates while they run for president, but after election, we see policies that are completely opposite of *any* form of principled faith.

Regardless of whether you completely align with the current U.S. leadership or not, there is a very apparent contrast between new leaders and how our forefathers embodied their faith in God. We can see the morals, ethics, and primary principals of new era leadership do not revolve around God; they actually revolve around one man. To be fair, though, many do revere him as a god—instanity!

One Nation Under God, or Under … god?: Obama, the Foremost American Idol

The U.S. has progressed far away from its roots and foundations, which were firmly established by and dependent upon
faith in a holy and sovereign God. Through its more than 200-
year history, America has been led by the original founders and
framers, war heroes, military men, democratically-elected presidents, and now one who some esteem as a manifestation of god
in the flesh!

People like Nation of Islam leader Louis Farrakhan, MSN-
BC's Chris Matthews, *Newsweek*'s Evan Thomas, and numerous media outlets—there have been over 1,000 articles depicting Obama in messianic terms—have spoken about our leader as
someone to be worshipped and adored. Obama has been characterized as one who causes goose bumps to run up and down the
legs of media people. He has been noted to bring about fantasies
and explicit dreams, and through his charm and charisma has
prompted even the most devoutly religious people to express adulation that was previously strictly reserved for God alone. There
is no doubt that our president is the epitome of an American idol!

The irony about the blatant and wanton idol worship we
have so gratuitously extended to our president is that our faith
strictly forbids this kind of worship to anyone or anything except
God Himself! It doesn't matter whether people are Christian,
Jewish, Muslim, etc.; idol worship is not condoned by any of
these faiths. Since over ninety percent of the U.S. professes to
be of some kind of religious faith, how could we have been so
swayed to participate in this new era of idolatry? Who or what
has bewitched or enchanted us? We have been under the spell
of instanity.

Many will try to dismiss their state of instant insanity
by saying they were primarily looking to be part of a historic
moment. People will use their true desire for hope and wishful
thinking as their primary motivations behind aggressive pro-

motion of Obama and his agenda. This may be an palatable excuse to a point, but, how do we then explain a 2009 Harris poll that asked Americans who they admire enough to call a hero? Barack Obama was ranked number one, and Jesus was ranked number two. We even go as far as to heap constant worship on our president, even after obvious patterns of gross missteps, the desire to weaken and undermine our constitutional freedoms, and the obvious desire to control every aspect of our lives, including life and death! We need to be realistic about our worship of Obama, because we can be set free if we embrace the truth.

The truth about our worship of our president is that, as a result of one man's personal charm and popularity, we desire to cover up mistakes and make irrational excuses for his entire leadership team. Even as our freedoms are at risk and our foundations of faith are seriously undermined, we worship President Obama! How is this obvious act of worship rational, logical, or prudent for people who, by vast majority, purport to be people of faith?

We have seen well-known religious leaders, ministers, rabbis, imams, etc. paying almost sacrificial homage to our new president by prominently wearing shirts and caps with his likeness and buying any number of pictures, dolls, bumper stickers, and other trinkets that display his image. Our kids have even been enlisted (or, more appropriately, indoctrinated) in the never-ending barrage of idol worship as they are often encouraged to sing, praise-dance, and offer pledges to Obama as part of school activities. Isn't idol worship described as the worshipping of the image and likeness of anything other than God? Again, as a nation with a majority of people of faith, how do we justify the brazen idol worship? There should be an outcry by all people of faith pronouncing the need and call to repent. Current government actions force us to answer a critical question: Are we one nation under Obama, or one nation under God? Though our president and leaders may not consider their actions antithetical to faith, we should firmly bemoan that the sovereign God of our nation "shall not be mocked."

During the brief tenure of this new era administration, it has become clear that our president does not identify with the country's strong foundation of faith in God. He has not only implemented policies that directly conflict with foundations of faith, but he has demonstrated a reckless and condescending disregard for people of faith. While speaking with world leaders, President Barack Obama smugly asserted, "We are not a Christian nation." What? Does he have *any* understanding of the role Christian faith played in our rich U.S. history? He went on to later comment to world leaders, "We are one of the largest Muslim countries in the world."

These statements are not only blatantly, factually incorrect, but they are brutally dishonest.

The facts confirm that the U.S. cannot seriously be considered one of the largest Muslim countries; most recent data suggests that based on total number of Muslims, the U.S is not even in the top thirty countries as far as Muslim population. Christianity is still one of the fastest-growing religions in America. By any measurement, our president's statement is a lie. Why would our president feel the need to make such a dishonest remark? While there are positive attributes we tend to heap on our president, we should also know he has a penchant for intellectual dishonesty and appeasement. Statements about the U.S. not being a Christian nation—that it should be thought of as a Muslim country—are a demonstration of dishonesty and appeasement. It seems almost un-American! This is a good, clear example of having reached the pinnacle of instanity.

The Truth Shall Set Us Free

Jesus spoke to His disciples, "If you obey my teaching, you are really my disciples; you will know the truth, and the truth will set you free" (John 8:31–32). This teaching is a poignant reminder of the virtue of truth. It helps us to know that as a universal law, it is truth alone that has the capacity to set people free.

Think about it—if we know and understand the various vantage points and all angles behind the thinking about new era policies and initiatives, we would be left with a general sense of real freedom. Freedom comes from understanding the truth because it provides the ability to make genuine choices. Our founding fathers seemed to understand this, since they strove for maintaining a foundation of truth as they purposely set boundaries between citizenry and the states, and further between the states and the federal government. They seem to have clearly understood that if government had the majority powers over citizenry, it would be in a position to manipulate the truth, which would create a system of bondage and tyranny for the citizens of this country. A knowledge and understanding of truth is fundamental to being able to experience freedom and liberty.

With political land mines surrounding issues of faith, we are spoon-fed suppositions and careful positioning, along with platitudes and clichés from our president and leaders. The president purports to be a Christian man of faith, and most, if not all, in Congress also say they practice some form of faith. This raises the question, why does there seem to be such strident effort to remove faith in God, or anything attributing existence of God, from U.S. foundations and from the public square? This new era seems almost antagonistic toward God and people of faith.

Our forefathers knew that America could be built, and they provided a pathway to success while fully maintaining their faith foundations. Our forefathers demonstrated that reasonable and principled men of faith would naturally view the world and govern in ways indicative of faith. Even while writing the U.S. Constitution, our leaders faithfully authored the First Amendment in a way that preserved the integrity of individual religious freedoms while also maintaining appropriate reverence and decorum for God. Needless to say, things have changed over the years.

Instead of our leaders properly conveying the spirit and intent of the First Amendment to mean what it clearly states—that "Congress shall make no laws respecting an establishment of religion or prohibiting the free exercise thereof"—we have heard many excuses from our leaders as they hide behind the establishment clause and the separation of church and state in order to preclude prayer in schools, in courts, and practically any other public place. How can our government leadership take a huge leap to go from "Congress shall make no laws respecting establishment of religion" to an all-out removal of any religious language, imagery, or symbolism from American society? Allowing religious imagery does not constitute an act of government establishing a religion. The most glaring part of this insane logic is that they completely disregard the weight and duty of the second part of this sentence, which reads, "or prohibit free exercise thereof."

The First Amendment was not written to take God out of our lives; it was written to make sure God remained a vibrant and active part of our lives without coercion from government. It provided space for religious freedoms, so we would come to know the truth, and the truth would make us free!

It is quite ironic to see our new era government seemingly doing all it can to rely on a very strict—albeit misguided and certainly progressive—interpretation of the Constitution as justification for further reducing God from the public square. The irony is that we see our leadership hiding behind their strict and dishonest interpretation of constitutional limitations on religion, while feeling completely justified proposing policies in direct opposition to other fundamental aspects of our Constitution. Why do we see the rigor to feign strict adherence in one instance to exclude God, yet the complete casual disregard of constitutional limits in another, to encourage new era policies? Based on patterns and behavior, it seems our government wants to transition from being a country dependent and founded upon faith in God to a country of unhinged neo-secularists.

Our president is wholly complicit in the dismantling of faith in this country. When Obama decided to cancel traditional participation in the National Day of Prayer at the White House—the first time in over a decade the sitting president has not attended—and cancel participation in the God and Country Festival—the first time in over forty years a sitting president has not participated—we should have paid attention. When he then forced removal of any Christian symbolism before speaking at events, we began to see a definitive pattern. Then, when all our president's actions culminate in a consistent pattern of blatant disregard for human life—including embryos, babies, and the elderly—we should just know that it signals he is unabashedly a neo-secularist. Secular progressives tend to have little to no regard for issues of faith, generally resorting to stances consistent with moral relativism instead of moral truths.

Pegging someone who says he is Christian and a man of faith as a secularist may seem too harsh to some. Instead of rushing to judgment, perhaps we should reflect on specific actions to help confirm a fair and appropriate assessment. As it relates to participation in faith-based meetings, the truth is that all other U.S. presidents, for at least the past forty years, participated in these faith-based events. It is intellectually dishonest to try to assert some form of faith neutrality through nonparticipation. The truth about our Constitution is that, as long as a particular religion is not established by the government, it condones and encourages everyone to freely participate in faith-based activities.

Provisions preventing government from establishing or forcing religion were put in the Constitution because our forefathers wanted Americans to experience true freedom, unlike what they endured under the Church of England. In a nutshell, this is the purpose of the establishment clause and subsequent ruling for separation of church and state. To be sure, the Constitution was designed to limit any possibility of government-mandated intrusions in personal issues of faith, but it was not intended to eliminate participation in faith-based public events, or to remove prayer from schools, courts, and other public places.

Some will try to argue a general lack of protocol and respect for faith-based events can still be marginally excused; they will try to make the case that our president is new and perhaps unprincipled, but that doesn't mean he is purely secularist. Well, what are we to make of our president forcing removal of anything religious before speaking at events? Can or should this be excused as just lack of experience or naive understanding?

First, we should recognize that our president is not naive about the Constitution; he taught constitutional law at the University of Chicago law school! Ignorance about what is constitutionally acceptable behavior cannot be used as his excuse or defense. A purposeful, determined, and calculated commitment to secularism is the only logical reason why a sitting president would require religious items be taken down before speaking. Case in point: Before coming out to speak at a Georgetown University event—an event held at a Catholic university—our president had his team remove or cover anything depicting Christianity. By all accounts, this was completely unnecessary, as no other U.S. president has ever insisted on removal of instruments of faith before speaking at events. This approach is highly irregular and is indicative of an overreacting secularist.

The U.S. Constitution does not, by any stretch of the imagination, present any potential conflicts or provisions which preclude heads of state from speaking within church settings. There is absolutely no justification for initiating such an egregious act—taking down or covering sacred instruments of faith—without coming to the rational conclusion that there is some kind of inherent disdain for such instruments. I have no doubt our founders would view these actions as a direct affront to faith. There is a caveat to this notion, however, since our president visited a mosque in Turkey and wore an Islamic cap while praying, clearly adhering to their artifact and instruments. Perhaps his actions are not so much an assault on faith as much as they are an assault on Christianity.

Maybe this would explain why our president can be seen on YouTube videos, arrogantly scoffing at the interpretation, efficacy, and intention of the Sermon on the Mount. For Christians, the Sermon on the Mount is one of the most revered of all Jesus's sermons, and our president is on video, presenting blatant condescension of Biblical truths. We have hit new lows; now, we see a blasphemous form of instanity!

A pattern of secularism has clearly emerged, and it seems the people have been wholly entranced by it. Through our determined adulation and support of our newly-elected leadership, we have become fully complicit with a creeping and destructive loss of the foundations of faith. We should know that secularism produces major, negative implications to people of faith. Since we are, by vast majority, people who practice some kind of faith, a healthy skepticism of the secularist agenda is required. For instance, central to all faiths is the encouragement and preservation of life. Even if inclined to give our president the benefit of the doubt for not participating in faith-based events, we should know no religion justifies his apparent disregard for life. All religions are proponents for life.

Since many avowed secularists have a similar mind-set to that of agnostics, atheists, communists, Marxists, statists, and eugenicists, most progressive secularists do not view life as a precious moral issue. They see life in relative terms and primarily hold it as a social issue that could and should change consistently with the progressive mind-set. An understanding of the secularist mind-set provides clues as to why our president would endorse the unnecessary destruction of embryos under the guise of research and endorse and promote killing the unborn around the world. It also allows us to understand why he would propose policies that will result in significantly reducing life expectancy of the elderly.

With documented foundations in faith provided to us by our forefathers and our own personal commitments to faith as our guides, does it still seem logical and prudent to idolize someone who holds such a blatant disregard for life? Political expediency based on ideology is one thing, but for people who are not ideologues, it would be completely irrational and illogical to continue to make excuses and provide defense for a president that has clearly demonstrated his beliefs and agenda through purposeful anti-faith actions. For our U.S. forefathers, faith was a lifestyle. It seems that, for President Obama, faith and religion are compartmentalized as something you *do,* not something you *live.* He sees the world through a lens that is largely secular; therefore, his policies are primarily and fundamentally secular—at the expense of faith.

Instead of looking for excuses, we should again hearken to the wisdom of the verse noted throughout this book: "For the mouth speaks what the heart is full of. A good person brings good things out of a treasure of good things; a bad person brings bad things out of a treasure of bad things" (Matthew 12:34–35, GNB).

We should know by now that strict attention needs to be paid to the actions and policies of U.S. leadership, not their words. As we have seen, the words are misleading and steeped in intellectual dishonesty.

Regardless of what our leaders say, it is secularist policies that have the most profound effect on shaping our new era, not reliance on fundamental constitutional freedoms regarding religion and faith. For at least the past fifty years, the American Civil Liberties Union and liberal activist judges—who attempt to rewrite legislation based on their personal views instead of strict interpretation of the Constitution—have launched a concerted effort to reshape American society by trying to eliminate God from our culture. When it satisfies their activist agendas, they try to insist on strict and misleading interpretations of the Constitution as their weapon, but make no mistake, their reasoning and interpretation of the Constitution is motivated by agenda, not constitutional fact. Unfortunately, though, they have had some success, and some court rulings, like those surrounding First Amendment rights, have been ruled upon with misguided premises and interpretations.

Activist judges, and especially those of progressive mindset, can really cost the people their freedoms. Unless we commit to hiring leaders who have professed a determination to only appoint judges of strict, constitutionalist mind-sets, we will see many more devastating and erroneous judgments handed down. As we can see from the homosexual marriage issue, there are a good number of judges at the state level who legislate from the bench and pass rulings based on agenda and mindset instead of strictly relying on our founding documents. Even though judges are supposed to rule based on the supreme laws of the land—the Constitution, and appropriate cases demonstrating foundational precedence—we will have to endure many more cases like this unless we proactively get involved in scrutinizing the motives and intents of our leadership.

The secular progressive mind-set is now quite pervasive throughout our new era leadership. As noted, our president has already named czars who are avowed communists, eugenicists, and others who have written and proposed ways to quantify the value of human life according to usefulness and instrumental value. In this system, the elderly are assessed as having nominal value. This provides government a way to value one human life over another and will no doubt be relied upon in a system of rationing under government-run health care.

There are a number of specific anti-faith policies and agendas being proposed as part of the secularist agenda. Of the many initiatives, there are a few that pose major and direct affronts to our faith foundations and associated freedoms. These initiatives can be summarized as follows:

Government Funding of Stem Cell Research

Under the guise of science, President Obama immediately over-turned President Bush's ban on government funding of embry-onic stem cell research. This means that, though embryonic stem cell research has been wrought with incalculable ineffi-ciencies and has been proven morally and ethically wrong, our president has chosen to use our money to help fund it.

There are many issues introduced by government funding and support of embryonic stem cell research. One of the major issues is that the process entails the casual destruction of life. This research uses cells derived from fertilized human embryos that are only a few days old—destroying the human embryo in the process. With the moral and ethical issues combined with the gross inefficiency of harvesting stem cells, government funding of this research should not even be a consideration. The Heritage Foundation's analysis found, for example, that "if we were going to try treating the approximate 17 million diabetes patients in the United States, it would require a minimum of 850 million to 1.7 billion human eggs. Collecting 10 eggs per donor will require a minimum of 85 to 170 million women. The total cost would be astronomical, at $100,000 to $200,000 for 50 to 100 human eggs per each patient."

Although committed secularists have tried to ignore it, there is a very good stem cell research alternative through adult skin cells; this process can be modified in a way that gives sci-entists all the properties of embryonic stem cells. With adult stem cell harvesting proving successful in treating Parkinson's disease, juvenile diabetes, and spinal cord injuries, it is appalling that our president would insist on government funding of inef-ficient research that allows the continued destruction of human embryos.

The blatant disregard for life does not end with stem cells. Human cloning is also an open door through which secular progressives can begin funding and experimentation. According to Ken Blackwell of *World Magazine,* "In the same speech where he authorized the new stem cell funding, he announced he would also not allow human cloning for purposes of reproduction. He clearly left the door open to allow cloning for medical research purposes. In a way that was considered unthinkable during every American administration in the past, President Obama refuses to rule out allowing scientists to actually grow human beings in a laboratory, to harvest their body parts, and conduct research for the benefit of other human beings. No human being should ever be killed to benefit another human being. Such a policy would put America on a path that would lead to terrifying results. The door to human cloning should not only be shut, it should be slammed shut and locked forever."

Our forefathers would not only be shocked at the apparent governmental overreach to fund such controversial programs, but they would also be stunned at the casual lack of regard our government has toward life. Our forefathers viewed America from a moral and ethical perspective, governed by their faith and "life, liberty, and the pursuit of happiness."

Policies Regarding the Unborn

The God who gave us life, gave us liberty at the same time; the hand of force may destroy, but cannot disjoin them."
—Thomas Jefferson

When the U.S. government proposes expanding programs that, instead of encouraging life, actually help to end life, it reveals that perhaps the moral foundations established through our forefathers have been replaced by the secular progressive mindset.

One of the first major changes our president made when he came into office was to reverse President Bush's policy to block U.S. funding of international family planning groups that provide abortion or abortion counseling. President Obama's reversal means the U.S. government will again sponsor and promote killing of the unborn around the world through use of $400 million taxpayer dollars per year. If our president feels it is prudent to spend almost a half billion taxpayer dollars to fund abortions around the world, it must be a heartfelt initiative. This is especially telling, since this policy change and expenditure were immediately implemented during a time in which the U.S is enduring its worst budget crisis. It seems odd to have a president display such passion and fervency over the delicate issue of abortion. Even though his fervency seems completely illogical, his background and history should have provided some clues into his feelings about this issue.

While he was a senator, Obama was big supporter of Planned Parenthood; he made many promises and commitments to this organization about preserving abortion rights. Since Obama studied and taught constitutional law and has a fervent commitment to minority rights, social justice, and human rights, his stance on this issue presents some interesting irony. We should recognize that when our forefathers wrote, "We hold these truths to be self-evident, that all men are created equal, that they are endowed by their Creator with certain unalienable Rights, that among these are Life, Liberty and the pursuit of Happiness," abortion was not a policy they would have even contemplated. To be sure, we can just observe their language, which highlights that there are unalienable rights, and first and chief among them is *life*. From the standpoint of our forefathers and their heartfelt conviction about life, how did America stray into such a blatant disregard for life by encouraging abortion on demand?

Our president is on record as a proponent for minority rights; his advocacy is noble and justified. However, his rhetoric and actions are again in conflict, as abortion is one of the most devastating tragedies unleashed on minorities. Many elitists and social progressives will try to say that abortion is a woman's fundamental right, but the truth confirms that this brutal and immoral practice evolved from a strategy that had little to do with women's rights; it evolved from a strategy to control and reduce minority populations.

Planned Parenthood offices are located in areas heavily populated by minorities, and this was not by happenstance. Margret Sanger, Planned Parenthood's founder, has been described as a racist because of her stance as a proponent of various methods of population control and the use of eugenics—in essence, the desire to create a pure and ever-improving human race by weeding out the "undesirables." Because she had concerns about population growth of minorities, she had a scheme to strategically reduce the number of minorities through her Planned Parenthood offices; unfortunately, her strategy has proven successful, as minorities—especially African-Americans—have been disproportionately killed as a result of abortion. In one of Sanger's books, *The Pivot of Civilization,* she wrote about eliminating "human weeds" and the need for sterilizing "genetically inferior races." She went further to proclaim, "the mass of significant Negroes, particularly in the South, still breed carelessly and disastrously, with the result that the increase among Negroes, even more than among whites, is [in] that portion of the population least intelligent and fit and least able to rear children properly. Before eugenicists and others who are laboring for racial betterment can succeed, they must first clear the way for birth control. Like the advocates of birth control, the eugenicists, for instance, are seeking to assist the race toward the elimination of the unfit. Both are seeking a single end but they lay emphasis upon different methods."

What is extremely troubling about this is that the very people we have deemed heroes and trusted with leading are the most strident defenders and supporters of Sanger's tactics, strategies and racial injustice. That's right—people we have deemed brilliant, notably President Obama, and Secretary of State Hillary Clinton, have lauded Ms. Sanger by heaping much praise on her and the entire Planned Parenthood organization, even though there is clear evidence this organization was bent on making abortion available so minorities would inevitably limit their growth. A 2008 Guttmacher report states black women are responsible for 37 percent of abortions—well above our percentage of the population in general! According to the Centers for Disease Control, 472 black babies are aborted for every 1,000 live births in 2004—roughly one black baby killed for every two born! Susan Cohen, writing for the Guttmacher Policy Review in 2008, noted, "The abortion rate for black women is almost five times that for white women."

Some may still try to defend our leaders by claiming the truth is unfair or somehow taken out of proper context. Well, we should just listen to the words of our ultra progressive Supreme Court Justice Ruth Bader Ginsberg as she—also an ardent Planned Parenthood supporter—explains about abortions: "Frankly, I had thought that at the time *Roe* was decided, there was concern about population growth, and particularly growth in populations that we don't want to have too many of." Justice Ginsburg confirms knowing, and still ardently supporting, the race purification and eugenics strategies of Planned Parenthood founder Margaret Sanger. It is interesting to note that Sanger has also been labeled a socialist and a progressive, and she was known for having a healthy disdain for Christians.

To add to the diabolical and unfathomable injustice perpetrated by Planned Parenthood, hundreds of millions of our tax dollars are given to Planned Parenthood every year. This is sick! With our money, this organization encourages and perpetuates brutal killing of the most innocent and seemingly preventing our innocents of their basic human rights. On this issue, we are experiencing a hemorrhage of our very souls without so much as a peep about our heartache and pain due to this incredible injustice. So, is this how our government is providing change in the area of social justice and human rights? Outrageous! This is how our government and our African-American president provide increased minority rights? Where is the outrage, and where are people of faith on this issue? Remember, over ninety percent of us profess to be people of faith.

In "World Magazine," Dr. Martin Luther King, Jr.'s, niece, Alveda King, correctly assessed abortion as follows: "Abortion is the white supremacist's best friend." To some, this may seem a gross overstatement, but the statement is the painfully brutal truth. Here are the stark realities about this issue.

- Estimates say approximately 90 % of Planned Parenthood clinics are placed in target urban/minority neighborhoods.

- While African-Americans make up only approximately 13% of the U.S population, a 2008 Guttmacher report confirms African-American abortions account for 37% of the total.

- According to the Centers for Disease Control, 472 black babies are aborted for every 1,000 live births in 2004, amounting to roughly one black baby killed for every two born.

- Since estimates range from between 45 to 50 million abortions having been performed since *Roe v. Wade* in 1973, somewhere between 16 and 18 million innocent black children have been strategically denied their right to life, liberty, and pursuit of happiness.

- Abortion is number one killer of blacks in America, not AIDS, as President Obama has repeatedly asserted.

Ms. King admonished all Americans to "tell the president of this land and all of Congress: It is not okay to kill the weak. It is not okay to kill the babies in the name of science. It is not okay to kill the youngest." Since America has many people who proudly describe themselves as proponents of social justice, human rights, and minority rights, in light of this new information about abortion, will people have the courage to acknowledge that the zeal for abortion should be tempered with their a bigger and more purposeful zeal for the right to life?

For many, the truth about abortion will present major dilemmas and a disruption of their existing paradigm; it strikes a raw nerve with many. There is a clear and wide divide between people who are either firmly for it or against it—there is rarely a middle ground. To help further confirm how strategic and yet diabolical this issue really is, here are more truths to weigh, pray, and consider.

The Fourteenth Amendment to the U.S. Constitution states, " ... nor shall any state deprive any person of life, liberty, or property, without due process of law, nor deny any person within its jurisdiction the equal protection of the law."

While considering Roe v. Wade, the Supreme Court admitted, "If ... personhood (for the unborn) is established, the appellant's case, of course, collapses, for the fetus's right to life is then guaranteed specifically by the (Fourteenth) Amendment."

In *Roe v. Wade,* the U.S. Supreme Court declared it could not resolve "the difficult question of when life begins." And, on that basis, it declared a new right to abortion based on right to privacy.

Most people who are pro-abortion purposely feign ignorance when it comes to answering the question about when life begins. They tend to answer with nebulous responses like, "That's beyond me," or, "Only God knows." This is similar to how Obama chose to answer a Rick Warren question about "when does life begin." The fact is that the scientific community accepts that life begins at conception; they conclude that at conception there is unique DNA indicating a new creation at that very moment. The only way pro-abortion people can keep their logic and any semblance of integrity is if they can convince themselves that somehow the unborn are subhuman—some form of pre-life.

This argument really falls apart when you consider that Congress passed the Unborn Victims of Violence Act, which states someone who "intentionally kills or attempts to kill the unborn child...be punished...for intentionally killing or attempting to kill a human being." Even Congress now acknowledges that the unborn are human beings. Since this is now acknowledged as the truth, that human beings deserve human rights and protections provided by Constitution, it's fundamental to our guarantees and protections. Science is clear that human life begins at conception.

According to Webster's dictionary, "kill" is defined as "to deprive of life in any manner; cause the death of; slay." Likewise, "murder" is defined as "to kill brutally or inhumanly."

It shocks the conscious to come to understand that we, the people, who have been given the opportunity to life, liberty, and pursuit of happiness, have participated in the killing and murder of innocents, according to the definitions for life, kill, and murder—especially when we consider much of this movement evolved as a result from a strategy to rid society of the overcrowding of minorities. Insanity!

More appalling is the thought that our president has consistently refused to acknowledge the plight of the innocents and is actively fighting for even more injustice by expanding funding and promoting these practices around the world, mostly to the detriment of his own minority race. I am sure our president knows the facts concerning abortion, but he chooses to sacrifice his sensibilities while exercising a clear lack of moral fortitude in order to further the secularist agenda. One good example is when, as a state senator, Obama was the only Illinois senator to speak against a bill which would have protected babies who survive late-term abortions. His justification for speaking against such a vital bill was that in some cases, the law would possibly forbid abortions to take place. He went further to confirm he did not want the bill to turn into an anti-abortion statute. To further his lapse of conscious and morality, our president has vowed to sign the Freedom of Choice Act into law, which would negate the effect of the recent Supreme Court ruling upholding the partial-birth abortion ban. Wow—unbelievably irresponsible and insane!

Obama's abortion stance is steadfast and without repentance. During a rally, he said about his own daughters, "If they make a mistake, I don't want them punished with a baby."

To demonstrate his commitment to abortions and to members of Planned Parenthood and its affiliates, our president appointed Kathleen Sebelius as Secretary of Health and Human Services. Sebelius has a long record of support for abortion; her support extends to include indefensible and heinous late-term abortions—aborting a near full-term baby. She was friends with the late-term abortion doctor, George Tiller. The late Dr. Tiller provided significant campaign contributions to Ms. Sebelius— so much, in fact, that she couldn't keep count. She seriously underestimated his contributions to her while she underwent her Senate Confirmation Hearing; she received nearly three times more money from Tiller than she originally revealed.

There is obviously no justification for the abhorrent practice of abortion, but whether you agree with the practice or not, there should be some agreement that the soul of America is being poisoned by this practice, as Planned Parenthood reported more than one billion dollars in revenue in 2007–2008, while being heavily funded by American taxpayers!

According to its most recent annual report, in fiscal 2008, Planned Parenthood Federation of America, the nation's largest abortion provider, had annual revenue of more than $1 billion. Of this, about 34 percent was made up of government grants. This means, approximately $350 million of American taxpayer dollars supported the work of Planned Parenthood from October 2007 to September 2008. And, according to tax records, this 501(c)(3) nonprofit organization had a net income $85 million greater than its expenses. The taxpayer-funded "non-profit" is actually generating a profit at the expense of the huge loss ... *of life!*

At some point, we have to come to the realization that there would be unrestrained and vehement outrage if even puppies were aborted. Honestly think about it—we would have more collective outrage because of abortion on dogs or other animals; People for the Ethical Treatment of Animals would hold endless vigils and protests if we demonstrated the wanton disregard for animals that we do for unborn humans. Yet, we allow the casual abortion of human beings at the rate of approximately 1.5 million per year. Instanity.

Indefensible insanity is what drives the illogical and irrational defense of abortion. As demonstrated, just by stepping back and observing the issue from new vantage points can help shine the light on the truth. True freedom is within reach if we can gain clarity of thought and understand truth behind the aforementioned outrage.

What if we come to realize the entire abortion battle is being waged based on purposeful deception and false premises? What if abortion is just a masterful marketing scheme purposely intended to play on our emotions in order to further an agenda? In his brilliant book, *The Marketing of Evil,* David Kupelian helps unravel gross manipulations and deviant misconceptions surrounding the abortion argument. Through candid admissions from the very people credited with pioneering the abortion movement, this book exposes how abortion evolved into a "right" through a purposeful scheme filled with lies and deception. A clever strategy was unleashed that gained considerable traction by brilliant marketing shrouded as an extreme crisis in women's health; the pioneers of this movement have now admitted that the crisis never really existed. The unfortunate results are, however, that we have now accepted abortion as an issue of freedom. In actuality, however, abortion sprouted through a seed of corruption, and has led us into gross immorality and bondage.

Mr. Kupelian's book details how Dr. Bernard Nathanson can be credited with helping create the mass deception. He was co-founder of NARAL Pro-Choice America and later the Center for Reproductive and Sexual Health (CRASH). He was a pioneer in the pro-choice movement and has admitted to personally aborting over 75,000 babies. Nathanson, as a pioneer and principle strategist for the movement, explained that he needed a catchy phrase that would act as an emotional rallying cry for women so abortion could be brought into mainstream. He laughed about making up "pro-choice," "freedom of choice," and the notion of women controlling their own bodies. Nathanson admitted these were purposely cynical slogans, but they worked. Aren't these the primary slogans our president uses to defend abortion? Our brilliant leadership, along with the rest of us, has just been sucker punched by slick marketers trying to push a progressive agenda.

According to Nathanson, he "persuaded the media that the cause of permissive abortion was a liberal, enlightened, and sophisticated one." He fabricated to the media that he and some colleagues had taken polls and sixty percent of Americans were in favor of abortions. Nathanson and his colleagues also fabricated the number of illegal abortions performed annually—they gave the media the figure of one million, but it was approximately 100,000—and the number of women who supposedly died every year as a result of abortions—they said 10,000, but the actual figure was around 200. These false figures took root and seared the consciousness of Americans, who felt something had to be done about the 10,000 women dying in the back alleys. To make sure abortion arguments would stick, Nathanson and others fed the media false hope that once abortion was legalized, it was just going to be done to allow women getting them done illegally to get them legally. The sad reality is, however, that abortion has been adopted as just another choice—an alternative form of birth control—as we have seen abortion rates rise over 1500% since legalization. It doesn't matter where one stands on this issue; we should realize we have propagated the killing of the most innocent based on completely fraudulent data.

After innovations like ultrasound and other technologies, Nathanson realized that a fetus was a human life, and not just the blob or mass he hoped. He could no longer deny that every abortion he performed ended a human life. This realization caused him to rethink his pro-choice positions and change his ways; he has now become advocate for life.

Not only did Nathanson realize his instanity about ushering in a culture of death with this issue, but "Jane Roe" of the landmark *Roe v. Wade* case also later admitted that the case was a fraud. Roe admitted she was complicit in being used by abortion rights attorneys to get abortion legalized. Roe's fraudulent testimony, coupled with Nathanson's false figures, lies, and misrepresentations, were admitted into the courts as evidence, and our judges made their decisions based on the apparent crises. The premises were false; the truth is that we have allowed almost fifty million babies to be killed due to an elaborate scheme based on false information.

Where is the collective outrage? Even after evidence and admission of rampant lies, fraud, and deceit used in abortion testimony, our culture is still seemingly entranced by clever marketing. Abortion has not yet been revisited by the courts. Just think—because of mass deception and clever slogans, to this day we continually render a death sentence on mostly minority babies at the rate of 1.5 million per year. Again, approximately fifty million babies have been killed because we were cavalier about checking facts and allowed lies and deceit to be entered in as official testimony of record. It is almost unthinkable to know that this destructive and immoral practice is enthusiastically applauded by our leaders as they encourage the spread of it around the world.

Think about this: We are Americans, citizens of "the land of the free," and committed to life, liberty, and the pursuit of happiness. We're not a primitive, barbaric, or uncivilized society. We have, unfortunately, become the ultimate picture of instanity.

A recent medical study confirms that unborn babies can taste, hear, and remember during the very stages when it's still legal to end their lives. According to *World Magazine*, researchers form Maastricht University Medical Center and the University Medical Center St. Radboud in the Netherlands have shown clear indication that unborn babies have short-term memory and even memory improvement as they progress toward birth. Other research has shown unborn babies can recognize rhythms of speech and their mothers' voices and taste the food passing through the placenta. They respond to their mothers' prenatal emotions and, unfortunately, feel pain.

The facts are brutally painful when it comes to unborn babies, as we continue to encourage the utter destruction of the most defenseless among us. To add further insult to the tragedies endured by the unborn, our new era government hopes to escalate this incredible farce by including abortions as part of the government-run health care plan. They attempt to use intellectual dishonesty when saying abortion will not be included in the health care bill. Unless abortion is specifically excluded as an amendment to the bill, it will be covered without restriction and on demand. Unless we intervene, the instanity will continue. We, along with our "progressive" government, will be wholly responsible for contributing to a culture of death.

If there is any good news in this abortion travesty, it is that, for the first time since *Roe v. Wade,* a slim majority of Americans consider themselves pro-life (according to a Gallup poll from May 2009). Perhaps the veil has lifted and truth will begin to reign; freedom will again result.

Life *is* truth. "You will know the truth, and the truth will make you free," provides new inspiration for setting our unborn babies free by allowing them to live as God ordained and as our forefathers intended. The issue of abortion is just another good example that proves we have come to a point in history where we have allowed our culture to degenerate to the point of becoming desensitized to death. We have enthroned a culture dominated by progressivism; the secular progressive culture allows the devaluing of human life. From the most innocent and earliest of stages of life to the defenseless elderly, we have unleashed taxpayer-funded policies that are simply anti-life.

Policies Regarding the Elderly

There has already been much written about our government's irrational and audacious desire to manage health care. Certainly, there is nothing inherently wrong with a government with the noble intent to make health care accessible and cost-effective for everyone. Before signing on to this, however, there is sound logic that should be considered to prevent another bout of instanity.

Logically speaking, before wholly adopting government-run health care, there should be serious consideration of whether it is justifiable to disregard the many governmental limits our forefathers wrote into the U.S. Constitution for our protection. We need to be willing to disregard the individual power we have over our own lives and hand that power over with the intent of extending power to government so it can fundamentally take responsibility for our life and death decisions. This extension obviously requires immense trust, as this action is likened to giving the government power of attorney over our lives. If we get sick, it will be up to the government to render appropriate treatment or referrals. If we experience trauma in an accident, our government will decide what treatments and remedies to render. If the elderly require medical attention, it will be up to our government to decide whether their lives are still worth additional investment. Government-run health care will have a serious and sometimes devastating impact on our lives, so the question is, do we trust government to this extent?

There is a pattern of complete incompetence in all vital aspects of our economy, currency, budgets, spending—almost everything our government has touched! When we factor incompetence with their obvious gullibility to falsehoods—consider the deception surrounding *Roe v. Wade* and controversial appointments of people with backgrounds and foundations in eugenics—and casual and callous disregard for life, how can we trust our government will do right by us and our elderly citizens? The sacrifice of the people will be gut-wrenching, as we will have to go to government officials with "broken and contrite hearts," offering sacrifices and hoping government bureaucrats will have compassion and empathy toward us. There have already been concerns raised about rationing, even as our president and his leaders have emphatically and publicly stated it will not take place. Again, this notion is insane!

All the other governments that have implemented this model of health care have admitted to partaking in some form of rationing, especially for the elderly. There is no way around this reality, as there are a finite number of health practitioners. Common sense confirms there is absolutely no way to fully employ a far-reaching, government-run health care system without a rationing body to oversee and manage allocation and usage. Believing the emphatic stance about no rationing is another example of the people extending blind trust to a government that has already been proven deceitful—instanity!

In September 2007, then-Obama adviser Robert Reich stated, "We are going to have to- if you're very old, we're not going to give you all that technology and all those drugs for the last couple of years of your life to keep you maybe going for another couple of months. It's too expensive.... so we are going to let you die." Hmm ... how's that for compassion for the elderly? To further expound on our leaders' heart and intentions, in April 2009, President Obama stated, "You get into some very difficult moral issues when considering whether to give my grandmother or everybody else's aging grandparents or parents a hip replacement when they are terminally ill. The chronically ill and those toward the end of their lives are accounting for potentially 80% of the total health care." Humph! Well I guess that says it all.

Here's another truth: If we allow government takeover of our health care, they will decide who lives and dies based on costs, benefits, and statistics. As the elderly use larger percentages of care as they approach death, government will necessarily look to implement strategies to limit costs, and the elderly will be monitored closely in an attempt to maximize efficiency.

It is easy to envision that creating efficiencies and necessary cost reductions will come in the form of delays or denial of treatment to the critically ill and elderly because of costs. Health care rationing must necessarily take place because of the sheer number of new health recipients; our government's ambitious plan will try to incorporate approximately fifty million people, including over twelve million illegal immigrants, into a health system with a fixed number of practitioners. In the other countries that offer government-run health care, the elderly are severely restricted, as they tend to have more ailments that come with the normal aging process.

To balance out medical facilities and fairness in care, the elderly will experience restrictions. Again, some of our president's closest health care advisors, like Ezekiel Emanuel, are on record confirming the need to ration by saying that some services should not be guaranteed. Emanuel stated, "An obvious example is not guaranteeing services to patients with dementia."

In Great Britain, there are committees that provide cost analysis of someone's medical needs and mete out care up to a maximum value based on factors including age and usefulness. If people go over the maximum, the government may offer additional counseling and sponsor euthanasia-type support. They provide end of life counseling sessions, like the proposed U.S. plan, and allow the elderly to determine their ultimate demise. When you consider the prospect of extreme pain and suffering due to long waits, delays, and unclear dispositions with a government-run plan, many will opt for the end of life. This should not be—this is America! If our forefathers were here, they would suffer complete outrage at how we value—or devalue—life.

The sanctity of life has been reduced to such a small hurdle in this country that we seem to quite easily make the leap over it. Our lack of action means we are complicit in the absolute devaluing of our traditions and the overall value we now put on life. I guess if we can feel completely justified in utter destruction of life by killing embryos and babies, we can certainly feel justified in killing—or allowing end of life—for the elderly.

Most social progressives probably feel that it's just a life, and that it's not a big deal. Well, for those who may have difficulty understanding, the big deal is just that—life! As our forefathers so clearly outlined, life is an unalienable right given to us by God, our Creator; it is completely His decision when our lives start and end. With the expanded role of government, we take matters into our own hands, and we are making a tremendous mess of things.

Since we *are* fundamentally a Christian nation, we should listen to the wisdom one of C.S. Lewis's famous quotes: "If you read history, you will find that the Christians who did most for the present world were precisely those who thought most of the next. It is since Christians have largely ceased to think of the other world that they have become so ineffective in this."

Life for every American is not an optional courtesy; it is a fundamental, God-ordained right that cannot and should not be interfered with, especially by government.

Left Behind—Literally!

We have absconded the faith of our forefathers while making allowances for escalating levels of moral decay and permitting government intrusion and control in the U.S. Our situation looks eerily similar to the prophetic storylines written in the *Left Behind* book series.

Left Behind is a dynamic book series authored by Jerry Jenkins and Tim LaHaye that has garnered a large and faithful audience around the world. Tens of millions of readers have been captivated by clever stories with artfully-constructed storylines about the end-times prophesies of the Bible. While reading, one can't help think about what those times will be like and contemplate how the U.S. could ever devolve into the society depicted in the series. With our new era, we are seeing the real feasibility of these scenarios emerge in our lifetime.

Things have so greatly accelerated that we now live in a time when our government leaders are open to having dialogue about adopting a one-world currency. Judges and other Obama appointments have mentioned a willingness to defer to world courts, therefore making our Constitution irrelevant. There has been dramatic escalation of government intrusion and control, and our president and other leaders look to appease by bowing to other nations. This new, pliable structure establishes a framework very similar to America as it is depicted in *Left Behind*. It also, unfortunately, aligns with Biblical prophesies—scary! God forbid we experience a devastating national or worldwide crisis, but if one occurs, we will begin to live in truly prophetically significant times.

Left Behind is not only analogous to the path down which we seem to be heading, but it is also acutely accurate in describing the radical left ideology. The radical Left can be described as those of the Democratic Party mindset who boldly wear the banner of pure ideologues—purposely and willfully enjoying the fruits of instanity. These people are also ardently progressive and proudly characterize themselves as secular progressives. If we consider the words "left behind," we see there is an interesting literal meaning and parallel that can serve as a reminder of current predicaments and the general state of affairs.

For example, we can see the radical Left is behind:

- Increased momentum and a move away from constitutional guarantees and freedoms.

- Increased encouragement of abortions.

- Increased support for government-run health care and, if necessary, euthanasia.

- Move toward one world government.

- Move toward one world currency.

- Increased government oversight and control of major dependencies for everyone.

- Increased intellectual dishonesty— corruption, lies, deceit, intrusion, and control,—without any transparency.

- Increased poverty and oppression of the poor.

Fundamentally, the Left *is* behind! Even in the specific domains they would purport to lead, like education, abortion, and health, they are behind. The educational systems wholly supported by the Left, and the abortion schemes they whole-heartedly defend, are the very systems that disproportionately decimate minorities, especially blacks. The Washington school system is just one example of many. Facts surrounding abortion promulgated in and through minority neighborhoods are unde-niable. The facts also confirm the largest cites with long histories of progressive Democrat leadership maintain disproportionally high unemployment and poverty rates. For instance, while the unemployment rate stands at approximately 10% for the whole country, the unemployment rate for blacks is a whopping 15.7 percent (over 18% for African American males).and 13.1 percent for Latinos compared to 9.5 percent for whites. These rates are significantly higher in inner-cities like Detroit, Philadelphia, and Chicago. My sociology background makes me quite sensi-tive to the plight of inner cities, and my instincts confirm minor-ities, and especially African Americans, are severely harmed by an increasing unemployment and dependency on government programs. It is a fact that government dependency is synony-mous with poverty, so why would we encourage it? Common sense should actually dictate that, just based on facts, the Left should be seen as the foremost oppressors and purveyors of bigoted social policies that carry vile and nefarious intentions and outcomes. Yes … the Left is behind!

Common sense should confirm that we, the people, must get in front. The goal is to slow or turn back the momentum of the progressive affront to our values, principles, and liberties. Whether prophetically or literally, we surely don't want to get left behind; in either case, it produces devastating consequences.

Summary

> The hottest place in hell is reserved for those who remain neutral in times of great moral conflict.
> —Dr. Martin Luther King, Jr.

The evidence of rampant instanity is overwhelming. America, and the people of faith that comprise her, are at a critical crossroads. We must "choose this day whom we will serve." Even as people of faith, we have allowed our political affiliations and their respective ideology, not our principles, to influence our decision making. This is a huge mistake; we have now ushered in a pervasive climate of secularism that is the antithesis of our collective faith and foundations.

If there is any good news in all that has been uncovered, it is that we are not powerless. Whether we like him or not, when it comes to issues of life and death, we do not have to exercise blind faith and stand by our president. It is our option to compartmentalize our allegiance and limit our support to only policies and initiatives that do not betray our beliefs and principles. The people still have majority power—though it is shrinking fast—and as a Republic, we have representative government that allows our elected officials to act on our behalf or be voted out of office. As we raise our collective voices, we can cause dramatic change, regardless of radical ideology and the agenda of our president and his administration.

We can and should put a stop to progressive secularism, as it is representative of everything we, by majority, are not. Its rampant spread throughout various presidencies has not only encouraged policies that completely undermine the U.S. Constitution and Declaration of Independence, but has also directly resulted in tens of millions of deaths and the destruction of human lives. By reviewing the faith of our forefathers and understanding their complete dependence on God, we can see this country needs repentance and healing, not more death and destruction. The state of instanity must cease now. We have heard about the travesties and now understand that complacency is equal to complicity. As we progress, we must engage, because we are the only true hope for producing the desired change. We, the people are the only remedy to bring about real hope and change; our history confirms we are a divinely-inspired people with a collective spirit of resilience.

Our forefathers provide great inspiration. The supernatural providence that led to foundations of faith, and the subsequent lapses that led to their erosion, can be summarized as follows:

- Our forefathers were providentially led to establish this United States as one nation under God, and they proceeded to construct foundational documents, monuments, government seals, and even all currency that revered God and reflected their commitment to faith.

- Through principled commitment to their faith, our forefathers wrote in the Declaration of Independence "that all men are created equal, that they are endowed by their Creator with certain unalienable Rights; that among these are Life, Liberty and the pursuit of Happiness."

- As time moved on, progressivism began to emerge with the mind-set that God should be removed from the public square.

- In conjunction with the ACLU, the progressive movement asked that the courts further define the establishment clause of the First Amendment to also include the complete separation of church and state.

- This ruling ushered in decades of methodical removal of God from schools, courts, and government offices; it threatens to completely undermine faith foundations in U.S. society.

- While we celebrate a historical presidency, our new leadership has apparently embraced the very mind-set that eroded our faith, and while being idolized, worshipped, and adored, our new president demonstrates antagonism toward faith and the foundations of our forefathers.

- While providing new government funding for stem cell research, our leadership encourages destruction of embryos and unborn babies. While spewing rhetoric and clichés about his faith, our president completely defers to the progressive agenda, to the detriment of our historical foundations and the right to life.

- Even though there is overwhelming evidence that abortion has been perpetuated based on lies and deception, our leadership is wholly complicit with it.

- With the advent of new health care policy, our government is positioned to make decisions about life and death for all citizens.

- With the necessity to ration care, the elderly will be adversely affected, which means the pattern of casual disregard for life of the most innocent and defenseless—unborn babies—will likely translate to a casual attitude toward the elderly as well.

Secular progressives will prevail unless we become active participants in our democratic Republic. The choice is clear, and the choice is ours.

CHAPTER THIRTEEN

Book Summary

In his book, The Great Divorce, C.S. Lewis said, "There are two kinds of people: those who say to God, 'Thy will be done,' and those to whom God says, 'All right, then, have it your way.'"

Based on pattern and track record, it is not logical to want or expect our new president to provide what we would deem a state of hope and the necessary and desired change. I fervently pray to our God we do not forget the wisdom of our president and forefather John Quincy Adams: "You will never know how much it has cost my generation to preserve your freedom. I hope you will make good use of it." As noted throughout this book, for too long, too many Americans have been absolutely complacent about liberty. Most Americans have never had to fight for liberty and, thus, have little concept of its value or any sense of gratitude for its accumulated cost—a cost paid by generations. This has lead to a false sense of security in the belief that freedom is their birthright and heritage, not understanding the fact that we have enjoyed the fruits of liberty and freedom because of the brave and heroic actions of others. We can no longer take our rights and freedoms for granted. We must connect with, and fully embody all necessary vigilance for maintaining the blessing of freedom(s).

I plead that we do not forget this vital truth.

MEMO

To: All Board Members
From: Fellow Board Member
Subject: We have identified its existence, and now it is time to remedy it!

Our quest to determine whether instanity exists required critical analysis of our thought processes and understanding of U.S. government. An objective analysis of our thought processes was needed to determine whether our president and his leadership team were elected based on competencies and experience or purely personality and party ideology.

In the end, we confirmed that zeal for incoherent policies and practices that directly undermine our collective interests and usurp authority enumerated in our Constitution prove instanity exists and is a prevalent force. Though our leadership has bouts of instanity, it is fundamentally an issue exacerbated by the people, since our leaders were hired to work for us. We are the primary enforcers and overseers of their performance, or lack thereof, and of our collective destiny.

Observation of various vantage points provided thoughtful analysis of America as a business enterprise, America as a historical heritage, and America as a country founded in faith. To our astonishment, America is experiencing a major transformation that has been underway for decades, and our collective state of instanity has fundamentally enabled this precarious transformation.

In the beginning, we started evaluating America as a business enterprise. Through this vantage point, we were able to confirm that America has been grossly mismanaged. This is the only logical conclusion we could derive, since the leadership we have hired is sworn to uphold our collective public interests and to honor and uphold the U.S. Constitution, yet they have repeatedly failed to meet this essential job duty.

After reviewing patterns and inclinations of our leaders, we can validate that they are not only inexperienced at fulfilling their respective job duties, but they also possess a zeal for ideology emanating from personal political agendas, radical social philosophies, and political gamesmanship rather than our expectation of a commitment to service. Again, they are hired as our public servants, and this should be taken seriously. A commitment to serve the interests of the board of directors is a fundamental characteristic of good leadership. Unfortunately, this commitment is sorely lacking within our new leadership.

Current patterns confirm that our leaders believe it necessary to assert and expand authority in order to bring about a remake of America. The general feeling is that the people are just not enlightened enough to know what's in our best interest. The leadership we hired would like us to continue to extend an uncompromising and blind trust to them because they supposedly know what's best for us. With no executive management experience, no proven core competencies, and no track record of success, extending blind trust to current leadership would be irresponsible and dangerous. When combining Obama's obvious lack of experience, notable incompetence, and a lack of fiscal accountability, along with a background of Marxist and socialist leanings, we have a tenuous situation requiring our maximum vigilance—not blind trust.

Through the past several presidents, we have seen a subtle shift toward an unchecked expansion of our business enterprise. Currently, we have ushered in a popular president with a zeal for socialized governance; he believes that social justice can be accomplished through government control over all major services—health care, energy, food, finance and banking policy, transportation, and education. While this may seem benign, it inevitably expands government well beyond the enumerated limits consistently articulated in our

Constitution and Declaration of Independence. It creates a system of government dependence, and therefore limits freedom. This establishes a "nanny state." Under a nanny state, extreme poverty flows freely at the expense of independence and entrepreneurship.

A true nanny state cannot evolve unless we allow it. As confirmed throughout this book, our government has been hired to work for us. Practically speaking, servants are bound and obligated to only do those things their "masters"—in this case, the board of directors, or the people of the U.S.—tell them to do. When observing the hurried zeal of our leaders to quickly remake America while going well beyond the boundaries of the Constitution, they look completely irrational—even just plain silly. If they succeed, however, they will look brilliant.

By strict definition, brilliance is not a characteristic indicative of our government. Since brilliance involves exceptional skill and keen foresight, our leadership doesn't qualify for this distinction. Instead, we see lack of leadership, a penchant for appeasement and apologies, a lack of experience and competence, arrogance, Marxist and socialist agendas, numerous missteps and mistakes, and a host of broken promises. Further, instead of growing in competency, our leaders seem to relish blindness as they feign ignorance of a clear focus and the need for strict restraint on finance. These are the fundamental characteristics of good leadership; without tending to these basic tenets, we are left with pure arrogance.

The second vantage point allowed observation and investigation into how, when, and where we became complicit with the new era of arrogance and elitism that characterizes our current leadership. The review of the Constitution and Declaration of Independence graciously provided confirmation of treasured promises and essentially confirmed that our forefathers established our great country with guarantees extended to all citizens. These great men put forth documents that, if administered properly, guarantee the preservation of a free America.

Through careful review of the Constitution and Declaration of Independence, we confirmed that the people possess majority powers, with strict, enumerated powers granted to government. For decades, our powers have precipitously eroded due to social and secular progressives and are now at risk of being completely and permanently undermined through the emergence of aggressive new tax schemes and government expansion and control. The pattern seems to indicate a need to control the progress and outcome of everyone and everything in order to bring about wealth redistribution; this is a direct affront to our Constitution. We are living in times that clearly conflict with the wisdom and established roadmap of our forefathers. Thomas Jefferson wrote, "If we can prevent the government from wasting the labors of the people, under the pretence of taking care of them, they must become happy."

Our leadership is zealous for implementation of its wantonly progressive agenda, seemingly at all costs. We should consider the wisdom of Ronald Reagan when he said, "The American dream is not that every man must be level with every other man. The American dream is that every man must be free to become whatever God intends he should become." He went further to confirm, "Nations crumble from within when the citizenry asks of government those things which the citizenry might better provide for itself.... [I] hope we have once again reminded people that *man is not free unless government is limited*. There's a clear cause and effect here that is as neat and predictable as a law of physics: *As government expands, liberty contracts."* By now, it should be painfully obvious that it is not governments job to control society in an attempt to mandate equal outcomes or accomplishment; every American has unique God-gifted talents and skills, and it is government's responsibility to just help ensure equal opportunity for achievement is possible, so talents and skills are gloriously manifested through great feats and accomplishments. This is a key tenet liberal progressives fail to grasp. Their agenda is fatally flawed and always ends in destruction.

Implementation of the progressive agenda seems to be the overriding objective for our president and his leadership team. Issues with discipline and control become apparent when our president appoints his own form of shadow government—czars and appointees who do not require confirmation from Congress. In just his first year, he has already appointed ten times more czars than any other president in history. With lack of accountability and guidance administered through the people, our "czar-struck" leadership is comfortably emboldened and seemingly beyond reproach, even as additional outlandish promises are made—most of which have largely gone unmet. Unfortunately, our president has become "Mr. Fibs," as there are many significant promises he has not kept.

We have seen a zealous pursuit of polices like stimulus spending, government-run health care, and cap and trade, all of which undermine the U.S. Constitution and the foundations our leadership swore to uphold. Ironically, these policies have been given priority instead of intense focus on directives established by the people to reduce taxes, reduce spending, and reduce deficits; this indicates a government that is clearly out-of-control and out-of-touch. The fact is we the people do not condone redistributive change. We believe like Benjamin Franklin did when he commented, "History affords us many instances of the ruin of states, by the prosecution of measures ill suited to the temper and genius of their people. The ordaining of laws in favor of one part of the nation, to the prejudice and oppression of another, is certainly the most erroneous and mistaken policy. An equal dispensation of protection, rights, privileges, and advantages, is what every part is entitled to, and ought to enjoy."

Fundamentally, progressive policies and actions have culminated to the point that we, the people, need to decide to stand up for our values and principles, grounded in common sense, or fully retreat in order to accommodate a neo-secular government and society.

Either we allow our leadership to remake our country, as our president pledged to do, or we turn back to the path of our forefathers. We cannot forget that our forefathers established a solid foundation for America. However, at a campaign stop, Michelle Obama said, "Barack knows that we are going to have to make sacrifices. We're going to have to change our conversation. We're going to have to change our traditions, our history. We're going to have to move into a different place."

God forbid! Changing our precious history and foundations is not an option; we are here today as a proud, determined, and mighty nation as a result of our history. We must not acquiesce on our principals; to do so would be unpatriotic. We can overcome the obvious state of instanity and stave off secularism if we commit to holding firm to the foundations laid by our forefathers. They established "one nation under God," designed to be "indivisible." History confirms that this nation has had greatness and success because of God's divine providence and the faith of our forefathers.

As a third vantage point, we looked intently at our faith foundations to clarify and confirm their role in establishing our great nation. Our forefathers allowed faith to guide their thinking and actions within all areas of government and society. Unfortunately, our forefathers' passion for and reliance on God have undergone erosion precipitated by secularists, erroneous rulings, and faulty judicial interpretation, culminating in the separation of church and state and a callous disregard for life.

Over the past several decades, eroding faith has resulted in our nation embracing practices that seem almost antagonistic toward guarantees of life established by the Fourteenth Amendment and the Declaration of Independence. For instance, we now see that through deception, we have been hoodwinked on the issue of abortion. Our gullibility has not only caused the loss of approximately fifty million innocent lives, but it has also desensitized us to the necessity to uphold the enumerated guarantee of life. We have grown cynical

about life, as we embrace—or at least accept—a culture complicit with death instead of life. Despite, however, rampant
abortion and diminishing care for the elderly, we are still a
majority nation of faith (approximately 90%).

The clarion call for people of faith is to reject secularism and
progressivism and return to what should be our first love—
the God of our fathers. Learning to lean on faith foundations will help us come to know the truth, and it is the truth
that will make us free. The goal is to maintain and perpetuate freedom and liberty, not to adhere to zealous ideology or
political agendas.

Thoughtful analysis of faith foundations, when compared to
the direction of our current government, leads us to conclude
that by ignoring the need to cut budgets and spending, our
current leadership is wholly complicit in *stealing* from future
generations—our children and grandchildren will bear the
brunt of tax burdens. As a result of the secular progressive
agenda to keep the farce of abortion-on-demand—the ultimate minority "equalizer"—available, we have devolved into
a society that tolerates *killing* of the innocent. Additionally,
by overlooking the need to uphold the Constitution as the
supreme law of the land, we are *destroying* rights, guarantees,
and freedoms. Steal, kill, destroy—is this the new model for
American government? Have we evolved from foundations
representative of one nation under God to a nation characterized by new era foundations—to steal, kill, and destroy?

We are in a fight against the weapons of mass deception
being wielded by progressive liberals and their agenda for
change. The cornerstone of their agenda is their version of
government-run health care reforms, increased abortion-on-
demand, education reforms (that limit and restrict school
choice), and energy reform in the form of taxation. As has
been thoroughly documented in this text, these are all tactics of deception that severely harm the poor, people of color
(and especially African Americans), and our inner-cities. The
deception is that liberal progressives tout these programs

helping the poor and people of color. Let's consider, does it help the poor to ration, restrict or limit care by forcing them to change doctors and by disallowing medical procedures to their elderly loved ones? Does it help the poor to encourage killing of their unborn by strategically bigoted schemes that reduce their population thereby reducing their economic value? Does it help the poor and under-served communities to limit them to rotting, dilapidated, and (in many cases) dangerous public schools that have been proven tremendously lacking in academic achievement? Does it help the poor to "necessarily" increase their energy bills, and produce an economy with even greater unemployment? Fundamentally, does it help the poor when we encourage dependence on the government thereby relegating (current and future) generations to poverty? These deceptive policy shams are what progressives have packaged in terms like "social justice" and "human rights," but as we can see, these are just more examples of rhetorical labels and empty words that sound compelling but deliver outcomes that are verifiably opposite of their claims. Further, these types of policies limit freedom and liberty while promoting intense levels of tyranny and oppression upon the very people most in need of our help and compassion. Instanity!

Fundamentally, we have come to a point that requires we objectively discern whether our liberties and freedoms are real or myth, fact or pretense. Citizens are the sole guardians of the Constitution; there are no other stopgaps. Our forefathers declared us to be the ultimate balance of power. At the end of the day, we are responsible for what has happened and what could happen within our Republic in the future. If we agree that our liberties and freedoms are real, guaranteed, and worth preserving, we must actively become engaged in order to protect them. Current leadership has demonstrated a pattern of recklessness and irresponsibility through horrible choices in appointees and nominations, radical czars, and policies that fundamentally oppose our Constitution; since we are the board of directors, we must act. The facts and overwhelming evidence confirm that the desire to pursue unrestrained progressivism is an act of insanity. This is especially troublesome when we consider the fact that the U.S. has been wildly successful over the past 200 years by creating more new wealth than the rest of the world combined, while never suffering a famine, and being (by far) the most charitable philanthropic country on the planet. Our existing free-market capitalistic system working under the confines of the U.S. Constitution may not be perfect, but it absolutely works!

We must refrain from the temptation of casting our votes for people who have enabled and embraced and are wholly complicit with this new era of irrational, illogical, and irresponsible mode of progressive governance, regardless of party. With that in mind, the following is a list of candidates who we should actively campaign against when they come up for reelection:

- Rep. Pelosi, Nancy (D-CA-8th)
- Rep. Filner, Bob (D-CA-51st)
- Rep. Waters, Maxine (D-CA-35th)
- Rep. Waxman, Henry (D-CA-30th
- Rep. McNerney, Jerry (D-CA-11th)
- Rep. Lee, Barbara (D-CA-9th)
- Rep. Stark, Fortney (D-CA-13th)
- Rep. Sanchez, Linda (D-CA-39th)
- Rep. Speier, Jackie (D-CA-12th)
- Rep. Watson, Diane (D-CA-33rd)
- Sen. Boxer, Barbara (D-CA)
- Sen. Feinstein, Dianne (D-CA)
- Rep. Miller, George (D-CA-7th)
- Rep. Woolsey, Lynn (D-CA-6th)
- Sen. Reid, Harry (D-NV)

- Rep. Grijalva, Raul (D-AZ-7th)
- Rep. Pastor, Ed (D-AZ-4th)
- Sen. Sanders, Bernard (I-VT)
- Sen. Leahy, Patrick (D-VT)*
- Sen. Durbin, Richard (D-IL)*
- Sen. Burris, Roland (D-IL)*
- Sen. Whitehouse, Sheldon (D-RI)*
- Sen. Casey, Robert (D-PA)*
- Rep. DeFazio, Peter (D-OR-4th)
- Sen. Gillibrand, Kirsten (D-NY)*
- Rep. Hinchey, Maurice (D-NY-22nd)
- Sen. Schumer, Charles (D-NY)
- Rep. Nadler, Jerrold (D-NY-8th)
- Rep. Weiner, Anthony (D-NY-9th)
- Rep. Rangel, Charles (D-NY-15th)
- Rep. Velazquez, Nydia (D-NY-12th)
- Rep. McDermott, Jim (D-WA-7th)
- Rep. Conyers, John (D-MI-14th)
- Rep. Dingell, John (D-MI-15th)
- Rep. Kilpatrick, Carolyn (D-MI-13th)
- Rep. Pascrell, Bill (D-NJ-8th)
- Rep. Frank, Barney (D-MA-4th)
- Sen. Kerry, John (D-MA)
- Rep. Olver, John (D-MA-1st)
- Rep. Markey, Edward (D-MA-7th)
- Sen. Dodd, Christopher (D-CT)
- Sen. McCaskill, Claire (D-MO)

- Sen. Specter, Arlen (D-PA)
- Rep. Scott, David (D-GA-13th)
- Sen. Franken, Al (D-MN)
- Rep. Wasserman Schultz, Debbie (D-FL-20th)
- Sen. Snowe, Olympia (R-ME)
- Sen. Collins, Susan (R-ME)
- Sen. Baucus, Max (D-MT)

A * denotes that though all of these representatives have performed poorly in consideration of their duty to uphold and protect the Constitution and have been irresponsible and derelict of duty when it comes to voting logically and responsibly by reading bills before voting on them; those with an asterisk grossly maligned justice by voting to continue taxpayer funding of egregiously fraudulent and corrupt organizations like ACORN. Their deliberate embrace of insane "politics" over logic reason and prudence absolutely precludes them for *any* further consideration of office. (An immediate recall election would be an ideal remedy for these individuals.)

Please understand that this list is not at all comprehensive, as there are many more leaders who should be on this list. In general, anyone who voted for the stimulus spending plan, cap and trade, government-run health care, or any other policies that undermine our constitutional guarantees to freedoms and liberty, must be replaced. According to our forefathers, this is our individual duty and responsibility! As Samuel Adams said, "It does not take a majority to prevail ... but an irate, tireless minority, keen on setting brushfires of freedom in the minds of men."

The choice is ours; we must choose now this day! God bless us all!

Fellow Board Member

CHAPTER FOURTEEN

Concluding Thoughts

"If the inexpressible cruelties of slavery could not stop us, the opposition we now face will surely fail. We will win our freedom because the sacred heritage of our nation and the eternal will of God are embodied in our echoing demands."
—Dr. Martin Luther King Jr.

After reading this book, I pray that there was much brought to light, and that by God's grace, we can now see. I truly believe that regardless of political affiliation or persuasion, there is much about which we can now stand in agreement. Even if we disagree on some things, my earnest prayer is that we do not allow a state of instanity, propagated by political ideology, to continue to dominate our society and overwhelm and pervade us individually.

I hope you agree that this book was not an exercise in futility; merely a good read; or a fictional, political thriller that brought about nightmares. The goal was to distinguish and confirm existence of a new, contagious, and dangerous paradigm; we achieved that goal, as we can now observe and distinguish that there is a disempowering paradigm known as instanity!

Since much of this information may be overwhelming, a review of the various topics and ideas is important. To confirm existence of the state of instanity, we used our government and leaders as primary examples. We observed the entire body of U.S. leadership from multiple vantage points, with each presenting a unique perspective. In the end, we clearly identified insane policies, initiatives, and a pattern of radicalism in and around the White House; these completely undermine our collective standards and principles and the historical foundations firmly set by our forefathers. This provides verification that we, the people, are participating in a cycle of a pervasive state of instanity.

The good news is that, by way of the various vantage points and new observation, we can recognize that we are still in charge of our destiny. We still have the majority powers guaranteed to us by way of the Constitution and Declaration of Independence. If the government adheres to these documents, we can regain our full rights and liberties. Conversely, if we allow our out-of- control and out-of-touch government to pursue personal agendas, we will see further erosion of our freedoms and liberties to the point where America becomes unrecognizable as an independent and successful nation; instead, it will be a compromised world nation.

For many, including most in our current leadership, being viewed as a world nation—fully subservient to world laws and powers—seems to be palatable. In their minds, America's independence and "excptionalism" are passé, and as such, its society should be remade to reflect the collective consciousness of the world. While this is quite idealistic and a noble thought, it would ultimately result in tyranny and oppression like that which led to America's formation in the first place. Therefore, this cycle should again remind us of Einstein's definition of insanity—doing the same thing over and over again and expecting different results.

Einstein's definition is directly relevant when considering that all the new era social policies have been tried, and time after time they have failed. Consider this: In the thirties, we tried to spend our way out of economic turmoil, and it failed. We also saw Marxism, communism, and socialism fail repeatedly. We have seen tax and spend policies and strategies fail repeatedly, and we have seen societies wrought with class struggle, redistribution of wealth, and class conflict inevitably collapse. Again, per Einstein's definition, it is clearly insane to pursue failed policies, yet expect different results.

We cannot afford to pursue instanity; we must choose this day which path we will follow: the path of truth, logic, and reason, or an insane commitment of blind trust in a corrupt and contemptuous government.

Remedies

This book is not authored as a referendum on Barack Obama and his administration; it is fundamentally about us—"we the people." This book is about what we have allowed ourselves to become. Through our compliancy and lethargy, we have allowed our country to forge a new era path that seems to be going against the very values and principles for which our forefathers fought, bled, and died. Our new era policies actually rob the soul of America. One primary culprit of our relative state of instanity is complete trust on the political system, which is readily encouraged by political parties. If we are to end instanity, we must end blind trust in either of the two major political parties.

Our explosive political climate has highlighted the fact that our current political system and parties have set brother against brother, children against parents, and neighbors against neighbors. We have become jaded, hateful, and intolerant of one another due to political parties. This is not indicative of

America, and it should not be tolerated. Blatant hypocrisy borne out of the narrow-minded two-party political system shocks the consciousness of people with common sense. Our president tried to address this, but even though he ran as a unifier, our nation has never been more polarized than it is now. Though many may attempt to blame him, our current state cannot be blamed solely on the president. Our state is exacerbated by increased dependence on the petty, adolescent, and incredibly irrational two-party political system.

Let's face it—our system forces polarization and seeks to demonize and silence opposing points of view. People we would consider to be rational can quickly devolve into throwing tantrums and spouting tirades as a result of their party affiliation. What have we become—a bunch of babies? Passionate dialogue is one thing, but this does not describe the aggressive attacks about politics. If we are going to take control of our government and future, we have to find ways to unite around politics; this will help us return to a state of civility. Civility will help end the state of instanity, but we must end our fervent commitment to one end of political spectrum versus the other. If we are going to end the pattern of antagonizing one another because of political affiliation, we must be willing to actively support alternative political parties; this is a primary weapon for keeping all politicians honest and accountable while helping put an end to instanity.

Most Americans agree with things from both political parties, so if a third-party candidate emerges with a good combination of values, principles, and positions more closely aligned to our individual beliefs, we should wholeheartedly support him or her. If more people are willing to go outside of party politics, we will see the emergence of viable third-party candidates. For the people, more candidates mean more choices and, ultimately, potential preservation of our provisions and guarantees. More candidates will also effectively break the partisan logjam that currently dominates Washington politics; they would allow us to again hold our government fully accountable for their actions or inaction. All leaders will begin to take seriously their service to the collective, as they will have a short leash; they will have to either fulfill the jobs we hired them to do, or they will face getting recalled or not reelected. Thomas Jefferson said, "Were we directed from Washington when to sow, and when to reap, we should soon want bread."

We are the sole guardians of the binding contracts between ourselves and our government. Though our leadership may mean well, in some cases they do not refer to our contracts before making policy decisions. We are the sole enforcement for preservation of liberty and freedom, and we therefore must provide them with guidance for any new policy that would infringe. Our forefathers conferred this responsibility to us because they knew we could lose all they fought for if not properly energized and engaged in the political process.

Often attributed to Alexander Hamilton, "Those who stand for nothing fall for anything" is an absolute truth. When we consider the responsibility before us, this truism is especially poignant, as we will either *stand* for guarantees of liberties and freedom via our Constitution, or we will find ourselves *falling* for increased levels of socialism, Marxism, or other forms of government that conflict with our guarantees.

Though there is much to dread about our new era politics, we have a lot to be thankful for as well! The people have awakened, and we are now engaged, enthused, and looking forward to returning our Republic back to its rightful owners. We now know that we are the only true catalysts for hope and change. We are the ones who can and will make this country great again. It is unbelievable that we have come to where our leaders refuse to listen to the will of the people, but we must force them to listen. This is absolutely imperative, because, as Thomas Jefferson said, "When the people fear the government, there is tyranny, but when the government fears the people, then there is liberty."

The fundamental remedy is this: We have to take back control of our government and end the relative state of instanity. This requires that we commit to patronize the media outlets that tell the truth, are fair and balanced, and are committed to reporting facts and allowing citizenry to decide. Media outlets without these standards for reporting are just propaganda outlets and need to be avoided. Additionally, we must continue peaceful demonstrations—town hall meetings, Tea Party protests, 912 protests—and rallies, while also taking definitive action at the ballot box through our votes. Our vote must no longer be taken for granted; it is an extremely powerful weapon, and it is at our full disposal. It will decimate the threats to our freedom as long as it is used just as it was designed. If we would forgo party politics and cast our votes strictly based on candidates' commitment to uphold the Constitution and preserving all freedoms, we would end instanity! Of course, this would mean a complete turnover of our personnel in Washington, but so be it.

According to September 2009 Rasmussen polls, data suggests that "if Americans could vote to keep or replace the entire Congress, 57% would throw out *all* the legislators and start over again." Just 25% would vote to keep the Congress; this is huge. The overwhelming majority of us would replace all incumbents! This is very encouraging, as it demonstrates there is an end in sight to the state of instanity. For probably one of few times in history, most people are no longer complicit with the policies of their political affiliations and would rather just start over with fresh perspectives from newcomers to the political arena.

Based on their irresponsible patterns and behaviors, some of our leaders should already be on notice and face the prospects of immediate termination. Based on what we've learned about our political responsibility, we should seriously consider actively helping any new candidates running for political offices and campaign against all multi-term incumbents, regardless of party. All leaders who have not taken their respective jobs seriously by reading the bills before voting and carefully performing all the duties we hired them to do must be fired.

I pray we do not forget that freedom is not free. Our freedom was very, very expensive; it was costly beyond measure and comprehension. Our forefathers and the millions of brave and heroic men and women who have served or are serving in the armed forces did their best to ensure our freedom. There have been many lives lost in support of our freedom, and we must not let them and the countless untold sacrifices committed on our behalf to have been in vain. Now, it is our time to stand up. It is our time to engage by becoming active and holding all leadership accountable. We must become the final check or balance and enforce the provisions of our contract with our government. Future generations are depending on us to do our part to protect their freedoms.

Freedom is a very expensive and quite unique treasure. In it, we will find the capacity for life, liberty, and pursuit of happiness. From it, we will find free market capitalism leading to increased innovation and entrepreneurship, and through it we will have the ability to uncover truths, as it is truth alone that upholds freedom.

"You will know the truth, and the truth will set you free."
John 8:31–32

Dear Reader,

I am humbled by and very grateful for you. There are millions of books you could have chosen to read, and yet you chose to read this one. I do not take this for granted, and I extend my sincerest thanks to you.

In complete transparency, I have to confess I am not an emotional guy, so imagine my utter surprise when—at several points while writing—I was literally brought to tears. I was greatly impacted while writing the section on the Constitution and the section on our faith foundations. I can assure you this will come as a big surprise to anyone who knows me, especially my wife and kids. I am not generally thought of as emotional, but everyone knows I am very passionate about what I believe. It was my passion for righteousness and truth that brought me to tears, and they still come.

The primary impetus for this book came from a couple of Bible verses that resonate very strongly with me:

> "For the zeal of thine house hath eaten me up; and the reproaches of them that reproached thee are fallen upon me" (Psalms 69:9).

> "Fear not, thou worm Jacob, and ye men of Israel; I will help thee, saith the LORD, and thy redeemer, the Holy One of Israel" (Isaiah 41:14).

> "Behold, I will make thee a new sharp threshing instrument having teeth: thou shalt thresh the mountains, and beat them small, and shalt make the hills as chaff" (Isaiah 41:15).

As I wrote, these verses consumed me. It should be quite apparent by now that I am unapologetically a Christian. I have a quest and fervent desire to serve God and be considered a great instrument in His hands. Matthew 23:11 states, "The greatest one among you must be your servant." The zeal to be great for God and His kingdom compels me, and my earnest prayer is that this book will in some way serve you—at the very least, I hope it delivers the truth, which has capacity to set us free. Since there are far too many issues to be comprehensively discussed in one book, I want you to know I am available to you; I commit myself as your servant, willing to serve in whatever way I can to help further clarify and confirm any of the topics discussed herein.

God bless you, fellow patriots,
Kevin

BIBLIOGRAPHY

America's Providential History, Providence Foundation © 1989 Mark A. Belilies & Stephen K. McDowell

"And don't call me racist!", Argonaut Press, © 1998 Ella Mazel

C.S. Lewis Society, www.lewissociety.org

Fox News, foxnews.com

Good News Bible, American Bible Society, Good New Translation-Second Edition ©1992

Holy Bible, King James Version, © 1972 Thomas Nelson Inc.

Innovation and Entrepreneurship, Harper & Row Publishers © Peter F. Drucker 1985

Investors Business Daily

Leaders, Harper & Row Publishers, © 1985 Warren Bennis and Burt Nanus

Newsweek magazine

New York Times

Oxford Concise Dictionary of Politics, © Oxford University Press, Iain McLean and Alistar McMillan-Second edition 2003

Pathway to Leadership, Peace House Publications, Gbile Akanni, © Living Seed Media 2003

Patriot Post, www.patriotpost.us

The 5000 Year Leap: A Miracle That Changed the World, © 1981 by W. Cleon Skousen, National Center for Constitutional Studies

The Age of Unreason, Harvard Business Schools Press, © 1989 Charles Handy

The Bill of Rights Does Not Grant You Any Constitutional Rights, Robert Greenslade & Claude Ellsworth, Nitwit Press

The New Realities, Harper & Row, © Peter Drucker 1989

The Marketing Imagination, Collier Macmillan Publishers, © 1986 Theodore Levitt

The Marketing of Evil, Cumberland and House Publishing, Inc. © 2005 David Kupelian

The Message Bible, Navipress, © 1995 Eugene H. Patterson

The Story of the Constitution, House Office Publishing, © 1937 Sol Bloom

Wall Street Journal

World Magazine and WorldMag online (www.worldmag.com)

Other offers from Author

Book-*Lifestyle of the Rich in Kingdom* © 2003

Workshops, Training, and "Boot-camps" for new and emerging political leaders

In-depth analysis and discussion designed to help participants

1. *Thoroughly explore,* understand and articulate the issues impacting our current political climate

2. *Develop clarity* and strategies for solving social issues across the political spectrum

3. *Gain* in-depth understanding and appreciation for the Constitution, Declaration of Independence, and other important historical documents

4. *Ignite* renewed political zeal and patriotism

5. *Apply* new commitment to take action and to begin making immediate transformational impact within respective communities

Some topics include:

- The "ultimate" standards for Social Justice and Human Rights: Life, Liberty and the Pursuit of Happiness

- Know thyself: Establishing a "platform" of a principled, focused foundation for political leadership

- Re-framing the" arguments": Constructive de-construction of the social issues of our time

  o Poverty
  o Education
  o Healthcare
  o Abortion

o Climate change

- Confronting and combating "new era" economic paradigms
- Forging Constitutional discipleship
- The "Independent": The ultimate tool for political empowerment transparency and accountability

Speaking engagements and seminars

Some of the topics include:

- Faith and Freedom matters
- Healthcare matters
- Socio/economic matters specifically impacting "people of color"
- Education matters
- Human Reproductive Rights matters

Find *Instanity* online!

www.instanity.com
email: kevin@ instanity.com
facebook page: facebook/kevin mcgary
facebook fan page: facebook/instanity.com